# American
## Gold and
# Platinum Eagles

President Ronald Reagan signed the legislation that created the American Eagle bullion program.

# AMERICAN
## GOLD AND
## PLATINUM EAGLES
### A GUIDE TO THE
### U.S. BULLION COIN PROGRAMS

# Edmund C. Moy, U.S. Mint Director (ret.)

*Foreword by Representative Michael Castle*

www.whitman.com

# AMERICAN
## GOLD AND PLATINUM EAGLES
### A GUIDE TO THE U.S. BULLION COIN PROGRAMS

www.whitman.com

© 2014 Whitman Publishing, LLC
3101 Clairmont Road • Suite G • Atlanta, GA 30329

ISBN: 0794839738MS
Printed in the United States of America

Whitman Publishing is a leader in the antiques and collectibles field.
For a catalog of related books, supplies, and storage products,
visit Whitman Publishing online at www.Whitman.com.

# CONTENTS

# ACKNOWLEDGMENTS

Being a first-time author, I could not have written this book if it weren't for the help and encouragement of too many people to mention here. However, a few deserve special recognition. Miles Standish, Elaine Chao, Deen Kaplan, and Ron Christie opened my mind to new possibilities after my tenure as director of the U.S. Mint, including writing this book. I am grateful to Mike Barnes, my agent, for securing this opportunity for me. Mike has the trifecta of qualities I want on my side: a great lawyer with sound judgment and a large network. Thanks for looking out for me.

Special thanks go to Dennis Tucker and his great team at Whitman Publishing for having confidence in me and coaching me in the mysterious art of book writing. And while I am on the topic of this mysterious art, I am indebted to my collaborator Katherine de Silva. Writing a book was a daunting task for me, but her research, editing, patience, and wise suggestions made it a very enjoyable experience.

I am grateful to several friends who read various chapters and gave me helpful feedback: Andy Brunhart, Mike Stojsavljevich, and David Kim. Thanks also to Tom Jurkowsky, director of Public Affairs at the U.S. Mint, for fact checking some key portions of the book, and to Jeff Minear, counselor to the chief justice of the Supreme Court of the United States, for assisting with the use of some photos and documents.

I had the privilege of serving with talented and dedicated people during my tenure at the Mint, and together we were able to accomplish great things. Thank you to my political appointees David and Mike, Aaron Johanson, Allison Simms Parmiter, Brendan Adams, Christine O'Hara, and Cliff Northup, may he rest in peace. Cliff was my head of legislative affairs and helped me navigate Congress. I'm sure that he would have enjoyed helping me with this book. And thanks to the entire U.S. Mint family. It was a privilege to serve alongside you.

This book would not be possible if I hadn't been director of the Mint, a position appointed by the president of the United States and confirmed by the U.S. Senate. Thank you, President George W. Bush, for your confidence in me. Serving you at the White House and at the Mint is an honor for a lifetime. Thanks also go to Treasury secretaries John Snow for recommending me and Hank Paulson and Tim Geithner for being my bosses during a very consequential time. Deputy Treasury Secretary Bob Kimmitt provided me with wise counsel and mentoring. Senate Banking Committee Chairman Richard Shelby and ranking member Paul Sarbannes held an expeditious hearing on my nomination, asked tough questions, and recommended me to the full Senate. Senate Majority Leader Bill Frist led the process that confirmed me unanimously. Thank you, Mike Castle, not only for writing the foreword, but for being so great to work with in Congress.

Finally and most importantly, I'm grateful for my family. Thanks, Mom (may she rest in peace) and Dad, for the sacrifices you made to raise Donna and me. And to Karen, who has stuck by me for richer or poorer and in sickness and health. Your love and the marriage we built together sustain me and give me strength. I thank my daughters for their unconditional love, and all their hugs and kisses that make me remember what is important in this life.

Whitman Publishing would like to thank the U.S. Mint for contributing images from its archives for this book; Deputy Mint Director Richard Peterson and Director of Public Affairs Tom Jurkowsky and their teams were very helpful. Katherine de Silva, Lindsey Mitchell, and Whitman Publishing staff contributed research and editorial assistance. Various historical images are courtesy of the Library of Congress, the U.S. Department of Defense, and the U.S. Department of the Treasury. Numismatic Guaranty Corporation of America (NGC) shared images of various bullion coins. Q. David Bowers reviewed the manuscript.

Special thanks to Representative Michael Castle of Delaware for contributing the foreword to this edition, and to Mike Fuljenz for contributing appendix E, for which Miley Tucker-Frost kindly shared her memories.

In chapter 1, photographs of the Treasury Building's modern-day Cash Room, a Mint worker inspecting dies, and coinage dies awaiting production are by Shaina Mishkin, and used with permission of the U.S. Mint.

The ancient coins in chapter 2 are from *Money of the World: Coins That Made History* (Goldberg and Goldberg, editors). Certain photographs in chapter 2 are licensed as follows. The safety-deposit box photograph: kali9 / Getty Images. The image of gold coins spilling out of a sack: Stockbyte / Getty Images. The photo of gold bars in a West Point Mint vault: Scott Eells / Bloomberg via Getty Images. The image of gold ingots, bars, and coins: © 2012 Anthony Bradshaw. The Massachusetts note image is courtesy of the Peabody Essex Museum.

In chapter 3, the photograph of Tutankhamen's burial mask is courtesy of Bjørn Christian Tørrissen, and the image of the Mycanae "Mask of Agamemnon" is courtesy of Rosemania. The portrait of Augustus Saint-Gaudens and the sketches and plaster of the artist's double-eagle design are from *Striking Change: The Great Artistic Collaboration Between Theodore Roosevelt and Augustus Saint-Gaudens* (Moran). The U.S. Mint group portrait featuring Sherl Joseph Winter is courtesy of John Mercanti, from *American Silver Eagles: A Guide to the U.S. Bullion Coin Program*. Certain photographs in chapter 3 are licensed as follows. Portrait of James Baker: Diana Walker / Time & Life Pictures / Getty Images. Portrait of James Exon: Terry Ashe / Time & Life Pictures / Getty Images. Portrait of Ron Paul: John Prieto / *The Denver Post* via Getty Images. Portrait of Henry Morgenthau Jr. and John Maynard Keynes: Alfred Eisenstaedt / Time & Life Pictures / Getty Images.

In chapter 4, the photograph of platinum-coin dies is by Shaina Mishkin, used with permission of the U.S. Mint. The photograph including Chief Justice John Roberts is courtesy of Steve Petteway, Collection of the Supreme Court of the United States. The photograph of Michael Castle and Carolyn Maloney is by Chris Greenberg / Bloomberg via Getty Images. The portrait of Thomas D. Rogers Sr. is courtesy of the artist.

# ABOUT THE AUTHOR

**Edmund C. Moy** is a 1979 graduate of the University of Wisconsin with majors in economics, international relations, and political science. He was a sales and marketing executive for Blue Cross Blue Shield United of Wisconsin from 1979 to 1989. Moy served in the administration of George H.W. Bush, within the Department of Health and Human Services, then worked eight years in the private sector with venture-capital firms, entrepreneurs, and corporate and nonprofit boards. In the George W. Bush White House he was special assistant to the president for presidential personnel. In this capacity he recommended candidates to President Bush for the most senior political appointments for 11 Cabinet departments and Cabinet-rank agencies, 32 independent federal agencies, and 14 part-time presidential boards and commissions.

It was during a dramatic period in American history—from September 2006 to January 2011—that Ed Moy served as 38th director of the U.S. Mint. This important position within the U.S. Treasury Department put Moy in charge of the largest coinage factory and bullion "company" in the world, with responsibility over the main Philadelphia Mint and branch mints in Denver, San Francisco, and West Point, as well as the gold depository of Fort Knox. During Moy's directorship, demand for American Gold Eagles more than quintupled from 328,000 ounces in 2007 to 1,803,000 in 2009. Silver and platinum bullion production saw similarly dramatic surges.

Today Ed Moy is an executive, strategist, and advisor in economic policy and finance/investment, and a frequent speaker and commentator on these topics. He lives in Seattle with his wife, Karen, and their daughters.

# FOREWORD

For many decades the minting of American currency was quite static, with very few changes of individuals or scenes depicted on our coins. It was American coin collectors who came up with the concept that coinage could be *interesting*, with rotating depictions of each of the 50 states. They argued that the coins (quarter dollars, in this case) would become collectibles and through seigniorage (the difference between a coin's face value and the cost to produce and distribute it) additional revenue would be available for use by the Treasury. As the chairman of the House subcommittee with jurisdiction over the U.S. Mint, I was approached by some of the leaders of the coin-collecting community. After initially saying "no" to them, I was persuaded by my staff and by a return visit by the coin collectors, who advised me that the quarters could be issued in the order in which the various states were admitted to the Union. We discussed the idea with the head of the U.S. Mint, Philip N. Diehl, who was very supportive, and with the Treasury secretary, Bob Rubin, who, as I had been, was somewhat skeptical. A study was ordered and was positive and the legislation was prepared and eventually passed. The new State quarters were struck and the program succeeded beyond our wildest imagination—a new generation of coin collectors was born, and the government profited greatly without additional taxation. Since then, our Mint directors have been quite supportive of farsighted coin programs.

**Representative Michael Castle**

Programs for American Eagle gold and silver bullion coins have also proved to be very successful. The Mint, knowing the intrinsic and commodity value of platinum, and knowing platinum coins had been issued in other countries, strongly supported the concept of a new line of U.S. platinum bullion coins of a size which would be affordable to the public, but which would also provide profit to the Treasury in the form of seigniorage. Legislation was drafted and eventually passed by Congress in 1996 and the first American Platinum Eagle bullion coins were issued in 1997.

Following the initial launch, variations on design have been issued working with the Citizens Coinage Advisory Committee and the exceptional Mint artists. Our Mint directors, including the author of this book, Edmund Moy, have been helpful at every turn with the expanded coinage programs of the United States. We are all deeply indebted to them for making everyday coinage interesting, turning so many Americans (particularly children) into coin collectors, and aiding in opening a new stream of funding for the United States government that does not involve taxation. Their role in converting ideas and dreams into legislative reality, overseeing the actual designs to be implemented, and seeing to the final production of our coins has been exceptional. Politics may, from time to time, rear its head on Capitol Hill, but the Mint directors with whom I worked, Democrats and Republicans alike, always put their job ahead of whatever their politics may be, and the country has been well served for it.

**Michael Castle**
**Wilmington, Delaware**

Michael Castle, a graduate of Georgetown University Law Center, practiced law and served as deputy attorney general of Delaware and in the state legislature in the 1960s and 1970s. He was Pierre "Pete" du Pont's lieutenant governor in the early 1980s, then served as governor himself from 1985 to 1992. This public service was followed by nine terms as Delaware's sole member in the U.S. House of Representatives, where Castle worked on the House Financial Services Committee (with jurisdiction over the banking, securities, and insurance industries) and chaired the Subcommittee on Domestic and Monetary Policy. He coauthored the legislation that created the highly popular State quarters program, as well as the Mint's platinum bullion coinage.

# PREFACE

The U.S. Mint launched its groundbreaking American Eagle bullion program in 1986. Its coins rank at the top among the world's best-selling precious-metal investments, and yet for more than 25 years there was no definitive reference and history book on the subject. That changed in 2012 with the publication of John M. Mercanti's *American Silver Eagles: A Guide to the U.S. Bullion Program*, covering in detail one of the program's three precious metals.

Now Edmund C. Moy, retired 38th director of the United States Mint, takes us behind the scenes to explore the other two metals, in *American Gold and Platinum Eagles*.

As with their silver sisters, the Mint's gold and platinum bullion coins have been hugely popular with collectors and investors in the United States and around the world. More than 41 million of the coins have been purchased since 1986—in a dazzling variety of sizes, weights, surface finishes, packages, and designs. They are stockpiled by investors who value their stability, collected by hobbyists who seek the finest examples and strive to build complete sets, and treasured by aficionados who appreciate their fine artistry and historic design themes.

American Gold Eagles have been issued by the Mint since the bullion program's debut in 1986. Their sales give us a lens through which we can study broader threads of the U.S. economy and society. Investors bought a whopping 1.9 million ounces of the program's gold bullion in the first year, illustrating the pent-up demand for a good old-fashioned *American* source of government-guaranteed, investor-quality gold. Sales decreased—considerably—during the economic doldrums of the early 1990s, as American families cautiously held onto what money they had. Why did sales skyrocket back up into the millions of ounces in 1998 and 1999? Because people feared a much-ballyhooed economic meltdown at midnight, January 1, 2000—the infamous "Y2K"—and they flocked to a commodity immune from computer malfunctions and infrastructure failures. Sales boomed again in 2008 and 2009, after the American housing and banking markets collapsed; gold looked better and better as the U.S. dollar got weaker and weaker.

Platinum entered the scene in 1997 as the third metal in the American Eagle bullion program. Since their debut, American Platinum Eagles have offered collectors some of the most innovative designs in modern coinage. The series has also produced some of the *rarest* of U.S. coins, giving enthusiasts elusive targets to hunt for in their quest for a great coin collection. As has its gold coinage, the Mint's platinum products have given investors worldwide a solid, well-established commodity backed by the full faith and credit of the government of the United States.

One measure of the significance, popularity, and influence of a coinage series is how many entries it has among two indexes: the 100 Greatest U.S. Coins (for "classic" series), and the 100 Greatest U.S. Modern Coins (for more recent types).[1] The American Eagle bullion program boasts an impressive 22 rankings among the 100 Greatest U.S. Modern Coins—10 American Silver Eagles, 7 American Gold Eagles, and 5 American Platinum Eagles. This is a testament to the importance of these beautiful coins.

Until now, there has been no encyclopedic book-length study made on our nation's gold and platinum bullion programs. In *American Gold and Platinum*

*Eagles*, your guide is no less an authority than Edmund C. Moy—38th director of the U.S. Mint, who captained the nation's bullion-coin production during a turbulent period of unprecedented growth, when silver, gold, and platinum sales skyrocketed during the Crash of 2008 and the beginning of the Great Recession.

This book is an overview for the newcomer to these coinage series—the collector who wants a detailed but engagingly readable education in history, rarity levels, popular varieties, and market values. It's also a book for the long-time collector who wants a single-source reference: a guide not to be read once and then shelved, but to be kept handy for frequent visits and consultations. It's a textbook for the serious numismatist who wants an insider's view of the intricacies of design, production, distribution, and other technical and artistic factors. And for the investor this book introduces and explains the lure of numismatics—the art and science of the hobby of collecting coins—adding another aspect to the desirability of these interesting bullion issues.

To create this book, Edmund Moy has drawn on more than 30 years of work in the public and private sectors. In addition to his experience as an executive, strategist, and advisor in economic policy, finance, and investment, Moy for more than four years oversaw a Treasury bureau that is the world's largest manufacturer of coins, medals, and coin-related products—a highly efficient enterprise with 1,900 employees and operations in five states and the District of Columbia, including the main Philadelphia Mint, branch mints in Denver, San Francisco, and West Point, and the bullion depository at Fort Knox. As director of the U.S. Mint, he was singularly positioned to observe and direct operations including the American Eagle bullion programs. His firsthand knowledge and experience—both broad and deep—make him the perfect author for *American Gold and Platinum Eagles*.

A foreword by Representative Michael Castle, a longtime friend of coin collectors and coauthor of the platinum bullion legislation, presents the book and its distinguished author. Chapter 1 discusses the "Gold Rush" of 2008 and Director Moy's push into uncharted territory as the bullion markets went off the map. Chapter 2 is Moy's look at bullion-coin investment, decision-making, and market forces. Chapter 3 presents a history of the modern U.S. gold bullion coin program, with an overview of gold in American and world history. Chapter 4 explores platinum in the same light, and lays out the birth of the American Platinum Eagle program. In chapter 5 you get a detailed year-by-year study of each gold and platinum American Eagle, plus varieties and sets, with high-resolution photographs, rarity information, values, surface and strike characteristics, market details, and more. Several appendices offer you a compilation of the book's data in convenient chart format for easy coin-to-coin comparisons; illustrated overviews of other coins in our nation's bullion programs, setting the gold and platinum American Eagles in the context of a larger constellation of precious-metal coins; an illustrated catalog presenting the large body of coinage designs produced under Edmund Moy's directorship of the U.S. Mint; a bibliography for further research; and an index providing a convenient and detailed resource for looking up the book's information.

These diverse elements—technical and artistic, historical and current, market-driven and hobbyist—combine to make *American Gold and Platinum Eagles* a valuable addition to any collector's or investor's bookshelf.

# 1

# The Gold Rush of 2008

It was another hot, muggy day in Washington, D.C., in the late summer of 2008. Treasury Secretary Hank Paulson's eyes weren't as lively as usual, which I found out later was a telltale sign that he wasn't getting much sleep. America's subprime crisis had been with us since the spring of 2007, and the economic contagion had begun spreading to other countries. Just a few months earlier, Bank of America had bought the troubled lender Countrywide Financial. Fannie Mae and Freddie Mac were getting wobbly and needed some government help; and rumors were flying that Merrill Lynch & Co. and Lehman Brothers were in trouble because of some big housing-derivative bets.

Adding to my worries as U.S. Mint director: demand for circulating coinage had begun taking a nosedive. Our Mint analysts and Federal Reserve economists were having a hard time understanding the big drop, and hypothesized that this might become "the new normal" due to credit and debit transactions supplanting the use of cash. This raised the specter of whether we actually needed all of our manufacturing facilities. (Later, our data analysis proved that circulating coin demand was an indicator of retail sales, and the slump in orders from the Federal Reserve indicated that retail sales were slowing. For the most part, electronic transactions have gained at the expense of checking.)

**A 1980 view of the Treasury Building's southern façade, showing sculptor James Earle Fraser's statue of Alexander Hamilton, first secretary of the Treasury.**

**Henry "Hank" Paulson served as secretary of the Treasury from July 2006 to January 2009.**

We were in the Secretary's Conference Room, which is adjacent to the secretary of the Treasury's office in the historic Treasury Building, built starting in 1836. Twenty of us were sitting around a twenty-four-foot-long table with another twenty sitting around the perimeter of the room. We were the principals who attended the secretary's regular senior-staff meetings: presidential appointees with Senate confirmation, and the career heads of some of Treasury's operational divisions. Two feeble window air conditioners struggled vainly to keep the large room cool. They made a lot of noise, so we waited until the last minute to turn them to low so we could hear each other in the meeting. All of us wore jackets, and you could see and smell our losing battle with humidity.

Hank, as the Treasury secretary liked to be called, walked into the room in his shirtsleeves and sat in his usual chair at the middle of the table, with the windows behind him. His offensive-lineman physical presence (and he *had* in fact been a lineman, at Dartmouth) combined with a scary-sharp mind and a mouth that spewed forth equally scary-sharp questions. With a glance, he could read you and instinctively know if you were the real deal.

I had known him for a relatively short time. It had been Paulson's predecessor, Treasury Secretary John Snow, and President George W. Bush who agreed to my selection as director of the U.S. Mint. I had been a handy, quick nominee because my FBI background check was current, and as divine providence would have it, the Senate Banking Committee had an impending hearing set up for several nominees and invited me to join them. Chairman Richard Shelby (R–Alabama) and ranking member Senator Paul Sarbanes (D–Maryland) had a good laugh, ribbing me that I pulled a "Cheney"—meaning that as a special assistant to the president for presidential personnel, I was supposed to find Mr. Bush a candidate, but ended up being the candidate myself! There were three other nominees at the hearing, but I received a large share of the questions, and afterward got more than my fair share of questions for the record. I cannot tell you how relieved I felt when Senator Sarbanes said that I was well qualified.

After the committee voted to recommend my candidacy, I was unanimously confirmed by the full Senate on July 26, 2006, to become director of the Mint. I requested an early September swearing-in, so my wife Karen and I could travel to China in August to adopt our first child, our daughter Nora. The date we set was September 6. By that time, Treasury Secretary Snow had resigned and Paulson had been confirmed as of June 28, 2006. So the first time Hank and I met was in his office just before he swore me in. He teased me about becoming the 38th Mint director since 1792, and I teased back that I had twice his life expectancy, since he was the 74th Treasury secretary over the same period. He shared that he was looking forward to swearing me in, as I would be his first, and he graciously spent a generous amount of time with my wife Karen, our daughter Nora, my parents Tom and Rosa (who were awestruck in his presence), and my sister Donna.

My swearing-in took place in the historic Cash Room, chosen by President Ulysses S. Grant for the scene of his inaugural reception. It is easy to see why! Designed to look like a traditional European bank (because it had originally *been* a bank, where gold, silver, and paper currency were delivered until 1900), it has rich marble walls, ornate bronze gaslight chandeliers, and a checkerboard floor of red Lisbon and Italian Carrara marble. Today it is used for press conferences, formal meetings and receptions, bill-signing ceremonies, and official swearing-in ceremonies like mine and, later, Treasury Secretary Tim Geithner's.

**President George W. Bush, and John W. Snow, the secretary of the Treasury (February 2003 to June 2006) under whom Ed Moy was nominated for director of the U.S. Mint.**

The treasurer of the United States, Anna Escobedo Cabral, presided. Hank did the oath of office while wife Karen held our Bible, and I made a few short remarks. So began my relationship with Secretary Paulson.

**Ed Moy being sworn in as director of the Mint by Secretary of the Treasury Hank Paulson. His wife holds the Moy family Bible.**

The historic Cash Room of the U.S. Treasury Building—shown as it appeared not long after the American Civil War, and as it looks today—was the scene of Moy's swearing-in.

Newly sworn U.S. Mint director Edmund C. Moy and his family, with Treasury Secretary Hank Paulson, 2006. (Left to right: sister, Donna; wife, Karen, and daughter, Nora; Moy; Paulson; parents Tom and Rosa.) They stand before an oil-painting portrait of Alexander Hamilton, founder of the nation's financial system and first secretary of the U.S. Treasury.

Hank usually started off his senior staff meetings with something funny or interesting. Then, on to a short briefing on the things that were on his plate that week, tasking some attendees, or asking questions. Then we would go clockwise around the table and report anything going on in our areas of responsibility that he needed to know about. Hank appreciated brevity, clarity, and accuracy, and did not tolerate fluff or self-aggrandizement. It was better to take a pass if you had nothing to report.

Today Hank skipped his briefing and nodded to Deputy Secretary Bob Kimmitt, who sat on his left. Kimmitt reported and then we went around the table. Instead of actively listening, Hank seemed to be lost in thought.

My turn was coming up. Doug Shulman, the commissioner of the Internal Revenue Service, was giving his report two seats to my right. No matter how many times I've given reports, I still have some butterflies in my stomach, and today was no different. Trying to stave off a drying mouth and a perspiring head, I mentally practiced what I was going to say. For 2006 and 2007, gold and silver demand had been pretty steady at roughly 200,000 ounces of gold and 10,000,000 ounces of silver annually. Through July 2008, my reports had steadily indicated that we would likely double gold and silver bullion sales by the end of the year. But things had changed suddenly.

"Sir, demand for gold bullion coins is surging," I said. "Our sales jumped from 50,000 ounces in July to 86,000 ounces in August. Silver demand remains high."

He looked at me. "What's your gold forecast for calendar 2008?"

"600,000 ounces." (In hindsight, I was wrong. We sold more than 800,000 ounces that year.)

"Keep an eye on this. And get a better handle on demand."

The Washington, D.C., headquarters of the U.S. Mint.

"Yes Sir."

Relieved that my part was done, I let my mind wander as my peers finished their reports. When I snapped to, I found myself looking eye to eye with George Washington—that is, the portrait of George Washington attributed to Gilbert Stuart that was hanging on the wall to my left. What would he do if he were president today? What would he think about what we were doing in that room that morning? For now, I would have to be satisfied that we were under his watchful gaze.

The meeting ended with Chief of Staff Jim Wilkinson's report. At the time, I didn't give Hank's demeanor a second thought, chalking it up to the cumulative effect of managing a growing number of economic surprises. But just a little while later, during the week of September 15, 2008, the world's economy teetered on the brink of system-wide failure: Lehman Brothers failed, Bank of America bought troubled Merrill Lynch, Goldman Sachs and Morgan Stanley became bank holding companies, the federal government rescued AIG, and Congress refused the first TARP proposal, causing the Dow Jones Industrial Average to drop more than 700 points in one day. *Then* Hank's bleary, tired eyes made sense to me.

I left the Treasury Building to head back to my office at the U.S. Mint headquarters building, located six blocks away, near the Gallery Place Metro Station. It's a modern office building that houses our general management and administrative functions for sales and marketing, finance and accounting, legal services, information technology, public affairs, legislative affairs, manufacturing, and the office of our chief of the Mint Police.

It was my practice to schedule my own senior staff meeting right after the secretary's, so I could task my team immediately with any action items coming from his. We met in a large conference room nicknamed the Board Room, located on the top floor, near my office. About two dozen people attended in person and, at my insistence, the plant managers from West Point, Philadelphia, Denver, and San Francisco joined via teleconference. I called the meeting to order and gave a detailed debriefing on the senior staff meeting with special emphasis on Hank's conversation with me. After a lively discussion, I concluded that we needed to raise our game.

I asked my chief of staff, David Kim, Chief Strategy Officer Mike Stojsavljevich, and Chief Financial Officer Marty Greiner to better analyze and forecast the demand for the Mint's precious-metal bullion coins. Why didn't our sales of gold bullion coins mirror the activity of the gold bull run we'd seen since 2000? What factors explained the steep increase in demand during July and August 2008? Were the investors domestic or international? Institutional or individual? If individual, was the gold going into precious-metal retirement accounts or personal portfolios? What does gold demand and spot price best correlate with—oil? exchange rates? interest rates? inflation?

I asked my deputy director, Andy Brunhart, to pull together a task force to tackle the operational issues. If demand for precious-metal bullion coins grew beyond our capacity to meet it, how could we expand our production capacity? Does a third shift make sense? Do we need additional coining presses? What will be the lead time, and where do we put them? What are the supply-chain

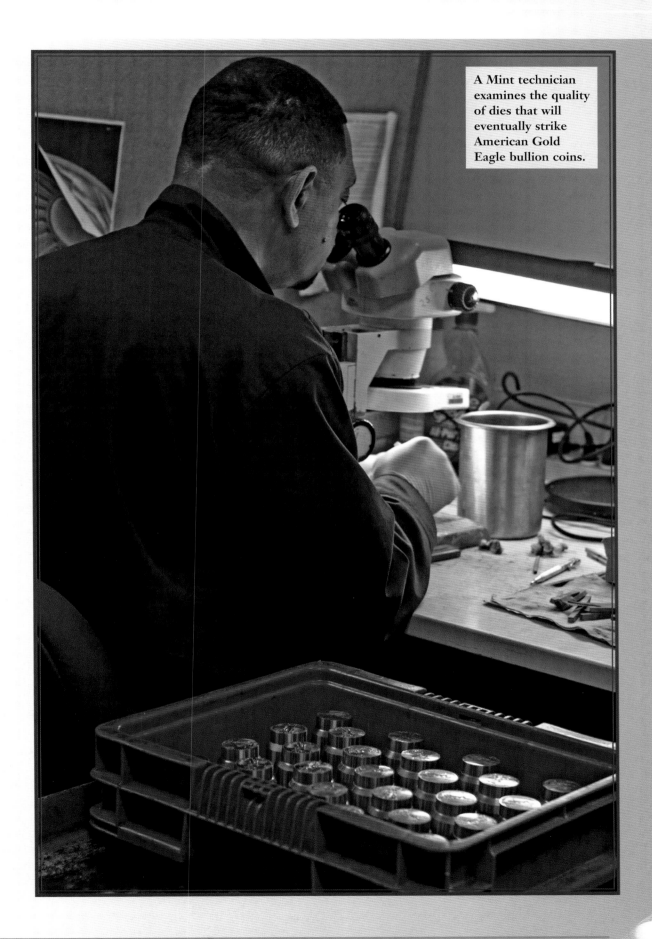

A Mint technician examines the quality of dies that will eventually strike American Gold Eagle bullion coins.

issues? How many vendors can produce the volume and quality we need? What is their lead time? Do they need long-term contracts, and if so, is that best for the taxpayer? Does the federal procurement process work quickly enough, or do we exercise our flexible authority; and if we do, can we write new policies quickly enough? What if demand drops and we're stuck with contracts to buy blanks that we are not going to use? What happens if demand exceeds supply? How do we allocate the existing supply fairly? Do we need more transparency in our pricing?

This was uncharted territory. The traditional theories and models that explained precious-metal bullion-coin demand weren't supplying adequate answers in this brave new world. What was needed was a much deeper and wider dive than ever before, extensive data-driven analysis, and new thinking to create a roadmap for the future. And because the United States Mint is the

**Coinage dies awaiting the production line— these will be used to mint 1/10-ounce $5 American Gold Eagles.**

largest mint in the world and has the responsibility to provide leadership to its industry, we needed to do this better than ever before.

As director of the Mint during that time, I am in a unique position to reveal some of what we learned. I've been immersed in the history and manufacturing processes of American gold-bullion coins, and I understand modern investors' interest in them, as well as the domestic and international factors impacting gold prices and demand. In this book, I will share my knowledge with you. My hope is to inform and educate, demystify gold investing for the uninitiated, help the gold investor (no matter how sophisticated) see a new thing or two, and add my inside knowledge to the historical, as well as the numismatic, record.

This book comes from my gratitude for the privilege I had of serving the American people during a consequential time in our country's history.

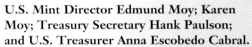

**U.S. Mint Director Edmund Moy; Karen Moy; Treasury Secretary Hank Paulson; and U.S. Treasurer Anna Escobedo Cabral.**

# 2

# Bullion Coin Investing: The Basics

**W**hen people find out that I was the U.S. Mint director, inevitably gold comes up in the conversation (platinum and silver, too). Typical questions range from "Isn't gold a barbarous relic in today's sophisticated financial world?" to "Why should I consider investing in gold?" to "If I wanted to invest in gold, what's the best way?" to "Does the Mint make gold bullion coins and where do I buy them?" In this chapter, I would like to answer the most common questions I get about bullion-coin investing.

Throughout recorded history, precious metals have been prized as a storehouse of value, and in recent centuries investors have rushed to them whenever governments, financial institutions, and currencies have shown signs of instability or uncertainty. Why is this? Most investments, like stocks, bonds, and cash, are based on the value of currency. As commodities and as currency, gold, platinum, and silver (and to a much lesser extent, palladium) have their own *intrinsic* value. Like a home or a work of art, they are tangible assets. And precious-metal coins have additional value coming from another direction: collectible value.

First, let's consider the *commodity value*.

Gold will always be in short supply in comparison with demand. Of course it is needed in jewelry making, coining, the decorative arts, and architectural ornament. Gold is even used for dental prosthetics. When I started seeing grills on rappers in the 1980s, I remembered the saying "what is old is new again," as I recalled a great-great-uncle who had several gold teeth. Since gold is impervious to chemical reaction with many other elements; reflects electromagnetic radiation; and is malleable, ductile,

**Gold miners with drilling equipment, Mogollon, New Mexico (June 1940).**

resistant to infrared penetration, and a good conductor, it has many practical uses. Protective coatings, printing, electronics, and shielding for space-bound vessels are just a few.

Platinum, too, has commodity value. It is likely that your car's catalytic converter and spark plugs contain some platinum, and a platinum compound could possibly save your life, since it is used in some cancer drugs. Platinum is even scarcer in the earth's crust than gold, and its physical and chemical properties, high melting point, and density make it superior for use in emission-control devices, electronics, and the chemical industry. Platinum's precious-metal value tracks consistently higher than that of gold, though its pricing has shown greater volatility.

Many precious metals have value as industrial commodities. Experiments in using platinum to make a type of photographic paper started in the 1830s and 1840s, when the metal was relatively inexpensive. The resulting paper was praised for its tonal range, permanence, and surface quality, and the platinotype print grew into a popular form of photograph through the early 1900s. Over time, however, platinum became more costly than silver, and it fell out of favor. By 1916 Eastman Kodak and other manufacturers stopped mass-producing platinum paper. The prints shown here were all made in the platinotype process; they date from the mid- to late 1800s and are archived in the Library of Congress.

Next is *currency value*.

For many centuries, alongside silver, gold served as the standard of value for currency. The first gold and silver coins, called *staters*, were issued by King Croesus, ruler of the kingdom of Lydia from 560 to 546 B.C. According to Harlan J. Berk in *100 Greatest Ancient Coins*, "Each gold coin had a corresponding silver coin of the same weight, with a value ratio of 13 to 1. Croesus's coinage thus became the first bimetallic, interrelated coinage and monetary system."[1]

A Lydian stater is shown here, enlarged. The coins were actually about the width of a modern Lincoln cent.

"**Croesus Receiving Tribute from a Lydian Peasant**" (**1629**), **by Claude Vignon, shows the wealthy king who introduced a type of gold coin called the** *stater.* **Croesus built his famous wealth from gold and electrum (a gold/silver alloy) found in the River Pactolus—where legend has it King Midas had washed away his cursed "golden touch," turning the river's sands into precious metal. (The 1893 painting by Walter Crane shows Midas despairing as his daughter transforms into a golden statue.)**

MIDAS' DAUGHTER TURNED TO GOLD

There is only one instance of platinum being used in circulating coinage: by Russia, between 1828 and 1845. Though Russia's platinum rubles were quite beautiful and more durable than their gold coins (because platinum is a harder metal), they looked a little too much like silver, and created confusion in the marketplace.

**During the reign of Czar Nicholas I, in the early 1800s, Imperial Russia used platinum in some circulating coinage—like this three-ruble coin of 1829. (shown 1.5x actual size)**

The U.S. Mint tinkered with platinum but never released any circulating coins struck in that precious metal. This mysterious Bust half dollar is one of only three such specimens thought to exist; according to *United States Pattern Coins*, 10th edition, "The circumstances of the production of the platinum 1814 half dollars are not known." In 1814 James Madison was president, the War of 1812 was in full swing, and that year the British would burn the U.S. Capitol building and the executive mansion in Washington, D.C.

When paper money was introduced to American history by the Massachusetts Bay Colony in 1690, it was intended to serve only as a convenient substitute for "hard money" and was redeemable at face value in gold or silver coins. When our Founders framed the Constitution, they recognized the need for a common currency and a government mint to make it, so they prohibited individual states from issuing their own currency ("bills of credit" or fiat money), but established that debts could be settled with gold and silver. Further, the weight of precious metal in the first federal coinage corresponded exactly to the value of the coin. The metal *was* the currency.

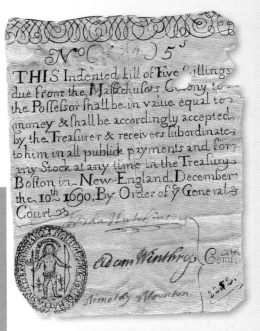

Massachusetts 5-shilling note of December 10, 1690.

## SIDEBAR: 21ST-CENTURY SPECIE

If you are a citizen of Utah, you can make purchases, pay taxes, and conduct business using gold and silver coins as legal tender. In March 2012, Governor Gary Herbert signed House Bill 157 to make his state the first in the country to allow it. The intent was not to supplant the dollar but to offer a constitutionally appropriate alternative currency. In the event of a sudden loss of faith in the dollar and other world currencies, Utah would have a legal basis at the ready for operating on another standard. The law also exempts the sale of gold and silver bullion coins from state capital-gains taxes. Individuals may store their bullion coins in a state-certified depository, which will issue a debit card to enable purchases backed by those coins.

Similar bills, or at least requests for studies to investigate the impact or necessity of such changes, have been forwarded to legislatures in 12 other states: Virginia, Colorado, Iowa, Minnesota, North and South Carolina, Tennessee, Georgia, Idaho, Indiana, Arizona, and Washington. Fiscal conservatives have led the charge. Some, like Virginia's Robert Marshall, are proposing these moves to ensure that alternative currency is available in the event a cyber-attack substantially disrupts everyday commerce.

In March 2013 Texas governor Rick Perry offered support for an initiative to create a Texas Bullion Depository, which would allow the state and its citizens to store gold bullion in a Texas-owned facility. Gold belonging to Texans would no longer be stored in federal depositories, and therefore could not be subject to, say, an executive order like President Franklin D. Roosevelt's, which required "all persons to deliver, on or before May 1, 1933, all gold coin, gold bullion, and gold certificates now owned by them, to a Federal Reserve Bank."

Opponents of these initiatives charge that setting up precious-metal currency standards for each state will erode the value of the dollar and potentially lead to exactly the kind of catastrophe their advocates are trying to guard against. Proponents counter with article I, section 10.1 of the U.S. Constitution, which asserts, "No state shall . . . issue bills of credit; coin money; or make anything but gold and silver coin a tender in payment of debts." The Utah bill does not compel citizens or businesses to spend or accept gold and silver in payment; it only gives them the power to do so immediately if needed.

Finally, precious-metal coins have *collectible value*. Factors such as antiquity, rarity, level of artistry, condition, and provenance can greatly enhance the worth of any precious-metal object, whether it is a tiara, tea set, ingot, bar, circulating coin, or bullion coin. Often, it is authentication and certification by a professional that establishes this increase in value. In the world of coins, we call this *grading*. (More on this later.)

No "barbaric relic" I know of has so many kinds of value! Considering that today's sophisticated financial world has given us such investment vehicles as credit default swaps and other derivatives that brought our global economy to its knees in 2008, many prudent investors are again looking to the time-tested investment of precious metals.

**Collectors value historic gold and platinum coins for far more than their precious-metal content. This 1839 British pattern coin shows young Queen Victoria as Una, a mythical character representing Truth and Purity, from Edmund Spenser's epic poem *The Faerie Queen*. Rich with historical importance, examples of this popular coin are worth tens of thousands of dollars—even though they only contain about an ounce and a half of gold. (shown enlarged)**

# MAKING THE INVESTMENT DECISION

Now that we've established that gold is a multi-faceted investment vehicle, is it right for you? What factors guide the decision to buy precious metals? Why not just own proxies for gold and platinum, like exchange-traded funds (ETFs), mining stocks, or gold futures and options?

My first consideration is that if I can't afford to lose all my investments, then I should jolly well invest in a product that has intrinsic value, and will always be worth *something*. There is no substitute for owning physical gold.

Stocks, futures, options, bonds, mutual funds, annuities, certificates of deposit, and similar investments all have a place in an investment portfolio, and they can bring great gains if you know what you are doing. But these are basically paper assets, and paper assets are only as strong as the market for them. To give them value, someone must be willing to buy. Metals will change in price, but their worth will never be completely wiped away by market conditions or panic (conversely, think of Lehman Brothers or MF Global Holdings).

This leads me to my second consideration. Precious-metal investment also reduces the risk of my currency-based investments becoming worth less because of inflation. Because gold has intrinsic value, historically it has tended to move in the opposite direction of the value of the dollar. If the value of the dollar goes up, the value of gold goes down, and vice versa. Most paper investments rely on paper currency. Paper currency's value is not intrinsic; it must rely on the full faith and credit of the government backing it. When confidence erodes in a government's ability to repay its debt, its currency falters. That's why so many investors view gold as an insurance policy. The suggestion here is not, like Scrooge McDuck, to amass a pool of gold coins deep enough for swan diving. I don't need an insurance policy that is bigger than my holdings. But I do like the idea of balance.

Gold has come to symbolize immense wealth in the popular imagination—an image that prolific American artist Carl Barks tapped into with his coin-hoarding character of Uncle Scrooge McDuck. (This 1952 comic book sold for $1,035 in a 2001 Heritage Auctions sale.)

My third consideration is what I call Plan B. We assume that we will always have the ability to carry out our lives under normal circumstances. But what if normal becomes abnormal? When Hurricane Katrina devastated the Gulf Coast, electricity was knocked out in some areas for weeks. ATMs, credit cards, and debit cards didn't work. The Federal Reserve ordered extra coinage from the Mint and had it delivered to terminals all over the impacted area, so that banks would have an adequate supply to meet the temporarily increased demand. Another potential threat to normalcy is the increasing number and sophistication of cyber-attacks on our interconnected banking systems. If these suddenly went offline and I couldn't access my account, I would have my Plan B stash of precious-metal bullion to bring me peace of mind. And for full disclosure, I was working in the White House on September 11, 2001, and one of the consequences of that experience was that it has made me ready for anything, which includes having a go-bag handy.

My fourth consideration is whether or not to own *physical* gold. Some investors favor gold exchange-traded funds (and their relatives, closed-ended funds and exchange-traded notes). The advantage of ETFs is that they benefit from the price of gold but the investor doesn't have to worry about storing the actual metal. Shares in ETFs rise and fall with the price of the physical gold the ETF is holding, while shares in ETNs rise and fall with the price of gold using derivatives in place of holding physical gold. While there are advantages to ETFs, their costs are generally higher than physical gold's, and they have greater risks (possible excessive leveraging by the custodian, some lack of transparency, and the potential to be worth nothing in the worst-case scenario). Ultimately, ETFs and their relatives are all paper proxies for gold. You can't redeem them for physical gold, and therefore they aren't useful as a currency or for a Plan B. ETFs can have a place in a portfolio but they do not have all the advantages of physical gold.

A personal supply of precious metal can bring peace of mind in case of manmade emergencies or natural disasters. In the aftermath of Hurricane Katrina, power outages disrupted normal banking and finance for weeks, and the Mint had to deliver extra coinage to meet demand in the affected areas. (In this photograph, U.S. Coast Guard Petty Officer 2nd Class Shawn Beaty looks for survivors in the path of the hurricane, over New Orleans, August 30, 2005.)

Finally, there are downsides to owning physical gold. The most obvious is theft. Physical gold requires physical storage, which should be safe, secure, and accessible, but there are associated costs. Buying or selling physical gold requires a physical transfer of the precious metal. It also requires a trustworthy seller who can ensure authenticity, quality, and a secure and discreet transaction.

Also, gold doesn't produce a dividend (it doesn't generate a profit and split with shareholders) or interest, nor does it create jobs. While gold has held its value better than stocks over the last decade, it has lost ground against stocks since the fall of 2011. Some say gold may have reached its peak in the summer of 2011 and can only go down. Eventually, the United States economy will recover and, as the dollar strengthens, gold prices will likely fall. And as an improving economy lifts the equity market over time, investors may jump back into the stock market in hopes of greater returns, which may cause gold prices to fall. Later in this chapter, I will discuss factors affecting the price of gold.

Buying gold coins usually involves a markup over the metal value, but at resale, only the metal value is recovered, so you lose the transaction and storage costs. Yet there are transaction costs for almost every investment, and gold should not be the majority investment in your portfolio.

If at some point my paper assets rise in value and my gold holdings take a corresponding dip in value, will I be kicking myself? Understanding the most advantageous ways to hold precious metals will certainly help in developing a strategy to mitigate those risks.

# WAYS TO HOLD PRECIOUS METALS

If you are going to own physical gold, what form is best? While there can be great pleasure in collecting and investing in jewelry, medallions, ancient coins, and U.S. gold coins produced before 1933, success in these arenas requires a fairly high level of expertise, years of study, and the inevitable period of trial and error.

Bullion in the form of bars and ingots is superior to jewelry as an investment and easy to obtain without a lot of expertise. These products benefit very-high-net-worth investors who want to buy thousands of ounces of physical gold and don't want the hassle of thousands of one-ounce bullion coins. But generally these formats are not produced or backed by governments. The level of confidence in their stated weight and purity correlates to the reputation of the manufacturer and supplier and must be corroborated with regular assay tests.

The easiest and most dependable way to enter the field for most investors is with bullion coins issued by government mints. Bullion coins are not intended for circulation, but are produced for the sole purpose of providing investors with the security and confidence of the official standards and specifications of a government treasury.

Not many people have the skills to identify, by eye, the metallic composition of an item, or the equipment to ascertain weight down to the milligram, or to perform some kind of assay test at home. There is no guesswork involved with bullion coins. They are guaranteed by governments, easily resold, and therefore are extremely liquid because they are readily convertible to cash or other assets.

While each government that makes bullion coins has its own appeal to certain investors, I have a bias toward U.S.–made gold and platinum bullion coins. To me, there is no other government whose guarantee means more, and for five years I was responsible for fulfilling that guarantee. I know the integrity of our procurement staff as they purchase only gold mined in the United States. I know the passion for accuracy of our assay team in testing the precious-metal blanks for purity, and the exacting standards for the blanks themselves. I know the dedication of our press operators who perform the precision minting of each coin, and the thoroughness of the quality-control staff that examines each coin before we release it to the public. In other words, when the U.S. government guarantees the weight, content, and purity of each bullion coin it makes, I know that investors can buy them with confidence.

## ALLOCATED VS. UNALLOCATED HOLDINGS

If you have decided to own gold or platinum bullion coins, there are more considerations to weigh before you buy.

Bullion can be held in two ways:

*Allocated holdings.* Say you bought five bullion coins from a dealer and put them in the safety-deposit box at your bank. Or you may have opened a special "allocated gold account" and paid a fee, and perhaps bought insurance, to have your purchases held at a

**Precious metals can be purchased in many forms, including bars, ingots, and coins. The "best" format depends on an individual buyer's circumstances and needs.**

depository. These coins are physically yours. They are secured against your name, account number, or other identifier that guarantees them as your property. When you open the deposit box, or make a withdrawal from the depository, you will retrieve the very coins you originally stored.

*Unallocated holdings.* This term defines a *value* in gold or other precious metal that is backed by physical precious metal held in trust by a bank or company on the account holder's behalf. You are purchasing a value equal to so many bars or coins, but specific bars or coins have not been set aside with your name on them. If you want to withdraw the value you have stored, you cannot redeem it as metal, since with the unallocated method you have not really purchased physical metal.

The obvious advantage, aside from peace of mind, with allocated holding is that it safeguards the *collectible* or *numismatic* value of your coins.

## TYPES OF BULLION COINS

Chapter 3 will go into depth on the history of the U.S. bullion coin program. But what are bullion coins, exactly?

As defined by authorizing legislation of a government, *bullion coins* are valued by their weight in precious metal and denominated in whole or frac-tional units of a troy ounce. Led by South Africa's 22-karat Krugerrands, first issued in 1967, today they are made in many countries. Our .9995 fine American Platinum Eagle bullion coins and 22-karat American Gold Eagle bullion coins are minted in four weights: one ounce, one-half ounce, one-quarter ounce, and one-tenth ounce. The weights of each coin may actually differ a little from the stated denominations: for example, the one-ounce platinum coin weighs 1.0005 ounce and the half-ounce gold weighs 0.5455 ounce. The standard is not in the scale weight but in the precious-metal content. These bullion coins contain the guaranteed weight in 22-karat gold (.9167 fine), or .9995 fine platinum. The addition of small amounts of silver and copper makes the gold bullion coin harder, reducing the potential for damage and wear. Until the last few decades, 22-karat gold bullion coins were the world standard.

Gold bars stacked in a vault at the West Point Mint (New York), June 2013; they will eventually be transformed into U.S. bullion coins.

**Bullion strike.**

**Proof strike.**

**Burnished ("Uncirculated") strike.**

Each coin has a corresponding face value proportionate to its weight. Some bullion coins have face values such as $5, $10, $25, $50, or even $100. These are largely symbolic because, by definition, a bullion coin is valued by the market value of its precious-metal content. But because they are legal tender, I suppose you could use a one-ounce gold bullion coin as a $50 coin if you'd like. I wouldn't advise it!

In the United States, authorizing legislation is needed to issue, or to alter the design, weight, composition, and/or face value of, any circulating or bullion coin. The same is true for *numismatic* bullion coins. Governments produce these variations to standard bullion coins for the pleasure of collectors, and by placing limitations on mintage, they unlock additional collectible value. For example, in 2006 the U.S. Mint issued a three-piece set of Proof $50 American Gold Eagles. This set included a novel numismatic variety, the "Reverse Proof." The mintage was only 10,000 and the sets quickly sold out. Today they are worth many times their original issue price. Varieties of U.S. gold and platinum eagles are:

*Bullion strikes.* This term refers to standard-issue bullion coins of the originally authorized design, which are struck at production speeds on regular, high-volume coining presses like circulating coins.

*Proof strikes.* The U.S. Mint began making special "Proof" strikes in the 1800s as special presentation pieces, and for sale to collectors. Today Proofs are made on highly polished dies at slower speeds and higher pressures than ordinary coins, and they are run through the press more than once. To keep them from picking up scratches or dents while passing through machinery or coming into contact with each other, the blanks are hand fed, one at a time, into the press. The resultant mirror finish allows design elements to stand out in crisp detail, and raised areas appear to have a frostlike surface. American Gold Eagle Proofs come in all four weights, while platinum Proofs are available only in the one-ounce size.

*Uncirculated or "Burnished" strikes.* Like Proof strikes, these bear the same designs as the original bullion coins and receive plenty of special handling, and in addition they carry a mintmark linking them to the facility where they were made. For American Gold Eagles, this is the West Point Mint (W mintmark). Uncirculated coin blanks are burnished (polished by buffing) before they are struck. Uncirculated American Gold Eagles are available only in the one-ounce size. The Uncirculated format is not available in platinum.

of each, have an impact. For example, as individuals, if we spend more than we take in, we go in the hole. If we go in the hole and no one gives us money, we are forced to either earn more money or spend less money. If we don't do either, we will go bankrupt. But if we are the biggest borrower of money at our bank, our bankruptcy will drag down everyone else. Banks cannot let this happen, so they make more loans to tide us over. This can buy time for us to work out a more balanced budget approach, but it doesn't help in the long run because it accommodates irresponsible behavior and gives no incentive for change. And the more money we owe, the bigger are our principal and interest payments, and the harder it is to pay them.

Now apply this individual example to our federal government. There is a further complication. Because the 14th amendment to the Constitution states that these principal and interest payments (the public debt) must be paid first (in order to maintain the full faith and credit of the United States, and therefore confidence in the dollar), solutions are needed for the huge problem of how to pay for the rest: that is, the very expensive activities of government. The stopgap recourse is to raise the debt ceiling. This in turn weakens faith in the dollar, which, as we have seen, drives up the value of precious metals. Hence the tight correlation between the level of the national debt ceiling and the price of gold.

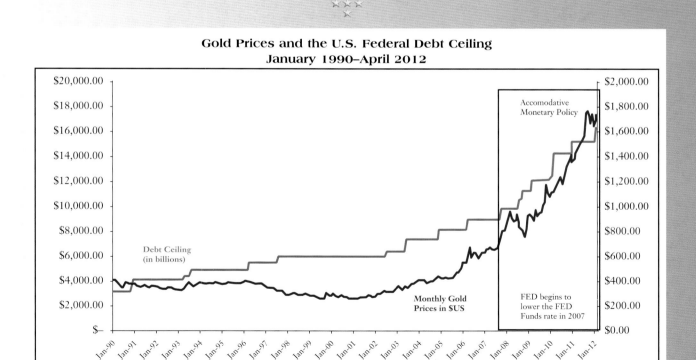

The chart above shows the correlation between gold prices and the Federal Debt Ceiling, with particular emphasis on the period of accomodative monetary policy starting in 2007. *Sources:* Fed, Bloomberg, Indexmundi, OMB, Congressional Research Service

Translating this back to personal finance: the best measure of how much you earn and spend and borrow (and how much you are really worth) is how close you are to maxing out on your credit line.

## WILL GOLD GO UP OR DOWN?

While some investment analysts have begun a public-relations effort to dismiss gold's value, one thing remains true. Sound fiscal and monetary policy is truly the only force capable of bringing the price of gold down, just as it did in the early 1980s. In today's economy, sound fiscal policy would include spending cuts, especially from entitlement reform, and increased tax revenues from tax reform and more tax receipts from a robust economy. That would enable the Federal Reserve to unwind the quantitative-easing programs with the smallest harm to the economy. Budgets that would be balanced or even showing a surplus in the near future would reduce the demand and price for gold.

However, if the economy's recovery is short of robust, and entitlement and tax reform is also short of robust, then the Federal Reserve will have to print more money to pay for spending (this is called "monetizing the gap"). More dollars chasing the same number of goods creates inflation. Inflation reduces the value of the dollar and serves as an accelerant to the price of gold.

Many economists forecast slow to mediocre economic growth in the United States for the foreseeable future. Few predict a dramatic improvement in our nation's fiscal or monetary policy anytime soon. Therefore, it is likely that the price of gold will continue to track with the level of the federal debt ceiling.

A point of caution: the likely rise in gold prices may be met with increasing short-term volatility. Because ETFs and hedge funds leverage their investments in gold with gold derivative products (coupled with a large number of investors attracted to gold prices and not physical gold), any changes in their paper gold holdings can have a proportionately large impact on gold prices. For example, the dramatic rise in gold prices beyond their correlated relationship to the debt ceiling was mainly caused by ETFs and hedge funds. Conversely, the dramatic drop in gold prices in April 2013 was similarly caused when momentum investors panicked. However, sales of physical gold actually increased to near-record levels.

Also, today's investors derive great meaning from any hint of change (earnings, unemployment, raising the debt ceiling, sequestration, a potential vacancy in the post of Federal Reserve chairman, etc.), and react accordingly. Watch, also, the instability of foreign currencies, especially compared to the U.S. dollar. Our economy may be on the road to full recovery (albeit a long and slow one), but the consternation in Europe over tottering budgets, drastic austerity measures, and the European Union's falling GDP has strengthened the dollar relative to the euro. Interest in the dollar as a safe-haven play may pause the rise in gold, providing an excellent buying opportunity for precious-metal investors. Finally, as some EU countries exhaust their bailout options, look for the possibility of countries such as Cyprus, Portugal, Spain, and Italy selling central-bank gold reserves to fund their bailouts. That will flood the market with large supplies of gold.

# How to Buy U.S. Mint Bullion Coins

The only American Eagles (silver, gold, and platinum bullion coins) you can buy directly from the U.S. Mint's online retail store (in limited quantities) are the numismatic versions like the one-ounce Proof and Uncirculated (Burnished) formats, and a few special boxed Proof sets. The half-ounce First Spouse series in Proof can also be purchased there in small quantities.

There is good reason why, as a private retail customer, you can't buy bullion strikes directly from the Mint. When establishing the program, legislators wanted to ensure a sustainable two-way market. The Mint maintains a small reserve fund as a hedge against losses in the purchase of precious metals (which is returned to the taxpayer through a transfer to the Treasury General Fund if not used), so it does not have the cash on hand to buy gold back on demand (nor does it have the authorization from Congress).

## The Authorized Purchasers Program

The Authorized Purchasers Program enables firms which *do* have the cash on hand (certain wholesalers, brokerage companies, precious-metal firms, coin dealers, and banks) to purchase the coins in bulk. They distribute them to retailers such as coin dealers and investment firms. They may also sell directly

*Numismatic* versions of the Mint's bullion coins can be purchased directly from the Mint's web site or catalogs. Bullion strikes, however, are available only through authorized resellers.

to the public. Firms must apply formally, and withstand a rigorous financial evaluation, to become Authorized Purchasers. The application criteria, limitations on volume, and pricing for each coin type are continuously updated at the Mint's web site, www.usmint.gov.

## Selecting a Retailer

So the sale of these government products is in the hands of the private sector. With more than 4,000 dealers and other retailers selling gold bullion, how do you select which one is right for you?

As director of the Mint, I saw first-hand the incredible growth of this market segment. While I had no direct regulatory oversight over gold-bullion dealers, I was ultimately responsible for overseeing the team that selected the Authorized Purchasers and made sure they were in compliance with our high standards. So afterward, when I began looking for a dealer for my own gold investing, you can imagine how picky I was. I wanted a dealer that scored high in all of my personal criteria: reputation, experience, volume, selection, and pricing.

Investors need to proceed with extreme caution. Gold's bull run over the last decade has attracted a lot of new customers, but it has also attracted a lot of new dealers. This has increased competition, which is good. But it has also brought to the market some unscrupulous sellers, some high-pressure sales tactics, and many inexperienced dealers. The U.S. Mint does not publish the list of its Authorized Purchasers, though it does provide a coin-dealer database while making it clear that it is only a sampling of local and national dealers and these dealers are not affiliated with nor are they official dealers of the Mint (because there are no such affiliations or official designations), nor is the Mint endorsing them.

A referral from a trusted friend who is satisfied with their bullion dealer can be a place to start.

Look for a firm that has a reputation for being transparent, fair, and honest. If they are not, complaints are usually a tell-tale sign. So research targeted firms with a consumer watchdog agency like the Federal Trade Commission and your state's attorney general. Objective third parties like the Better Business Bureau (www.bbb.org) for bullion coins and the American Numismatic Association (www.money.org) for numismatic gold and platinum coins can be helpful. Both the BBB and the ANA have an accreditation process for listing a company, and the BBB compiles ratings and reviews, and lists complaints. Find out about a firm's transaction policies and restrictions such as minimum amounts, accepted forms of payment (cash, bank wire transfer, cashier's check, personal check, company check, credit card, etc.), and how long you have to wait for delivery. Details of these policies should be clearly laid out for your examination. If older, numismatic versions of precious-metal coins are your true love, all the same dealer selection criteria apply. Begin with the ANA dealer list, at www.money.org/membership/dealer-directory.aspx.

AMERICAN NUMISMATIC ASSOCIATION

Trust your instincts. I'm turned off by high-pressure pitches ("buy now or you'll miss out on millions!") and claims that written risk disclosures are just a formality required by the government. Reputable sales professionals are clear about the risks. Beware of online dealers selling at big discounts (nobody stays in business selling to break even or lose money), pawn shops (how can you verify authenticity?), vending machines (mostly in Asia), and Craigslist ads. Be cautious with any dealer who has only an email address and no physical store or office. Avoid any online dealer who only accepts cash or bank wire transfers.

Reputations take a long time to build and can disappear in a moment, so consider experience too. I prefer a business that has been around since the last gold bull run (in the 1970s)—this ain't their first rodeo. If they've maintained a solid character through a boom and a bust, they will likely have the wisdom to handle the twists and turns of the bull run of the 2000s. Often, the reputation lies with an individual instead of a firm, so look over staff biographies for a well-established dealer with a long history of repeat clients. For a numismatic bullion-coin dealer, membership in the Professional Numismatists Guild (PNG, www.pngdealers.com) and/or International Association of Professional Numismatists (IAPN, www.iapn-coins.org) is a plus.

What is the sales volume of your targeted firm? It's easier to maintain a good reputation when there are only a few transactions per year. But to move hundreds of millions of dollars or even billions of dollars of precious-metal bullion requires excellent people, time-tested processes, and outstanding customer service.

What does the firm have for sale? Because I have high confidence in the authenticity and quality of bullion products of our Mint, I want to see a large selection of U.S. coins. Some international varieties (such as, but not limited to, Austrian Philharmonics, British Britannias, South African Krugerrands, Mexican Libertads, Canadian Maple Leafs, and Australian Kangaroos) are also welcome. More than a few dealers are now offering gold IRAs (see below).

## Pricing Factors

How do I know if a firm's pricing is fair? First, there is always a premium added above the spot price of precious metal in a bullion coin. This covers direct and indirect costs of making the coin. For example, the U.S. Mint charges 3% above spot for a one-ounce American Gold Eagle bullion coin sold to an Authorized Purchaser, which means if the spot price is $1,600, then its cost to the Authorized Purchaser is $1,648. The Authorized Purchaser then adds a slight premium above the $1,648 so they can make their money too. The retail dealer buying from the Authorized Purchaser must also tack on a slight premium.

Complicating this picture is the fact that the price of gold is changing every minute. Spot price affects your price in different ways, depending on the type of dealer. One dealer may hold inventory in house and ship directly to you. Another might broker the sale and have the coin drop-shipped from a larger wholesaler to you. There are also some dealers who do both, depending on what coin is purchased. The dealer holding inventory can hedge to reduce their risk of price fluctuations, while the dealer who brokers leaves hedging responsibility with their wholesaler. In either case, the dealer usually locks in the price to a customer at the time of a purchase. Both can be affected by price fluctuations and can lose money if the customer cancels an order. That's why some dealers require a signed, dated, binding agreement for the purchase of bullion coins.

It pays to comparison shop. Remember, you might not be comparing apples to apples. The highest prices could be from a gouger taking advantage of a new buyer, or they might reflect the addition of certain guarantees, premium shipping, and better customer service. Use a comprehensive approach, and especially beware of coins offered at spot price or slightly above spot. No one is going to sell you a bullion coin at the expense of the premiums they have paid, unless they have another angle for drawing your business—for example, you might have to commit to future purchases to get that initial discount, and later pricing will make up for it. Or the coins might have damage, wear and tear, or flaws that hurt their value.

**Do your homework before you buy. This will help you make wise purchases.**

Beware of buying bullion coins that will be delivered to a "secured facility" but not to you (with the exception of gold IRAs). Those coins might not be of the quality described, or worse, they may not exist! Beware of scam artists, whose preferred methods are significantly overpricing coins and/or trying to pass off ordinary bullion coins as rare numismatic coins. Some private mints and illegal mints have issued fake "bullion coins" that look like real bullion coins but have little or no precious-metal content. I have bought fakes (on purpose, as a reminder to be vigilant) of rare coins at street markets in China.

Remember, for one-at-a-time purchases of new *numismatic* versions of precious-metal bullion coins, the best place to buy is direct from the U.S. Mint. You need only visit the Mint's web site, www.usmint.gov. The procedures, official pricing, pricing criteria, volume discounts offered to Authorized Purchasers, mintages, and anticipated release dates of upcoming new issues are always posted for your review. Annual bullion and numismatic coin sales totals for each coin type are also reported. At the Mint, there can be no question about authenticity and there is no middleman markup.

## WHERE DO I STORE MY PRECIOUS-METAL BULLION PURCHASES?

Here are the typical options for bullion storage, on a sliding range from most secure to least secure (and conversely, least accessible to most accessible).

If you are a very large private investor, you probably already have accounts with a reputable private bank, have access to their vault services, and are storing their specified minimum value of bullion (usually $250,000) to qualify for vault space. Your bullion holdings might be not just in the United States, but also in London, Zurich, or Singapore, all well known for their bullion dealing and storage capacity. As the popularity of owning physical gold increases with smaller investors, more U.S. dealers are opening secure vaults or holding space at existing depositories to provide this service. On your behalf, they will transfer your gold to the storage facility, charge a fee for the space, and assess insurance based on the value of your bullion.

In smaller quantities, you can always store precious-metal bullion coins in your bank's safe-deposit box.

Those who want immediate access to their holdings are comfortable storing them in their home, usually in a hidden home safe.

**Precious metals can be stored securely in a bank vault, safe-deposit box, or home safe, depending on your situation.**

# WHAT IS A GOLD IRA?

The Taxpayer Relief Act of 1997 allowed for physical precious metals (gold, silver, and platinum) to be added to an IRA starting January 1, 1998. There are three key elements:

First, the law allows you to contribute gold bullion bars with a minimum purity of 0.995 fineness and NYMEX- or COMEX-approved refiner or assayer hallmark, and gold bullion coins with a purity of 0.9999 fineness (which includes the American Buffalo Gold Bullion Coin); and it includes an exception for the American Gold Eagle bullion coin (which is 0.9167 fine).

Second, your IRA custodian should be able to handle this transaction for you. If your plan does not allow you to contribute precious metals to your IRA, you will have to open a new gold IRA account, which an IRA custodian can help you do.

Third, you cannot be in physical possession of the precious metal in your IRA. The precious metal must be stored in an IRS-approved depository.

When I was the Mint director, I directed a team of analysts to come up with a better model to forecast demand for our bullion products. I specifically asked them to analyze the potential demand from gold IRAs, because I thought that many people would be attracted to this investment strategy. In the end, we concluded that while there were many advantages to gold IRAs, the administrative hurdles were too great for most investors. Buying the bullion coins was an easy step, but most IRAs do not allow contribution of precious metal. Once the investor located an IRA administrator willing to set up a "self-directed IRA," then that administrator had to handle the transfer of funds to the gold dealer and facilitate the physical transfer of gold from the dealer to an IRS-approved depository. It was a complicated transaction that only the most motivated and knowledgeable investors and IRA administrators could execute. No wonder none of the major brokerage or IRA administrators offers this product.

**American Buffalo and American Gold Eagle bullion coins may be added to an Individual Retirement Account.**

In the late 2000s, a few gold-bullion dealers began pulling together all these transactions into one simple one. The customer needs only select the bullion products desired, fill out some forms, and make a payment. The dealer, who has a standing contract with an IRA custodian, sets up the account, and coordinates the transaction, and the IRA custodian, who has a standing contract with an IRS-approved depository, physically transfers the purchased items. The custodian manages all the safeguard procedures, IRS filings, and administrative duties and reports them back to the customer. As a result, gold IRAs have quickly grown more popular as a form of allocated gold investment.

There are several investment advantages to a gold IRA. Because it is intended for the long term, the investor needs not monitor and/or worry through short-term spot-price volatility. The annual storage fees and fees to the IRA custodian are generally less than or equal to the management fees in a typical IRA. Finally, physical gold can be purchased by rolling over a portion of the existing IRA, which can be helpful if the investor has limited disposable income. What are the disadvantages? Gold prices may be down when it comes time for distributions, and IRA owners are usually on their own when selling their gold bullion coins for cash.

# SELLING YOUR PRECIOUS-METAL BULLION COINS

All of the criteria discussed in this chapter for selecting a dealer apply to *selling* your coins, as well, and if you have done your research at the outset, you already know your dealer's reputation as a bullion buyer. Most dealers will quote their buy prices over the phone, once you have supplied a description of the items you want to sell. Get multiple quotes if you wish, but make sure you have a very high level of confidence in each dealer you call.

Treat selling as seriously as you do buying.

The selling process is just the reverse of buying. At the time of sale you will enter a signed, dated agreement committing to a particular spot price no matter what direction the market might take during shipment of the metals and the corresponding return payment. Regular U.S. insured mail is an acceptable and safe shipment method, though some sellers prefer to deliver the goods in person.

An upside of selling off bullion-coin investments is that some transactions need not be reported to the IRS. While sales of kilo bars of gold, platinum, and palladium (containing 32.15 troy ounces) and 1,000-ounce quantities of silver coins or ingots are subject to reporting, many bullion-coin products are exempt. Get a clear understanding of the rules before you proceed to sale. Some good things to know:

One-ounce gold bullion and numismatic bullion coins only have to be reported in transactions of more than 24 coins, and this only applies to the South African Krugerrand, Canadian Maple Leaf, and Mexican Onza. The American Eagle, Australian Kangaroo, and Austrian Philharmonic gold coins are exempt.

There is no reporting on sales of gold bullion coins of less than one ounce in weight.

Among platinum bullion coins: American Eagles, Canadian Maple Leafs, and Australian Koalas are exempt in quantities under 25.

Russian palladium Ballerinas are also exempt in quantities under 25.

These rules are based on the commodity value alone. Numismatic value, of course, is assessed separately, and added to the bullion value as part of your dealer's price quote. The numismatic value of coins is also not reportable, and this has long made rare coins attractive to investors.

The earliest U.S. gold coins, minted under the presidency of George Washington, were of the *Capped Bust* design, featuring Miss Liberty and an American eagle. These motifs were used in the 1790s and early 1800s. (shown 1.5x actual size)

# 3
# History of the U.S. Gold Bullion Coin Program

**Y**ou might think Americans of the past had a much easier time of getting their hands on U.S. gold coins than we do today, because between 1795 and 1933 the Mint produced them for circulation, to be spent in everyday commerce. However, that wasn't necessarily the case.

## 1795 TO 1933: THE HEYDAY OF CIRCULATING U.S. GOLD COINS

The Mint Act of April 2, 1792, established our national monetary standard on both gold and silver (known as a *bimetallic* standard), setting the relationship between the two metals at 1 to 15: one ounce of gold was worth 15 ounces of silver. The first three denominations minted in gold for this system were the half eagle ($5), the eagle ($10), and the quarter eagle ($2.50).

From the start, the Treasury faced a problem: the $10 coins quickly sailed away on ships to Europe, where the gold-to-silver ratio was 1 to 15-1/2. Eagles disappeared as fast as they were minted, and half eagles after them.[1] Assurance of supplies for the use of American citizens was one of the reasons why the Act of June 28, 1834, reduced the authorized weight of gold coins to the point where their bullion value was just a little less than their face value. This act also fixed the value of gold at "ninety four and eight tenths of a cent per pennyweight," or $18.96 per troy ounce.

After the California Gold Rush of 1849, it seemed that everyone had one of the new $1 gold coins in their pocket, while the big wheels in California tossed about the prestigious new $20 double eagles. The San Francisco Mint opened in 1854, and in the same year a $3 gold coin was introduced. In 1863 the opening of the Denver Assay Office (which later became a mint) added capacity needed to absorb bullion from another gold rush in Colorado.

Examining mintage records for the various coining facilities, however, doesn't provide a clear picture of how many gold coins were in circulation at any given time. The intrinsic value of precious-metal coins caused a problem: it encouraged hoarding in times of financial disruption. Just as on a sinking ship when the least valuable articles are jettisoned first, people did business with fungible currency like paper notes, copper tokens, and scrip, or through barter, and held tight to their precious-metal coins. It happened during the "hard times" banking crisis of 1834 to 1844, and to a greater extent during the Civil War (1861 to 1865), when even U.S. postage stamps had to serve as currency.

In 1873, in spite of vigorous pressure from Nevada and Colorado silver-mining interests, Congress passed a coinage act that demonetized silver, to align with many world nations which, by then, had moved to the gold standard. Later, presidential candidate William Jennings Bryan ran (in 1896, 1900, and 1908) on a "Free Silver" platform in hopes of returning America to a bimetallic standard. In 1900, after defeating Bryan for the presidency, William McKinley effectively cut silver from the equation by signing the Gold Standard Act of 1900. It established gold as the official foundation for U.S. currency, and set the unit of value for the dollar as "twenty-five and eight-tenths grains of gold nine-tenths fine," which worked out to $20.67 per troy ounce. Paper currency, for example the dollar bill, could be freely converted into gold at this fixed exchange rate.

The flood of newly mined American gold that started in the late 1840s was channeled into several new coinage denominations—the gold dollar (first struck for circulation in 1849), the $20 double eagle (introduced for commerce in 1850), and the $3 gold piece (which debuted in 1854). (shown 1.5x actual size)

After being elected president in 1900, William McKinley helped to set gold as the nation's financial backbone.

## USE ME FIRST: SPENDING MONEY IN THE 1800S

Even in the best of times during the 1800s—but especially when finances were tight—Americans would first spend paper money, copper tokens, scrip, and base-metal coins (such as those seen here), saving their silver and gold coins as long as possible.

**Tablet 11 of the Epic of Gilgamesh, telling the story of Utnapishtim and how he saved his gold and silver treasure in the great flood. (British Museum collection)**

# SIDEBAR: GOLD IN HISTORY AND CULTURE

Our attitudes toward gold have been around at least as long as humans have known how to write. Clay tablets of the ancient Mesopotamian "Epic of Gilgamesh," thought to be the oldest written story on Earth, make reference to gold and silver. Versions exist that date from 2500 to 1000 B.C. In one part of the story, the painfully smitten princess Ishtar tempts her hero, Gilgamesh, to marry her with offers of a chariot of lapis lazuli and gold, "with wheels of gold and horns of electrum." Another part describes the building of a boat in preparation for a great deluge, similar to the one in the Noah's Ark story of the Bible. Here the shipbuilder was called Utnapishtim, and he loaded "all the living beings that he had," and "all the living beasts of the field," and "all of his gold and silver" into a boat made of rushes, reeds, and wooden poles, and survived the ensuing storm and flood with his family and his wealth intact.

More familiar in Western cultures is the Biblical description of the four rivers of Eden in the second chapter of Genesis: "The name of the first is Pishon; it is the one which skirts the whole land of Havilah, where there is gold. And the gold of that land is good." The New Testament has the account of the Magi, distinguished foreign emissaries or "wise men" who traveled to Bethlehem to pay homage to the baby Jesus. Arriving by night, they presented gifts of gold to Joseph and Mary, along with frankincense and myrrh. This gold was thought to have financed the holy family's flight to Egypt after the frightened parents learned that King Herod planned to kill their infant son.

Due to its excellent properties of corrosion resistance, gold survives unchanged for thousands of years, even if buried in soil, submerged in

**The adoration of the Magi is shown in this illuminated manuscript page from the *Book of Hours*, created in Zwolle, Netherlands, around 1470. *Illumination* in this context refers to a book page's decoration with gold.**

water, or exposed to extremes of temperature. In the 1870s German businessman and archaeological explorer Heinrich Schliemann excavated fabulous Bronze Age masks, belts, bracelets, cups, and daggers of gold at the sites of Mycenae in Greece and Hissarlik (ancient Troy) in Turkey. His finds proved that Homer's story *The Iliad* was based on real historical events, and attested to the extent of Aegean trade in precious goods between 1600 and 1100 B.C.

In 1922, Englishman Howard Carter astounded the world when every news service breathlessly reported the discoveries of his expedition to locate Egyptian pharaoh Tutankhamen's tomb. A passage from Carter's 1923 account of the tomb opening (from *The Tomb of Tut Ankh Amen*) kindles excitement even today:

The Mask of Agamemnon—a gold funeral artifact uncovered by Heinrich Schliemann in 1876 at Mycenae—is currently displayed in the National Archaeological Museum in Athens, Greece.

I suppose most excavators would confess to a feeling of awe—embarrassment almost—when they break into a chamber closed and sealed by pious hands so many centuries ago. For the moment, time as a factor in human life has lost its meaning. Three thousand, four thousand years maybe, have passed and gone since human feet last trod the floor on which you stand, and yet, as you note the signs of recent life around you—the half-filled bowl of mortar for the door, the blackened lamp, the finger-mark upon the freshly painted surface, the farewell garland dropped upon the threshold—you feel it might have been but yesterday.

That is the first and dominant sensation, but others follow thick and fast—the exhilaration of discovery, the fever of suspense, the almost overmastering impulse, born of curiosity, to break down seals and lift the lids of boxes; the strained expectancy—why not confess it?—of the treasure-seeker.

Surely never before in the whole history of excavation had such an amazing sight been seen as the light of our torch revealed to us—a roomful—a whole museumful it seemed—of objects, some familiar, but some the like of which we had never seen, piled one upon another in seemingly endless profusion. Gradually the scene grew clearer and we could pick out individual objects. First, right opposite to us, were three great gilt couches, their sides carved in the form of monstrous animals, curiously attenuated in body, but with heads of startling realism. . . . Next, on the right, two statues caught and held our attention; two life-sized figures of a king in black facing each other like sentinels, gold kilted, gold sandalled, armed with mace and staff, the protective sacred cobra on their foreheads. . . .

Long before Carter, treasure seekers had traveled the world looking for precious metals. Tantalized by Marco Polo's tales of Cipangu (Japan) and its endless wealth of golden objects, Christopher Columbus set off on a voyage to locate a Western sea route to the remote isle, and inadvertently discovered America. Legends of El Dorado launched the Age of Discovery (as well as the advances in navigation and cartography that made it possible). Once European governments fully realized the extent of the riches lying untouched in the West, wars for territory and supremacy followed. Continents were explored, natives were conquered, and gold was mined. Precious-metal discoveries have continued to drive population shifts. California, Alaska, Australia, New Zealand, South Africa, and Brazil have all seen their gold rushes, and even with today's strict nationalistic regulation of mining, where there are precious metals in the ground, there are thriving international communities nearby.

It is difficult to think of a world religion that has not shown reverence for its gods, mythical heroes, saints, or other holy figures with sculptures of gold. Gilded statues of the Buddha, the Hindu elephant god Ganesha or eight-armed goddess Kali, or the helmeted Joan of Arc on her rearing golden mount, spring to mind. Secular honors today must also be golden—like that coveted little Oscar awarded in California once a year, or the most prized Olympic medals.

Many cultural traditions revolve around the giving of gold as a gift. The 17th-century Hannukah gelt tradition of Polish Jews changed somewhat in 1958 when the Israeli government began minting collectible gold coins. These bore the Menorah symbol first used on the Maccabean coinage of the second century B.C. (Today, coin-shaped chocolate versions wrapped in golden foil proliferate.)

In the Chinese Spring Festival celebrating the Lunar New Year, families host a "reunion dinner," set off firecrackers, and make gifts of gold coins. Likewise, golden wedding gifts represent all the good things guests wish for the future of the married couple. The five-day Hindu festival Diwali (called the Festival of Lights) in India and South Asia is another occasion where golden gifts are considered a lucky omen, accompanied by the lighting of many candles and launching of fireworks.

**The richly decorated golden burial mask of the Egyptian boy-king Tutankhamen.**

# THE FABULOUS SAINT-GAUDENS GOLD COINS

Many words can be used to describe American gold coins minted during the century following our country's founding, but *beautiful* is not one of them. In 1905, President Theodore Roosevelt aimed to change that. He believed that the state of our coinage was "artistically of atrocious hideousness."[2] "TR" believed that coins were an extension of a nation's identity and our coins were telling the world that we were a European country. After 125 years, the boldest experiment in liberty had not only succeeded, but also had come of age. America was here to stay. Didn't it deserve coins that told the world what made the United States unique and a leader on the world's stage?

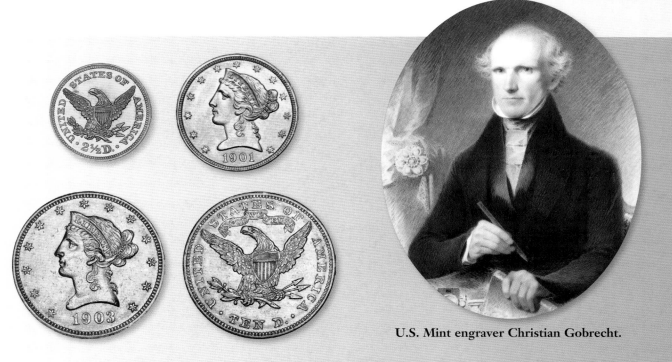

U.S. Mint engraver Christian Gobrecht.

**By the early 1900s, America's gold coins were aesthetically worn out and dated—Christian Gobrecht's Liberty Head design had been on the smaller denominations since the late 1830s, and James B. Longacre's Liberty Head on the double eagle since the 1850s. President Theodore Roosevelt felt it was time for more forceful, dynamic, and uniquely *American* designs. (shown 1.5x actual size)**

**Mint engraver James Barton Longacre.**

**President Roosevelt was inspired by the beautiful high-relief coinage of the ancient Greeks. (shown enlarged)**

It was a time of great innovation, patriotism, and flowering of the arts. Sculptor Augustus Saint-Gaudens's highly acclaimed work on various public memorials exuded vitality and excitement and a very American look, and awakened citizens to what could be achieved when a great artist made designs for the people. At the president's invitation, Saint-Gaudens sculpted what many believe is the most beautiful coin ever made: the MCMVII (1907) Ultra High Relief double eagle.

After studying the gold coins of ancient Greece, Roosevelt had concluded that the most beautiful ones were minted in high relief—that is, their design elements emerged from the background (field) to a level 50 percent higher than the coin's surface. Saint-Gaudens suggested the obverse of the double eagle depict Liberty as a strong and beautiful woman, "striding energetically forward as if on a mountain top," with her hair and "the drapery (of her gown) . . . flowing in the breeze."[3] The leading hand would hold "perhaps a flaming torch," and the other would hold aloft a shield with the word "Liberty" marked across it. In the final design, which was a compromise between the ideas of Saint-Gaudens and Roosevelt, Liberty holds an olive branch in her trailing left hand. Behind her shine the rays of the rising sun, and the U.S. Capitol dome can be seen in the distance. Ringing the field near the rim are 46 stars, representing the states of the Union at the time (two more stars would be added in 1912). On the reverse is a soaring young bald eagle flying at sunrise.

**Sketches and an early plaster of Saint-Gaudens's striding Liberty design as a work in progress.**

Saint-Gaudens's design succeeded in visually embodying America. Liberty is at the center of the coin and is the center of our country's values. Liberty is rooted in Western civilization, as represented by the Grecian/Roman gown she is wearing. (Depicting Liberty in her entirety and facing forward was a dramatic departure from European coins, which featured heads in profile.) The Capitol dome is the physical embodiment of our representative democracy, which Liberty has firmly established in the United States. She now is marching confidently into the rest of the world. The high relief of Miss Liberty makes her appear to be striding straight toward the viewer, further emphasizing that Liberty is moving forward. The torch would symbolize God for the Christian and other faithful and enlightenment for the secular, and the olive branch means peace. Wherever Liberty goes, when led by God or enlightenment, peace will follow. And on the reverse, a young America is soaring powerfully upward with the dawn of her day.

The president loved it, and the first coins of this design were struck in 1907.

Augustus Saint-Gaudens's original design for the double eagle was retained, with some alterations to the date style, the legends, the depth of relief, and the number of obverse stars, until 1933. The MCMVII (1907) Ultra High Relief version is ranked no. 2 among the 100 Greatest U.S. Coins (in the book of that title by Jeff Garrett and Ron Guth). (shown 1.5x actual size)

For the obverse of the $10 gold eagle, Roosevelt's concept and Saint-Gaudens's design were equally distinctive. Around this time, historians were coalescing around the theory that what had forged American democracy was the pioneer spirit embodied in the process of moving westward. America may have been launched in the European-looking neighborhoods of New York's financial district, Philadelphia's Center City, or Boston's Back Bay, but it had evolved to include the rough-and-tumble raw energy of Chicago, St. Louis, Denver, and San Francisco. Roosevelt believed it was the battles between the pioneers and the Indians that had forged a new people and thus he asked Saint-Gaudens to place a Native American war headdress on the head of Miss Liberty. On the reverse, a fiercely determined eagle stands guard, symbolizing America's passionate commitment to defend Liberty.

Both of these Saint-Gaudens gold-coin designs are beloved of coin collectors and bas-relief sculpture enthusiasts alike.

# THE END OF GOLD IN CIRCULATING U.S. COINAGE

America's minting of gold coins for everyday use came to an abrupt end in 1933. The change was triggered by the most devastating economic emergency in U.S. history, the Great Depression. The

**President Theodore Roosevelt took a personal interest in the work of August Saint-Gaudens, and encouraged him to turn his creative genius to the nation's coinage. The sculptor's Indian Head design for the gold eagle ($10 coin) was used from 1907 until the denomination ended in 1933. "The obverse . . . shows the head of Liberty crowned with an Indian war bonnet," notes the *Guide Book of United States Coins*, "while an impressively majestic eagle dominates the reverse side." Roosevelt was quite pleased. (shown 1.5x actual size)**

essence, to a fiat currency and launching the era of free-floating gold prices we have today.

Because the United States is still technically in default of payments to some foreign countries at the 1977 price, the federal government is obligated to record its reserve gold on the books at $42.22 per troy ounce.

Another outcome of the 1970s currency moves was that it no longer made any sense to prohibit private ownership of gold. To the relief of many, Congress under President Gerald Ford issued Public Law 93-373, finally revoking the 1934 ban. This opened the door for a renaissance in collecting and investing in precious metal.

**U.S. Treasury Secretary Henry Morgenthau Jr. and British economist John Maynard Keynes confer during the Bretton Woods international monetary conference to plan for postwar reconstruction, July 1944.**

**It was under the administration of President Gerald Ford that the gold-ownership prohibition of the early 1930s was finally lifted.**

South Africa launched its gold Krugerrand in 1967 as an international vehicle for investing in government-backed bullion. The coin features a portrait of President Paul Kruger (a hero of South Africa's late-1800s struggle against European control) and a leaping springbok antelope.

An early American foray into the gold-bullion market: examples of the American Arts Commemorative Series medals of the early 1980s.

# THE BIRTH OF THE BULLION MARKET

Today's competitive international market for precious-metal bullion coins was evolving well before U.S. Public Law 93-373. With the demise of the gold standard, South Africa became the first nation to produce gold coins valued for their metal content and specifically used for financial investment purposes. It released the popular one-ounce gold Krugerrand in 1967. Americans could not purchase Krugerrands until 1994, however, because our government's anti-apartheid sanctions against South Africa forbade such investments. Canada saw its opportunity and in 1979 launched a one-ounce gold Maple Leaf coin (which debuted at .999 purity, increased in 1982 to .9999). Americans were eager to get into the game, and Congress agreed, but was hesitant to create a new legal-tender gold coin in which the purity, weight, and quality would be guaranteed by the government.

In 1978, in spite of some opposition from the Treasury Department, Congress passed legislation sponsored by North Carolina senator Jesse Helms authorizing an "American Arts Commemorative Series" of gold medals. These half-ounce and one-ounce pieces were intentionally designed *not* to look like typical U.S. coins. Featuring portraits and scenes honoring 10 distinguished American contributors to the arts, they were available between 1980 and 1984, but sales performance was weak in comparison to monetized issues such as the Krugerrand, Mexico's Libertad (1981), and China's gold Panda series (1982).

Canada, seeing the success of South Africa's gold-bullion program, would introduce its own market entry, the Maple Leaf, in 1979.

# THE GOLD BULLION COIN ACT OF 1985

In the mid-1980s, America had just emerged from a recession so deep it added the term *stagflation* to our lexicon. During this time of great economic uncertainty, gold had a historic bull run as investors sought a safe haven from currency-backed investments eroded by inflation. Because the United States did not make any monetized gold coins and American investors were denied access to the Krugerrand, Congressman Ron Paul (R–Texas) led the effort to pass legislation authorizing the U.S. Mint to make a 22-karat gold bullion coin. President Ronald Reagan was enthusiastic about the potential for a true bullion-coin program and supported the development of a competitive U.S. product for the world bullion market.

Like most pieces of legislation considered by the United States Congress, the final version of this act was a few iterations removed from its first proposal. It began in the first three months of 1983. In January, Ron Paul introduced a bill known as the Monetary Freedom Act, which was intended to set the stage for the issuance of a monetized gold bullion coin. This ambitious proposal would amend the Gold Reserve Act of 1934 to require congressional authority to sell gold bullion, and would prohibit the government from having the power to seize gold or require its exchange for other U.S. currency (as had happened in the 1930s). It would direct the secretary of the Treasury to redeem in gold all Federal Reserve and U.S. notes, and make gold the money of account of the U.S. government. It would require all banks to keep sufficient money in their possession at all times to cover all outstanding promises to pay a sum of money on demand, and authorize any association of persons who filed an organization certificate to carry on the business of banking.

The bill was referred to the House Subcommittee on Financial Institutions Supervision, Regulation, and Insurance, and died there.

Undaunted, in February Paul submitted a bill he called the American Gold Eagle Act of 1983, which directed the secretary of the Treasury to mint two weights of gold bullion coins called *American Eagles*, and set forth their specifications. Coins minted under this act would not be legal tender for public debts, public charges, taxes, duties, or dues, but could be used for the payment of private debts. The proposal would also permit the exchange of gold bullion for American Eagle coins.

This bill, which had seven cosponsors, was referred to the House Committee on Banking, Finance, and Urban Affairs, where it died.

In March, Paul introduced a full alternative version, the Coinage Act of 1983. This authorized the secretary of the Treasury to mint and issue gold and silver coins in several denominations, and established the *silver dollar* as the unit of account of the United States. It sought to require by law all financial records to be maintained in terms of gold coins, silver coins, or the unit of account of the Federal Reserve System. It prohibited the United States or any state from: (1) imposing an excise, transaction, or capital-gains tax upon the use of gold or silver; or (2) restricting the convenient transfer of any ownership or equity interest in gold or silver; and provided that gold and silver should not be prohibited as lawful tender in payment of debts. Under this proposal, the secretary of the Treasury would establish a formula for determining on an hourly basis

**Congressman Ron Paul, a proponent of gold bullion and financial reform (pictured here from the 1980s).**

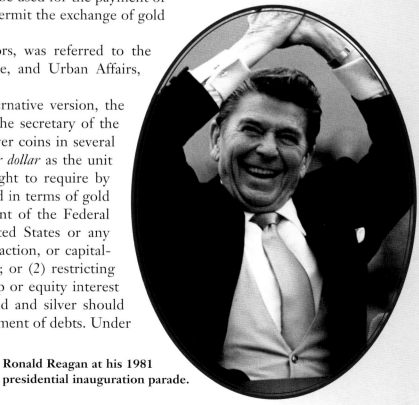

**Ronald Reagan at his 1981 presidential inauguration parade.**

the official conversion rate between gold, silver, and the unit of account of the Federal Reserve System, and would then allow the exchange of gold bullion, gold coins, silver, or silver coins for their equivalent fine weight in coins minted by the United States. Finally, the bill would prohibit both the secretary of the Treasury and the treasurer of the United States from issuing, or authorizing to be issued, any form of paper currency.

Ron Paul's proposals were so comprehensive and far-reaching that they stood little chance of making it into law. They did, however, draw attention to the need for revision of federal law regarding bullion-coin production and, at the very least, they highlighted the need for a bullion investment coin. In March 1985, Senator Jake Garn (R–Utah) and Senator J. James Exon (D–Nebraska) each introduced bills to the Senate to amend Title 31 of the United States Code, to authorize one ounce, one-half ounce, one-fourth ounce, and one-tenth ounce gold coins. Their bills also died in the hands of the Banking, Housing, and Urban Affairs Committee, but a later version of Exon's, Senate Bill 1639, made it to President Ronald Reagan's pen.

**Senators Jake Garn of Utah (seen walking with President Reagan) and J. James Exon of Nebraska both sought legislation that would authorize production of U.S. gold bullion coins.**

Complete text of the Congressional Act

**An Act**
To authorize the minting of gold bullion coins.

*Be it in enacted by the Senate and House of Representatives of the United States of America in Congress assembled.*

SHORT TITLE
Section 1. This Act may be cited as the "Gold Bullion Coin Act of 1985".

MINTING GOLD BULLION COINS

Sec. 2. (a) Section 5112(a) of the title 31, United States Code, is amended by adding at the end thereof the following new paragraphs:

"(7) A fifty dollar gold coin that is 32.7 millimeters in diameter, weighs 33.931 grams, and contains one troy ounce of fine gold.
"(8) A twenty-five dollar gold coin that is 27.0 millimeters in diameter, weighs 16.996 grams, and contains one-half troy ounce of fine gold.
"(9) A ten dollar gold coin that is 22.0 millimeters in diameter, weighs 8.483 grams, and contains one-fourth troy ounce of fine gold.
"(10) A five dollar gold coin that is 16.5 millimeters in diameter, weighs 3.393 grams, and contains one-tenth troy ounce of fine gold.

(b) Section 5112 of title 31, United States Code, is amended by adding at the end thereof the following new subsection:

"(i) (1) Notwithstanding section 5111 (a)(1) of this title, the Secretary shall mint and issue the gold coins described in paragraphs (7), (8,) (9), and (10) of subsection (a) of this section, in quantities sufficient to meet public demand, and such gold coins shall

"(A) have a design determined by the Secretary, except that the fifty dollar gold coin shall have –
"(i) on the obverse side, a design symbolic of Liberty; and
"(ii) on the reverse side, a design representing a FAMILY OF EAGLES, with the male carrying an olive branch and flying above a nest containing a female eagle and hatchlings;
"(B) have inscriptions of the denomination, the weight of the fine gold content, the year of minting or issuance, and the words 'Liberty', 'In God We Trust', 'United States of America', and 'E Pluribus Unum', and
"(C) have reeded edges.

"(2)(A) The Secretary shall sell the coins minted under this subsection to the public at a price equal to the market value of the bullion at the time of sale, plus the cost of minting, marketing, and distributing such coins (including labor, materials, dies, use of machinery, and promotional and overhead expenses).

"(B) The Secretary shall make bulk sales of the coins minted under this subsection at a reasonable discount.

"(3) For purposes of section 5132(a)(1) of this title, all coins minted under this subsection shall be considered to be numismatic items".

(c) Section 5116(a) of title 31, United States Code, is amended by adding at the end thereof the following:

"(3) The Secretary shall acquire gold for the coins issued under section 5112(i) of this title by purchase of gold mined from natural deposits in the United States, or in a territory or possession of the United States, within one year after the month in which the ore from which it is derived was mined. The Secretary shall pay not more than the average world price for the gold. In the absence of available supplies of such gold at the average world price, the Secretary may use gold from reserves held by the United States to mint the coins issued under section 5112(i) of this title. The Secretary shall issue such regulations as may be necessary to carry out this paragraph".

(d) Section 5118(b) of title 31, United States Code, is amended –
(1) in the first sentence, by striking out "or deliver"; and
(2) in the second sentence, by inserting "(other than gold and silver coins)" before "that may be lawfully held".

(e) The third sentence of section 5132(a)(1) of title 31, United States Code, is amended by striking out "minted under section 5112(a) of this title" and inserting in lieu thereof "minted under paragraphs (1) through (6) of section 5112(a) of this title".

(f) Notwithstanding any other provision of law, an amount equal to the amount by which the proceeds from the sale of the coins issued under section 5112(i) of title 31, United States Code, exceed the sum of –
(1) the cost of minting, marketing, and distributing such coins, and
(2) the value of gold certificates (not exceeding forty-two and two-ninths dollars a fine troy ounce) retired from the use of gold contained in such coins,
shall be deposited in the general fund of the Treasury and shall be used for the sole purpose of reducing the national debt.

(g) The Secretary shall take all actions necessary to ensure that the issuance of the coins minted under Section 5112(i) of title 31, United States Code, shall result in no net cost to the United States Government.

PUBLIC LAW 99-185—DEC. 17, 1985 99 STAT. 1179

EFFECTIVE DATE
Sec 3. This Act shall take effect on October 1, 1985 except that no coins may be issued or sold under section 5112(i) of title 31, United States Code, before October 1, 1986.

**The Gold Bullion Coin Act of 1985.**

## ACHIEVING AN EXEMPLARY GOLD BULLION COIN

Hopes were high, upon passage of the act, that the resulting coins would carry a design worthy of America's debut on the gold bullion-coin market. The design elements spelled out in the text of Public Law 99-185 left a certain amount of wiggle room: the coins would have a reeded edge (that is, with grooved notches on the edge of the coin to prevent it from being shaved), and would be composed of 22-karat gold (.9167 fine gold, .03 silver, and .0533 copper). The reverse would represent "a FAMILY OF EAGLES, with the male carrying an olive branch and flying above a nest containing a female eagle and hatchlings." Secretary of the Treasury James Baker would have the power to choose, from designs submitted by Mint staff and others, which artist's rendition would be used. The charming reverse scene he selected was designed by sculptor Miley Busiek (today known as Miley Tucker-Frost) and engraved by Sherl Joseph Winter.

In 1985 James Baker, in his role as secretary of the Treasury, had the honor of selecting the design of the nation's new gold coins.

U.S. Mint engraver Sherl Joseph Winter (center), a talented longtime member of the Mint's staff, engraved the American Gold Eagle's reverse from the design submitted by artist Miley Busiek (active today under the name Miley Tucker-Frost).

The only requirement specified for the obverse was that it bear a "design symbolic of liberty." To the delight of nearly everyone interested in the art of the "golden age" of United States coinage, Secretary Baker chose to return to Augustus Saint-Gaudens's iconic 1907 depiction of Liberty. The enabling legislation called for the usual required coin legends "In God We Trust," and "E Pluribus Unum," and a statement of the denomination and guaranteed bullion weight. All of these elements were placed on the reverse, so nothing whatsoever would detract from the simplicity and beauty of Saint-Gaudens's original design. Just like in the original, the year date on the first issue was expressed in Roman numerals, MCMLXXXVI, and this practice continued through 1992, when the switch was made to Arabic numerals. Two more stars were added to the ring to represent the states of Alaska and Hawaii.

Other specified characteristics of the coins, struck at the West Point and Philadelphia mints, are:

| Net Bullion Weight | Denomination | Actual Weight | Diameter |
| --- | --- | --- | --- |
| 1/10 ounce | $5 | 3.393 grams | 16.5 mm |
| 1/4 ounce | $10 | 8.483 grams | 22.0 mm |
| 1/2 ounce | $25 | 16.966 grams | 27.0 mm |
| 1 ounce | $50 | 33.931 grams | 32.7 mm |

The obverse of the 1986 American Gold Eagle was based on Augustus Saint-Gaudens's famous $20 gold design of 1907. Like its predecessor, the new bullion coin featured a date in Roman numerals. Because Alaska and Hawaii had entered the Union after the double eagle series ended in 1933, two additional stars joined the revamped design.

the coin, and inscribing the year of production (2009) in Roman numerals. The Citizens Coinage Advisory Committee, under the leadership of Chairman Mitch Sanders, recommended adding four more stars for a total of 50. The Commission of Fine Arts, under the leadership of the Honorable Earl A. Powell III and commission secretary Thomas Luebke, confirmed its recommendation of this final design and Secretary Paulson gave his final approval on April 28, 2008.

On November 24, 2008, I was privileged to personally strike the first 2009 Ultra High Relief double eagle gold coin, at the West Point Mint. This coin was transferred to the Smithsonian Institution's National Museum of American History, National Numismatic Collection. To forestall any accusation of creating a numismatic rarity as well as to be consistent with my principle of benefiting as many Americans as possible, we produced as many coins as anyone wanted to buy in 2009. When the UHR debuted it was, and remained throughout 2009, the most talked-about United States coin. Sales totaled 115,178 coins. All coins we did not sell were destroyed (which of course, means recycled).

The popularity of the 2009 UHR double eagle went beyond numismatists; it captured the imagination (and purchases) of art lovers, history buffs, gold bugs, and connoisseurs. Its sales did not cannibalize the Mint's other gold offerings. Congress thought it was an appropriate use of the legislative flexibility it granted the executive branch. It reestablished the U.S. Mint as a design leader and technological innovator. The challenge brought out the best from the employees at the Mint. As I reflect on the many accomplishments I had during my tenure as director of the United States Mint, this is one that gives me the most personal satisfaction.

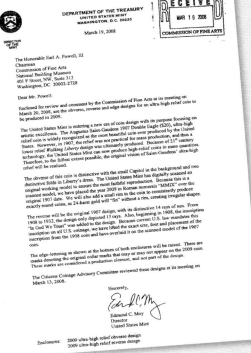

**Mint Director Edmund Moy's letter submitting the Saint-Gaudens Ultra High Relief design to the Commission of Fine Arts, March 2008.**

**Ed Moy discussing the 2009 Ultra High Relief gold double eagle— a triumph of modern minting technology.**

Coinage dies at the Philadelphia Mint, awaiting the production line: they will soon be used for striking American Platinum Eagles.

# 4

# History of the U.S. Platinum Bullion Coin Program

**A**s seen in chapter 3, the U.S. Mint's American Eagle gold and silver bullion coins were enormously successful, and consumer demand often reached the point where we could barely keep pace. In chapter 2 I described how platinum, just like gold and silver, has both intrinsic and commodity value, and how that value is affected by various factors including demand and scarcity.

From time to time in the early 1990s, public requests for a platinum bullion coin were received at legislative offices around the country. A growing number of financial investors showed interest in this metal because it is 15 times scarcer than gold in the ground, and nearly 33 percent of all platinum pulled from the ground is used in the production of catalytic converters for cars.

Several international mints began producing platinum bullion coins in the late 1980s—for example, Australia's platinum Koala in 1987, China's platinum Panda in 1987, and Canada's platinum Maple Leaf in 1988. The desire grew stronger to put the U.S. Mint on equal competitive footing in this expanding market, and Representative Michael Castle (R–Delaware) took matters in hand to make it happen.

Castle's concept for authorizing legislation arose during his tenure as chairman of the House Financial Services Committee's subcommittee on domestic and international monetary policy, which gave him jurisdiction over coinage issues. It was there that he came into contact with various collector/investors who convinced him to support the idea of a new line of platinum bullion (and platinum Proof) coins. Because a one-ounce platinum coin was too expensive for most buyers, they said, the United States should also create platinum coins in *fractional* denominations.

While creating coinage issues for investors was not Castle's first priority, he was very much interested in finding ways to reduce the federal deficit without raising taxes or cutting spending. Observing how the American Eagle silver bullion coins monetized much of the nation's silver reserves in an orderly and profitable way, and how circulating and numismatic coins could generate a profit, called *seigniorage*, deposited free and clear to the U.S. Treasury, he felt that adding platinum coins to the product line could only increase this form of revenue.[1,2]

In 1995 Castle drafted a bill called the Commemorative Coin Authorization and Reform Act, containing language enabling the secretary of the Treasury to mint platinum coins. Though the act easily passed the House, it did not clear the Senate. In 1996, however, a modified version made it through Congress as part of the annual omnibus appropriations bill for 1997 (H.R. 3610, Public Law 104-208). Because the entire market for platinum coins was relatively small compared to the market for gold or silver coins, the simple, direct wording of the pertinent clause in Public Law 104-208 gave the Treasury a great deal of latitude to nimbly execute a platinum bullion-coin program:

> The Secretary may mint and issue bullion and proof platinum coins in accordance with such specifications, designs, varieties, quantities, denominations, and inscriptions as the Secretary, in the Secretary's discretion, may prescribe from time to time, provided that the Secretary is authorized to use Government platinum reserves stockpiled at the United States Mint as working inventory, and shall ensure that reserves utilized are replaced by the Mint. (31 U.S.C. 5112(k))

**The American Platinum Eagle was not the only coinage program that Representative Michael Castle of Delaware would champion. Seen here in 2006, he unveils (with Representative Carolyn Maloney of New York) a rendition of the Presidential dollars that would debut the following year. (National Portrait Gallery, Washington, D.C., November 20, 2006.)**

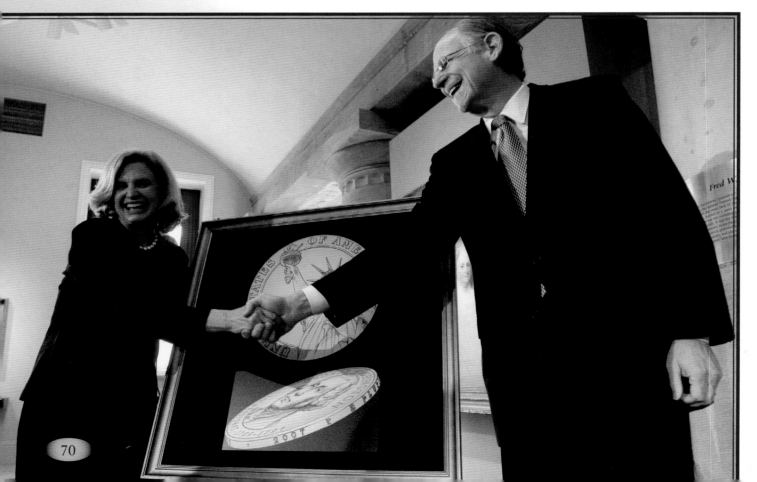

While "bullion and proof" were meant to be adjectives describing platinum coins, the law did not state explicitly that the bullion coins issued needed to be platinum coins. Representative Spencer Bachus (R–Alabama) authored the United States Mint Numismatic Coin Clarification Act of 2000 which struck the word *bullion* and replaced it with *platinum bullion coins*.

As you will see in the sidebar ("A $1 Trillion Platinum Coin?"), the word *denominations* and the phrase *Secretary's discretion* in the legislation could be played with in imaginative ways.

The first American Platinum Eagle bullion coins were issued in 1997. Like the gold Eagles, the coins came in four weights (one ounce, one-half ounce, one-quarter ounce, and one-tenth ounce), but their denominations differed from the gold coins at $100, $50, $25 and $10, respectively. Like all bullion coins made by the U.S. Mint, they are legal tender for all debts public and private at their face values. (The face value provides proof of their authenticity as official U.S. coinage, but as bullion coins, they are bought and sold for the intrinsic value of the platinum content, not their face value.) The Mint markup on American Platinum Eagles reflects their high production costs: platinum is a much harder metal than gold or silver, making it more difficult to coin.

The decision to issue American Platinum Eagles was a wise one: in the first six months, they claimed 80 percent of the world market for platinum bullion coins.

The bold obverse design is a full close-up of the Statue of Liberty's face, entitled "Liberty Looking to the Future," by U.S. Mint Chief Engraver John Mercanti. The reverse bears a design by Thomas D. Rogers Sr. of a flying eagle with wings extended for soaring (rather than in mid-flap, like so many flying eagle depictions). Regular bullion strikes in all four sizes with this obverse and reverse design continue to be produced each year with .9995 fineness.

The obverse and reverse designs of the bullion-strike American Platinum Eagle.

**Oversized plasters in the archives of the Philadelphia Mint.**

# SIDEBAR: A $1 TRILLION PLATINUM COIN?

The very simple wording of Public Law 104-208 (as codified at 31 U.S.C. § 5112[k]) gives the secretary of the Treasury the authority to order production of platinum bullion coins, of styles and denominations "in the Secretary's discretion." In late 2012, certain economists saw, in these little words, a way to avoid raising the federal debt ceiling: they suggested that the secretary of the Treasury use this loophole to mint $1 trillion coins and deposit them into one or more of our Federal Reserve Banks. In turn, the Federal Reserve Banks could then redeem these deposits to the Treasury, and—presto—the need to issue new federal debt (and the consequent need for a huge fight over the debt ceiling in Congress) would disappear.

This idea briefly surfaced in 2011 during the debt-ceiling crisis but before it could pick up steam Congress passed (and the president signed on August 2, 2011) the Budget Control Act of 2011; the idea quickly died from lack of need. However, in January 2013 the federal government projected that it was again going to exhaust its credit (by February or March), which led to another debt-ceiling crisis. Overnight, the $1 trillion coin idea became a social-media sensation and its hype spilled over into the mainstream media and the minds of policymakers.

Could the Treasury secretary direct the U.S. Mint to make a $1 trillion coin? The law does give the secretary "discretion." However, the author of Public Law 104-208, Representative Mike Castle, said that creating such a coin would be against the legislative intent of the law. In other words, it was possible but a big stretch and an unintended consequence.

Using a $1 trillion coin as money is an even more complicated matter. It hinges on the concept of *seigniorage*, which is the federal government's way of making "profit from coins." Seigniorage is the difference between the face value of a coin and the Mint's costs to produce and issue it. The Mint generates earnings from the issuance of coins in two ways:

1. When the Federal Reserve Banks order, say, a quarter-dollar coin for circulation and the Mint's cost to make that coin is 10 cents, the 15-cent difference is seigniorage. The Federal Reserve Bank pays 25 cents to the Mint for the coin, and the Mint transfers the 15 cents in seigniorage to the Treasury to use solely as a means of financing the national debt.
2. When the Mint makes a numismatic issue, like a Proof set or Proof bullion coin, and sells it to a collector or an investor, any price above the Mint's costs to make and sell the item is numismatic revenue. It may come as a surprise to many, but the Mint charges just enough to break even and have a small margin so that if it prices something accidentally at a loss, there is enough reserve to draw on to make sure taxpayers don't subsidize collector purchases. As with seigniorage, the Mint transfers to the Treasury any numismatic revenue it earns. However, unlike seigniorage, numismatic revenues may be used by the government for any purpose, including to pay for current operations, to offset a deficit, or to finance debt.

So how would a $1 trillion coin be turned into seigniorage?

# COMMEMORATIVE DESIGNS FOR THE PROOF AMERICAN PLATINUM EAGLES

In their first year of issuance (1997), the Mint issued bullion and Proof American Platinum Eagles (only in the $100-denominated, one-ounce size) using the Mercanti/Rogers design combination. In 1998 a distinguished new collectible series was launched. Bullion strikes of platinum Eagles would continue to feature the Mercanti/Rogers design combination. But for the first time in its history, the Mint would create a different reverse for each year's Proof issue, using design themes that would extend through five years. The first theme chosen was "Vistas of Liberty," and each year's reverse would feature a different scene of a bald eagle flying across an American landscape. The rationale behind the move was that first-year sales of a new coin were always strongest, and second-year mintages would generally drop by at least 30%. In the past, boxed sets and gift packs of various types were created to sustain collector interest and provide as many purchasing options as the public might desire. Now, it was hoped, each year's new variety would entice collectors to obtain another example.

At the launch of the first issue on May 18, 1998, Mint Director Philip Diehl announced, "The 'Vistas of Liberty' designs will profile the unique character and charisma of our nation's diverse landscapes, capturing the spirit and strength of America and its people."[3] The five reverses depicted the bald eagle in various ways: in flight over a New England coastal town (1998); passing by an alligator emerging from a Southeastern mangrove swamp (1999); soaring over a wide Plains farmstead planted with corn (2000); flying through a saguaro-studded Southwestern desert (2001); and scooping up a fish from a pristine Northwestern lake (2002). A special feature of the new reverses was

John Mercanti, designer of the American Platinum Eagle obverse and several Proof reverses.

Thomas D. Rogers Sr., designer of the "soaring eagle" reverse and a Proof reverse.

The law says that only bullion and Proof platinum coins can be made. A bullion coin's sales price is normally determined by the value of its metal content, though the bullion coin is also required to have a face value. Accordingly, to get seigniorage from a platinum bullion coin—for which the secretary of the Treasury has the discretion to assign any denomination—the secretary would merely have to assign it a face value in excess of the Mint's costs to mint and issue it (including labor, materials, dies, use of machinery, and promotional and overhead expenses). With the secretary of the Treasury's approval, the Mint therefore conceivably could lawfully mint, say, a one-ounce platinum bullion legal-tender coin with a face value of $1 trillion; therefore, if the bureau's cost to mint and issue the coin were $2,000, it would yield $999,999,998,000 in seigniorage. However, to monetize such a coin, it needs a buyer. The richest person in the world would be at least $930 billion short. The Federal Reserve chairman or one of the 12 presidents of the regional Federal Reserve Banks could order one, but it would be illogical for the Fed to hold a bullion coin with, say, one ounce of platinum and book it on their balance sheet as a $1 trillion asset. This is all theoretically possible using considerable legal gymnastics, but very improbable.

incuse sculpting, wherein a design element may be cut into the surface plane of the coin. This was used on the inscriptions for fineness (".9995 Platinum 1oz.") and denomination ($100). The Mercanti obverse design for the bullion strikes was used each year for the Proof version, with the variation that the legend E PLURIBUS UNUM was incused.

In 2003 through 2005, the Citizens Coinage Advisory Committee teamed with Mint artists and the Commission on Fine Arts to create more patriotic themes. As always, these had the bald eagle figuring prominently in the design. Alfred Maletsky's 2003 eagle held a branch of Rocky Mountain pine before the American flag. A depiction of Daniel Chester French's statue "America" from the U.S. Custom House in New York City, showing a seated Liberty with an eagle at her feet, graced the 2004 coin. In 2005 Donna Weaver's eagle design was a traditional heraldic one, with shield and cornucopia.

## SIDEBAR: WHAT IS THE DESIGN PROCESS FOR AN AMERICAN COIN?

The Citizens Coinage Advisory Committee recommended this design for the Proof 2013 American Platinum Eagle reverse: "Young America" amidst machinery wheels symbolizing the balance of governmental power.

Before 2003, coinage design concepts and motifs came from U.S. Mint staff and were informed by the requirements of a coin's enabling legislation. Representatives of the sales, marketing, and legal departments, the Mint director, and various other staff reviewed multiple drawings submitted by the Mint's artists, suggested revisions, and settled on preferred obverse and reverse design(s). These would then be submitted to the U.S. Commission of Fine Arts (CFA) for review. Since its creation by act of Congress in 1910, the CFA has overseen matters of design and aesthetics carried out in the nation's interest, from monuments, parks, public buildings, and memorials to commemorative and award medals and coins. This group of leading art experts often suggests alterations or requests entirely new designs. When all comments are incorporated and a final design is settled upon and approved by the CFA, creating the sculptural models may begin.

Since 2003, all coin designs need to also be reviewed by the Citizens Coinage Advisory Committee (CCAC). Unlike the Citizens Stamp Advisory Committee, which has had input into the design content of U.S. postage stamps since 1957, the CCAC has only been around since 2003. This group was established by Public Law 108-15 to advise the secretary of the Treasury about events, persons, and places to be honored by the issuance of commemorative coins. Its activity, conducted at public meetings, covers circulating coinage, commemoratives, bullion, Congressional gold medals, and national and other medals.

Both commissions make suggestions and recommend a design for actual coining. And while their suggestions and recommendations are advisory and non-binding, their input is taken seriously and the design team at the U.S. Mint does its best to incorporate their advice.

Once a final design emerges, the director of the Mint makes the recommendation via a decision memo to the secretary of the Treasury, who, if he agrees, signs off on it.

Reverse designs for 2006 through 2008 launched the three-part "Foundations of Democracy" theme, depicting the legislative, executive, and judicial branches of federal government. These designs symbolizing law, leadership, and justice—by Joel Iskowitz (2006 and 2008) and Thomas Cleveland (2007)—were well received.

In 2007 my sales and marketing team informed me that the Foundations of Democracy theme would end with the minting of the 2008 design and that I had the opportunity to choose the next theme. After some collaboration, my team came back with several themes, of which was chosen a six-year series exploring the core concepts of American democracy by highlighting the preamble of the U.S. Constitution. The Mint's acting deputy director at the time, Dan Shaver, suggested that we contact the chief justice of the United States, John G. Roberts Jr., and ask him to prepare a narrative for each of the six principles found in the Preamble. These narratives would be the story that inspired our artists' designs. The six principles are:

- "To Form a More Perfect Union" (2009)
- "To Establish Justice" (2010)
- "To Insure Domestic Tranquility" (2011)
- "To Provide for the Common Defence" (2012)
- "To Promote the General Welfare" (2013)
- "To Secure the Blessings of Liberty to Ourselves and our Posterity" (2014)

The following is Chief Justice Roberts's narrative on the Constitution's foundational objective, "To Form a More Perfect Union."

The 2012 design in the Proof platinum series honored the Constitution's promise to "provide for the common defence" (using the old spelling of the last word). The sketch shown here is the motif recommended by the Commission of Fine Arts—dramatically different from the coin's ultimate design.

## "To Form a More Perfect Union"

When the thirteen American colonies issued their Declaration of Independence from Great Britain in 1776, they recognized that the success of the American Revolution depended on unity in opposition to British rule. As the Revolutionary War progressed, those thirteen fledgling entities agreed, through "Articles of Confederation and Perpetual Union," to establish the United States of America. The Articles of Confederation proved inadequate, however, in creating an effective national government. After the Revolutionary War, the states convened a constitutional convention in Philadelphia to reconsider the terms of their confederation. During that fateful summer of 1787, America's leading statesmen drafted the Constitution of the United States of America with the avowed objective "to form a more perfect Union."

John Jay, who would later become the first Chief Justice of the United States, joined James Madison and Alexander Hamilton in authoring a series of essays, now known as The Federalist Papers, to urge the citizens to support ratification of the Constitution. In The Federalist No. 2, Jay explained that the Constitution's promise of "a more perfect Union" rested upon a unity of distinctly American ideals, interests, and experiences that joined the people of the United States together as one nation.

Jay noted that "independent America was not composed of detached and distant territories," but rather was "one connected, fertile, widespreading country" with "a variety of soils," "innumerable streams," and a "succession of navigable waters" that "forms a kind of chain round its borders as if to bind it together." Jay also recognized that "Providence has been pleased to give this one connected country to one united people" who, "by their joint counsels, arms, and efforts, fighting side by side throughout a long and bloody war, have nobly established their general liberty and independence." He discerned a connection between the land and the people:

> This country and this people seem to have been made for each other, and it appears as if it was the design of Providence that an inheritance so proper and convenient for a band of brethren, united to each other by the strongest ties, should never be split into a number of unsocial, jealous, and alien sovereignties.

John Jay believed that this "band of brethren" found unity in the English ancestry, heritage, and customs that many of the citizens of his era shared. But history has shown that the Constitution's aspiration of "a more perfect Union" rests more fundamentally on a unity of common beliefs that Americans of all backgrounds throughout history have embraced. As the United States has expanded across the continent, overcome internal conflict, and welcomed new states, the nation has found enduring strength in its people's diverse origins and perspectives.

The United States remains perpetually united by a shared dedication to the ideals of liberty, justice, and equality. Through these shared ideals, each new generation has sustained the Constitution's promise of "a more perfect Union."

*John G. Roberts, Jr.*

John G. Roberts Jr. (chief justice of the United States) with a presentation copy of the first reverse in the "Foundations of Democracy" platinum coinage series, in the chief justice's private chambers, Washington, D.C.

Common Proof Obverse. Designer: John Mercanti.

# SIDEBAR: PROOF AMERICAN PLATINUM EAGLE DESIGNS

Proof Reverse, 1997. Designer: Thomas D. Rogers Sr.

Proof Reverse, 1998: Eagle Over New England. Vistas of Liberty series. Designer: John Mercanti.

Proof Reverse, 1999: Eagle Above Southeastern Wetlands. Vistas of Liberty series. Designer: John Mercanti.

Proof Reverse, 2000: Eagle Above America's Heartland. Vistas of Liberty series. Designer: Alfred Maletsky.

Proof Reverse, 2001: Eagle Above America's Southwest. Vistas of Liberty series. Designer: Thomas D. Rogers Sr.

Proof Reverse, 2002: Eagle Fishing in America's Northwest. Vistas of Liberty series. Designer: Alfred Maletsky.

Proof Reverse, 2003. Designer: Alfred Maletsky.

Proof Reverse, 2004. Designer: Donna Weaver.

Proof Reverse, 2005. Designer: Donna Weaver.

Proof Reverse, 2006: "Legislative Branch." Designer: Joel Iskowitz.

Proof Reverse, 2007: "Executive Branch." Designer: Thomas Cleveland.

Proof Reverse, 2008. "Judicial Branch." Designer: Joel Iskowitz.

Proof Reverse, 2009. "To Form a More Perfect Union." Designer: Susan Gamble.

Proof Reverse, 2010: "To Establish Justice." Designer: Donna Weaver.

Proof Reverse, 2011: "To Insure Domestic Tranquility." Designer: Joel Iskowitz.

Proof Reverse, 2012: "To Provide for the Common Defence." Designer: Barbara Fox.

# 5

# Year-by-Year Study of American Gold and Platinum Eagles

This chapter sets each American Gold Eagle and American Platinum Eagle within its historical context and gives collectors an insightful market overview. Each coin is identified by its date, mintmark (if any), and format (i.e., *bullion strike* for the coins produced for bullion sales; or *Proof*, *Reverse Proof*, or *Burnished* for those formats). Mintages are specified. The mint facilities that produced each coin are noted. Enlarged photographs are provided, along with relevant close-ups and other related images. The charts include values in several conditions.

**A note about sales figures and mintages:** The numbers given herein are *mintages* of each coin—the quantity of coins struck and issued bearing a given year date. *Sales figures*, sometimes seen in a month-by-month format, may include coins dated from more than one calendar year. (In some years, the Mint's Authorized Purchasers—wholesalers, brokerage companies, et al.—were allowed to order the following year's coins in December, a month before their official release. These coins would count toward the earlier year's *sales*, while being counted in the next year's *mintage*.)

**A note about values:** In today's marketplace of professionally graded coins, retail prices (and auction prices realized) can vary, sometimes dramatically, for a given coin, depending on which third-party grading firm "slabbed" it.

American Gold Eagle year dates are in Roman numerals from 1986 to 2002.

# 1986

**Historical context:** The American economy in 1986 experienced only moderate expansion, as it had in recent years, and unemployment remained in the neighborhood of 7 percent. On the plus side, the relatively mild growth rate, plus a steep drop in oil prices (around 50 percent from the end of 1985 to the middle of 1986), helped keep interest rates down. The domestic inflation rate also dropped substantially, from 4 percent to less than 1 percent. The overall climate contributed to strong consumer spending—although Americans were saving less and taking out more in credit to support their spending.

Congress passed the Tax Reform Act of 1986 in an effort to simplify the tax code, close loopholes, and institute other reforms. Corporate tax rates went up, but the topmost income-tax rate dropped from 50 percent to 20.

NASA's shuttle, *Challenger*, was beginning its 10th mission in late January when it broke into pieces shortly after taking off, killing all seven astronauts aboard. It would be more than two years before NASA sent astronauts into space again. In April the Chernobyl Nuclear Plant just outside the town of Pripyat, Ukraine, exploded violently, claiming thousands of lives and forcing almost 150,000 people out of their homes permanently.

In American numismatics, in 1986 Dr. Richard Doty became the senior numismatic curator at the Smithsonian Institution's National Museum of American History. He would go on to transform numismatic research by "illustrating poignant human relationships reflected in the objects he thoughtfully analyzed" ("Richard [Dick] G. Doty, 1942–2013," Smithsonian press release, June 5, 2013). Doty's work resulted in published books (including *America's Money, America's Story: A Chronicle of American Numismatic History* and *Pictures From a Distant Country: Seeing America Through Old Paper Money*) and many honors and awards.

In addition to the debut of the American Gold Eagle, 1986 was the year that PCGS (the Professional Coin Grading Service) began operation as a third-party grader.

**Coin commentary:** The American Gold Eagles of 1986—their debut year—feature the date in Roman numerals, in the style of the coin that inspired their obverse design, the 1907–1933 Saint-Gaudens double eagle ($20 gold piece). Their mintages were high in all denominations, from one ounce down to one-tenth ounce. Not until late in the next decade would mintages approach those of 1986. The level of consumer demand in the bullion program's inaugural year is even more evident when you consider that the coins didn't go on sale until late October.

The new U.S. gold bullion program included four denominations: $5 (1/10 ounce pure gold); $10 (1/4 ounce); $25 (1/2 ounce); and $50 (1 ounce). Each shares the same obverse and reverse designs: a modified rendition of Augustus Saint-Gaudens's famous Striding Liberty motif, and a "family of eagles" scene by sculptor Miley Busiek (today known by the surname of Tucker-Frost). Busiek's initials, MB, appear on the reverse, above the G in the word GOLD. Another set of initials, JW, stands for Sherl Joseph Winter, the U.S. Mint sculptor-engraver who engraved the reverse based on Busiek's design. Saint-

Gaudens's stylized initials, ASG, appear in the sun's rays on the obverse, below the date and to the right of Miss Liberty's left foot.

The coins are legal tender—with weight, content, and purity guaranteed by the federal government—and are produced from gold mined in the United States. "American Eagles use the durable 22-karat standard established for gold circulating coinage over 350 years ago," noted the U.S. Mint. "They contain their stated amount of pure gold, plus small amounts of alloy. This creates harder coins that resist scratching and marring, which can diminish resale value."

The ceremonial launch of the American Gold Eagle came at a first-strike event at the U.S. Mint's West Point Bullion Depository on September 8, 1986. Planchets (coinage blanks) for the American Gold Eagles were supplied to the Mint by two firms, Leach & Garner Company and Engelhard Corporation. The West Point facility had four coinage presses in operation for the gold program, two of which were devoted to striking the largest (one-ounce) coins. Mainstream production began a few hours after the first-strike ceremony, and three shifts of Mint workers labored seven days a week to meet the Mint's goals. By the scheduled start of sales (October 20) a total of 800,000 ounces of coined gold (500,000 one-ounce coins plus 300,000 ounces total in the smaller sizes) was available. These coins were quickly bought up by the Mint's network of (at that time) 25 authorized purchasers. They were distributed into the numismatic marketplace, as well as through participating banks, investment firms, and other non-numismatic channels. Strongest demand was for the one-ounce and tenth-ounce coins (the largest and smallest sizes). Americans were eager for a convenient way to add gold to their holdings, and the American Gold Eagle program provided the perfect means. Even a substantial increase in the spot price of gold in the weeks leading up to the program's launch (breaking $435 from a year low of $326) didn't crush enthusiasm.

In addition to bullion-strike coins, collectors could purchase (directly from the Mint) Proof versions of the one-ounce 1986 American Gold Eagle. These collectibles, struck at West Point and bearing a W mintmark, were available only in the $50 denomination this year; fractional Proofs would not be offered until 1987. Sales neared 450,000 for these brilliant-finish presentation pieces, setting a mintage record for the series' Proof coins—and even eclipsing the mintages of many regular bullion strikes of later years.

# Bullion Strikes, Gold, 1986

**$5 American Gold Eagle (1/10 oz.), bullion strike**     *Mintage: 912,609*

| 1986 | Grade | Purchased From | Date |
|------|-------|----------------|------|
|      |       |                |      |

Bullion value at time of purchase: _____

**$10 American Gold Eagle (1/4 oz.), bullion strike**     *Mintage: 726,031*

| 1986 | Grade | Purchased From | Date |
|------|-------|----------------|------|
|      |       |                |      |

Bullion value at time of purchase: _____

The initials of Miley Busiek, the artist who designed the "Family of Eagles" reverse, are above the G in GOLD.

Sculptor-engraver Sherl Josef Winter's initials, JW, appear below the nesting eagles.

On the obverse, the monogram ASG stands for Augustus Saint-Gaudens, designer of the American Gold Eagle's predecessor, the $20 gold piece of 1907 to 1933.

**1986 average spot prices:**
silver, $5.47; gold, $368.24;
platinum, $461.59

**Total 1986 American Gold Eagle mintage (in ounces):**
1,935,202 (bullion);
446,290 (Proof)

**American Gold Eagles**
Date:   MCMLXXXVI (1986)
Mint:   West Point Bullion Depository (bullion strikes [no mintmark] and Proofs [W mintmark])
**Composition:**
.9167 gold, .03 silver, .0533 copper
Edge:   Reeded
**Weight:**
$5—0.109 oz.
(3.393 grams; 1/10 oz. actual gold weight)
$10—0.273 oz.
(8.483 grams; 1/4 oz. actual gold weight)
$25—0.545 oz.
(16.966 grams; 1/2 oz. actual gold weight)
$50—1.091 oz.
(33.931 grams; 1 oz. actual gold weight)
**Diameter:**
$5—16.5 mm
$10—22 mm
$25—27 mm
$50—32.7 mm
**Thickness:**
$50—2.87 mm
**Designers:**
Augustus Saint-Gaudens (obverse), Miley Busiek (reverse)

**$25 American Gold Eagle (1/2 oz.), bullion strike**   *Mintage: 599,566*

| 1986 | Grade | Purchased From | Date |
|------|-------|----------------|------|
|      |       |                |      |

Bullion value at time of purchase: _____

**$50 American Gold Eagle (1 oz.), bullion strike**   *Mintage: 1,362,650*

| 1986 | Grade | Purchased From | Date |
|------|-------|----------------|------|
|      |       |                |      |

Bullion value at time of purchase: _____

## Proof Strikes, Gold, 1986

**$50 American Gold Eagle (1 oz.), Proof**   *Mintage: 446,290*

| 1986 | Grade | Purchased From | Date |
|------|-------|----------------|------|
|      |       |                |      |

Bullion value at time of purchase: _____

# 1987

**Historical context:** U.S. economic growth from 1986 continued to increase into 1987 in what would be the longest peacetime upturn in the nation's history. Unemployment was somewhat reduced while inflation increased, and exports bolstered the strength of the economy by picking up the slack seen in the early 1980s. Oil prices rebounded, stabilizing employment in the oil and gas industries. However, in the fall of 1987 a sharp decline in stock prices sparked fears that recession was creeping up on the U.S. economy.

October 19, 1987, became forever known as "Black Monday" (recalling the Black Tuesday stock-market crash of October 28, 1929, which began the Great Depression). The Dow Jones Industrial Average dropped 22.6 percent of its value in one day—the equivalent of more than $500 billion for the index. Canada, Great Britain, Australia, Hong Kong, Singapore, Mexico, and other nations joined the United States in the crash. (In only two years the market would climb back up and even surpass its previous record high, continuing growth into the prosperous 1990s.)

On the international scene, the Berlin Wall had stood as a symbol of Communism and a divided Germany since 1961, separating the western Federal Republic of Germany from the eastern, repressive German Democratic Republic. In the midst of the Cold War, on one of his visits to Berlin, President Ronald Reagan gave a rousing speech that would quickly become famous as he challenged Soviet leader Mikhail Gorbachev to destroy the Berlin Wall in an act that could not only unify the two sides of Germany but also ease Cold War tensions.

1987 saw the founding of the Numismatic Guaranty Corporation of America (NGC), a professional third-party grading service for coins.

The bullion value of silver peaked above $10 per ounce during 1987, averaging near $7 for the year, an increase over 1986. Gold, too, was stronger overall than the previous year—about $70 higher, with an annual average of $447.95.

**Coin commentary:** The West Point Bullion Depository continued to make bullion-strike American Gold Eagles through 1987, keeping up with collector and investor interest, with four coinage presses devoted to their production. Demand dropped from the bullion program's inaugural year, but still was considerable: more than 1 million coins of the one-ounce $50 denomination were sold. The smaller denominations also saw diminished mintages. The $25 and $10 gold coin mintages dropped to about 40 percent and 20 percent, respectively, of their 1986 numbers, while the smallest size, the tenth-ounce $5 coin, held up better at about 64 percent.

The Mint again offered a Proof version of the one-ounce American Gold Eagle in 1987, while also introducing a half-ounce Proof. The $50 Proof coins were struck at West Point and bore a W mintmark, and the $25 at Philadelphia, with a P mintmark. In terms of sales the two collector-format denominations were closely matched in popularity, with only a few thousand more $50 coins sold than $25. The Proofs were available individually and also in two-coin sets.

# Bullion Strikes, Gold, 1987

**$5 American Gold Eagle (1/10 oz.), bullion strike**   *Mintage: 580,266*

| 1987 | Grade | Purchased From | Date |
|------|-------|----------------|------|
|      |       |                |      |

Bullion value at time of purchase: _____

**$10 American Gold Eagle (1/4 oz.), bullion strike**   *Mintage: 269,255*

| 1987 | Grade | Purchased From | Date |
|------|-------|----------------|------|
|      |       |                |      |

Bullion value at time of purchase: _____

**$25 American Gold Eagle (1/2 oz.), bullion strike**   *Mintage: 131,255*

| 1987 | Grade | Purchased From | Date |
|------|-------|----------------|------|
|      |       |                |      |

Bullion value at time of purchase: _____

**$50 American Gold Eagle (1 oz.), bullion strike**   *Mintage: 1,045,500*

| 1987 | Grade | Purchased From | Date |
|------|-------|----------------|------|
|      |       |                |      |

Bullion value at time of purchase: _____

**1987 average spot prices:**
silver, $7.02; gold, $447.95;
platinum, $552.58.

**Total 1987 American Gold
Eagle mintage (in ounces):**
1,236,468 (bullion);
219,197 (Proof)

**American Gold Eagles**

Date: MCMLXXXVII (1987)

Mints: West Point Bullion
Depository (bullion strikes
[no mintmark] and $50
Proofs [W mintmark]);
Philadephia Mint ($25
Proofs [P mintmark])

Composition:
.9167 gold, .03 silver,
.0533 copper

Edge: Reeded

Weight:
$5—0.109 oz.
(3.393 grams; 1/10 oz.
actual gold weight)
$10—0.273 oz.
(8.483 grams; 1/4 oz.
actual gold weight)
$25—0.545 oz.
(16.966 grams; 1/2 oz.
actual gold weight)
$50—1.091 oz.
(33.931 grams; 1 oz.
actual gold weight)

Diameter:
$5—16.5 mm
$10—22 mm
$25—27 mm
$50—32.7 mm

Thickness:
$50—2.87 mm

Designers:
Augustus Saint-Gaudens
(obverse), Miley Busiek
(reverse)

# Proof Strikes, Gold, 1987

## $25 American Gold Eagle (1/2 oz.), Proof          *Mintage: 143,398*

| 1987-P | Grade | Purchased From | Date |
|--------|-------|----------------|------|
|        |       |                |      |

Bullion value at time of purchase: _____

## $50 American Gold Eagle (1 oz.), Proof          *Mintage: 147,498*

| 1987-W | Grade | Purchased From | Date |
|--------|-------|----------------|------|
|        |       |                |      |

Bullion value at time of purchase: _____

# Proof Set, Gold, 1987

## $25 and $50 American Gold Eagle (1/2 oz. and 1 oz.), Proof

| 1987 | Grade | Purchased From | Date |
|------|-------|----------------|------|
|      |       |                |      |

Bullion value at time of purchase: _____

# 1988

**Historical context:** Throughout 1988 and into 1989, optimism was muted but the American economy continued to grow. After the financial crash of October 1987 the economy had slowed noticeably but did not decline as dramatically as some had feared. Inflation was unusually low despite strengthened demand for goods and services that further bolstered factory operations. Employment reached a record high.

After eight years of war between the countries of Iran and Iraq, a cease-fire went into effect on July 20, 1988, preventing additional casualties in a conflict that had already claimed at least half a million lives. In the Soviet Union, Mikhail Gorbachev, after forcing his predecessor, Andrei Gromyko, to resign, named himself head of the Supreme Soviet on October 1. He would quickly move the Soviet Union toward dissolution and play a significant part in ending the Cold War.

On the numismatic front, Aubrey and Adeline Bebee, longtime collectors and members of the American Numismatic Association, donated their expansive collection of more than 500 historical bank notes to the ANA museum. Arthur L. Friedberg, writing in "The Bebee Collection of the American Numismatic Association," ranks the couple as "trailblazers in turning paper money collecting into a major component of American numismatics." Meanwhile in March 1988 the U.S. Mint's West Point facility (erected in 1937 as a bullion depository and popularly called the "Fort Knox of Silver") gained official status as a full branch of the U.S. Mint.

Silver and gold bullion prices were both down a few percentage points in 1988 compared to their positions in 1987.

**Coin commentary:** The U.S. Mint expanded its offering of American Gold Eagle coins in 1988 by making all four denominations available in brilliant Proof format. The one-ounce Proofs were struck at West Point, and the three fractional sizes at Philadelphia. Proof mintages for the two smaller denominations were high, reflecting collector excitement over the new coins. The Proof coins were sold individually as well as in a four-coin set.

Demand for the gold bullion strikes continued its downward trend, with 1988's mintage of one-ounce coins dropping to less than 50 percent of 1987's. The $25 half-ounce and $10 quarter-ounce coins saw the most dramatic reductions in mintage, to fewer than 50,000 each.

## Bullion Strikes, Gold, 1988

**$5 American Gold Eagle (1/10 oz.), bullion strike**        *Mintage: 159,500*

| 1988 | Grade | Purchased From | Date |
|------|-------|----------------|------|
|      |       |                |      |

Bullion value at time of purchase: _____

**$10 American Gold Eagle (1/4 oz.), bullion strike**        *Mintage: 49,000*

| 1988 | Grade | Purchased From | Date |
|------|-------|----------------|------|
|      |       |                |      |

Bullion value at time of purchase: _____

**$25 American Gold Eagle (1/2 oz.), bullion strike**        *Mintage: 45,000*

| 1988 | Grade | Purchased From | Date |
|------|-------|----------------|------|
|      |       |                |      |

Bullion value at time of purchase: _____

**$50 American Gold Eagle (1 oz.), bullion strike**        *Mintage: 465,500*

| 1988 | Grade | Purchased From | Date |
|------|-------|----------------|------|
|      |       |                |      |

Bullion value at time of purchase: _____

## Proof Strikes, Gold, 1988

**$5 American Gold Eagle (1/10 oz.), Proof**        *Mintage: 143,881*

| 1988-P | Grade | Purchased From | Date |
|--------|-------|----------------|------|
|        |       |                |      |

Bullion value at time of purchase: _____

**$10 American Gold Eagle (1/4 oz.), Proof**        *Mintage: 98,028*

| 1988-P | Grade | Purchased From | Date |
|--------|-------|----------------|------|
|        |       |                |      |

Bullion value at time of purchase: _____

**1988 average spot prices:**
silver, $6.52; gold, $438.31;
platinum, $525.31

**Total 1988 American Gold
Eagle mintage (in ounces):**
516,200 (bullion);
164,292 (Proof)

**American Gold Eagles**
Date: MCMLXXXVIII (1988)
Mints: West Point Mint (bullion
strikes [no mintmark] and
$50 Proofs [W mintmark]);
Philadephia Mint ($5,
$10, and $25 Proofs
[P mintmark])
Composition:
.9167 gold, .03 silver,
.0533 copper
Edge: Reeded
Weight:
$5—0.109 oz.
(3.393 grams; 1/10 oz.
actual gold weight)
$10—0.273 oz.
(8.483 grams; 1/4 oz.
actual gold weight)
$25—0.545 oz.
(16.966 grams; 1/2 oz.
actual gold weight)
$50—1.091 oz.
(33.931 grams; 1 oz.
actual gold weight)
Diameter:
$5—16.5 mm
$10—22 mm
$25—27 mm
$50—32.7 mm
Thickness:
$50—2.87 mm
Designers:
Augustus Saint-Gaudens
(obverse), Miley Busiek
(reverse)

**$25 American Gold Eagle (1/2 oz.), Proof**     *Mintage: 143,398*

| 1988-P | Grade | Purchased From | Date |
|--------|-------|----------------|------|
|        |       |                |      |

Bullion value at time of purchase: _____

**$50 American Gold Eagle (1 oz.), Proof**     *Mintage: 147,498*

| 1988-W | Grade | Purchased From | Date |
|--------|-------|----------------|------|
|        |       |                |      |

Bullion value at time of purchase: _____

## Proof Set, Gold, 1988

**$5, $10, $25, and $50 American Gold Eagle
(1/10 oz. to 1 oz.), Proof**

| 1988 | Grade | Purchased From | Date |
|------|-------|----------------|------|
|      |       |                |      |

Bullion value at time of purchase: _____

# 1989

**Historical context:** The Canadian Free Trade Agreement, which was written to ease friction in economic relations between the United States and Canada, was enacted on January 1, 1989. It eliminated tariffs between the neighboring nations, reduced non-tariff barriers, liberalized investment practices, and addressed the trade of services.

In May of 1989, millions of Chinese students began a protest in central Beijing to demand democracy and the resignation of repressive Chinese Communist Party leaders. Almost three weeks passed without incident, until on June 4 government troops began to fire into the crowds. Estimates of the death toll reached into the thousands, and almost 10,000 students were arrested. The Tiananmen Square massacre shocked China's enemies and allies alike.

November saw at last the fall of the infamous Berlin Wall, which had separated East and West Germany for 28 years. Communism had already begun to lose its grip in East Germany, and the breaking down of the wall symbolized the changes. Soviet leader Mikhail Gorbachev's encouragement of the wall's destruction bolstered U.S. leaders to take further action toward a new international relationship that would lead to the end of the Cold War.

In numismatics, the 1913 Liberty Head nickels made national headlines when Aubrey and Adeline Bebee donated their specimen to the American Numismatic Association. The coin—one of only five known—was an instant draw for visitors to the ANA Money Museum in Colorado Springs. Meanwhile, the 200th anniversary of the U.S. Senate was celebrated with bicentennial postage stamps as well as gold, silver, and copper-nickel commemorative coins struck by the Philadelphia, San Francisco, and West Point mints.

Gold's annual-average bullion price dropped more than $50 from 1988 to 1989. The metal saw spikes above $400 per ounce early and late in the year, but these didn't offset lower values seen through much of 1989, and spot averaged just above $380 for the year.

**Coin commentary:** Mintage trends were mixed for the bullion-strike American Gold Eagle in 1989, with the two larger denominations slightly down, and the two smaller denominations more dramatically up.

The year's Proof offerings saw decreased mintages across all four denominations. Production of the Proof coinage was split between two mints: West Point struck the largest coin (the $50 one-ounce), and Philadelphia the smaller three (tenth-, quarter-, and half-ounce). These coins bear the W or P mintmark of their production facility.

The overall decrease in demand brought the year's sales below 500,000 total ounces for the bullion strikes, and below 100,000 ounces for the Proofs (the first time these thresholds weren't met in the American Gold Eagle program). The $25 half-ounce coin had the lowest mintages of the year—44,829 bullion strikes and 44,798 Proofs.

# Bullion Strikes, Gold, 1989

**$5 American Gold Eagle (1/10 oz.), bullion strike**　　*Mintage: 264,790*

| 1989 | Grade | Purchased From | Date |
|------|-------|----------------|------|
|      |       |                |      |

Bullion value at time of purchase: _____

**$10 American Gold Eagle (1/4 oz.), bullion strike**　　*Mintage: 81,789*

| 1989 | Grade | Purchased From | Date |
|------|-------|----------------|------|
|      |       |                |      |

Bullion value at time of purchase: _____

**$25 American Gold Eagle (1/2 oz.), bullion strike**　　*Mintage: 44,829*

| 1989 | Grade | Purchased From | Date |
|------|-------|----------------|------|
|      |       |                |      |

Bullion value at time of purchase: _____

**$50 American Gold Eagle (1 oz.), bullion strike**　　*Mintage: 415,790*

| 1989 | Grade | Purchased From | Date |
|------|-------|----------------|------|
|      |       |                |      |

Bullion value at time of purchase: _____

# Proof Strikes, Gold, 1989

**$5 American Gold Eagle (1/10 oz.), Proof**　　*Mintage: 84,647*

| 1989-P | Grade | Purchased From | Date |
|--------|-------|----------------|------|
|        |       |                |      |

Bullion value at time of purchase: _____

**1989 average spot prices:**
silver, $5.52; gold, $382.58;
platinum, $507.28

**Total 1989 American Gold
Eagle mintage (in ounces):**
485,131 (bullion);
98,976 (Proof)

**American Gold Eagles**
**Date:** MCMLXXXIX (1989)
**Mints:** West Point Mint (bullion
strikes [no mintmark] and
$50 Proofs [W mintmark]);
Philadephia Mint ($5,
$10, and $25 Proofs
[P mintmark])
**Composition:**
.9167 gold, .03 silver,
.0533 copper
**Edge:** Reeded
**Weight:**
$5—0.109 oz.
(3.393 grams; 1/10 oz.
actual gold weight)
$10—0.273 oz.
(8.483 grams; 1/4 oz.
actual gold weight)
$25—0.545 oz.
(16.966 grams; 1/2 oz.
actual gold weight)
$50—1.091 oz.
(33.931 grams; 1 oz.
actual gold weight)
**Diameter:**
$5—16.5 mm
$10—22 mm
$25—27 mm
$50—32.7 mm
**Thickness:**
$50—2.87 mm
**Designers:**
Augustus Saint-Gaudens
(obverse), Miley Busiek
(reverse)

## $10 American Gold Eagle (1/4 oz.), Proof

*Mintage: 54,170*

| 1989-P | Grade | Purchased From | Date |
|--------|-------|----------------|------|
|        |       |                |      |

Bullion value at time of purchase: _____

## $25 American Gold Eagle (1/2 oz.), Proof

*Mintage: 44,798*

| 1989-P | Grade | Purchased From | Date |
|--------|-------|----------------|------|
|        |       |                |      |

Bullion value at time of purchase: _____

## $50 American Gold Eagle (1 oz.), Proof

*Mintage: 54,570*

| 1989-W | Grade | Purchased From | Date |
|--------|-------|----------------|------|
|        |       |                |      |

Bullion value at time of purchase: _____

## Proof Set, Gold, 1989

**$5, $10, $25, and $50 American Gold Eagle
(1/10 oz. to 1 oz.), Proof**

| 1989 | Grade | Purchased From | Date |
|------|-------|----------------|------|
|      |       |                |      |

Bullion value at time of purchase: _____

# 1990

**Historical context:** July of 1990 saw the beginning of a U.S. recession that would last until March of the next year. The nation's poor economic health was "mainly attributable to the workings of the business cycle and restrictive monetary policy," according to the *Quarterly Review* of the Federal Reserve Bank of Minneapolis (Fall 1991), though the U.S. invasion of Kuwait was also labeled as a cause. The recession, however, proved to be mild, with unemployment rising only by half a percent and industrial production falling by only 3.7 percent.

After 27 years of imprisonment, South African anti-apartheid revolutionary Nelson Mandela was released from prison on February 11, 1990. Mandela had been arrested for treason after transitioning from peaceful resistance to guerrilla-warfare tactics in the wake of the massacre of peaceful black demonstrators. He was released under the orders of South African president F.W. de Klerk, who had begun dismantling apartheid in 1989. In August, in response to the Iraqi invasion of Kuwait, President George H.W. Bush ordered the organization of Operation Desert Shield, a force that would later join the international coalition of Operation Desert Storm. In Europe, Cold War tensions continued to relax, and Germany was reunified as a single nation.

That November President Bush signed Law 101-585, also known as the "Silver Coin Proof Sets Act," authorizing the creation and sale of annual silver coin sets from the U.S. Mint.

Gold's average annual price for 1990 remained steady compared to 1989, ending a couple dollars higher than the previous year.

**Coin commentary:** Across the board, mintages for bullion strikes in the American Gold Eagle program declined in 1990 compared to the previous year. Among all four denominations of Proofs, however, demand increased over 1989, with sales up about 14 percent. Once again Proofs were available individually ($50 one-ounce coins struck at the West Point Mint with a W mintmark, and smaller pieces struck at the Philadelphia Mint with a P mintmark) as well as in a four-coin set.

The 1990 half-ounce bullion strike hit a record-low mintage of just 31,000 coins—lower than the year's sales of half-ounce Proofs. Not surprisingly, the quantity submitted for third-party grading is significantly higher than for 1989; collectors recognize it as a key date/denomination of the series, and eagerly seek the Holy Grail of an MS-70 grade.

# Bullion Strikes, Gold, 1990

**$5 American Gold Eagle (1/10 oz.), bullion strike**    *Mintage: 210,210*

| 1990 | Grade | Purchased From | Date |
|------|-------|----------------|------|
|      |       |                |      |

Bullion value at time of purchase: _____

**$10 American Gold Eagle (1/4 oz.), bullion strike**    *Mintage: 41,000*

| 1990 | Grade | Purchased From | Date |
|------|-------|----------------|------|
|      |       |                |      |

Bullion value at time of purchase: _____

**$25 American Gold Eagle (1/2 oz.), bullion strike**    *Mintage: 31,000*

| 1990 | Grade | Purchased From | Date |
|------|-------|----------------|------|
|      |       |                |      |

Bullion value at time of purchase: _____

**$50 American Gold Eagle (1 oz.), bullion strike**    *Mintage: 373,210*

| 1990 | Grade | Purchased From | Date |
|------|-------|----------------|------|
|      |       |                |      |

Bullion value at time of purchase: _____

# Proof Strikes, Gold, 1990

**$5 American Gold Eagle (1/10 oz.), Proof**    *Mintage: 99,349*

| 1990-P | Grade | Purchased From | Date |
|--------|-------|----------------|------|
|        |       |                |      |

Bullion value at time of purchase: _____

1990 average spot prices:
silver, $4.82; gold, $384.93;
platinum, $466.93

**Total 1990 American Gold
Eagle mintage (in ounces):**
419,981 (bullion);
113,822 (Proof)

**American Gold Eagles**

**Date:** MCMXC (1990)

**Mints:** West Point Mint (bullion
strikes [no mintmark] and
$50 Proofs [W mintmark]);
Philadephia Mint ($5,
$10, and $25 Proofs
[P mintmark])

**Composition:**
.9167 gold, .03 silver,
.0533 copper

**Edge:** Reeded

**Weight:**
$5—0.109 oz.
(3.393 grams; 1/10 oz.
actual gold weight)
$10—0.273 oz.
(8.483 grams; 1/4 oz.
actual gold weight)
$25—0.545 oz.
(16.966 grams; 1/2 oz.
actual gold weight)
$50—1.091 oz.
(33.931 grams; 1 oz.
actual gold weight)

**Diameter:**
$5—16.5 mm
$10—22 mm
$25—27 mm
$50—32.7 mm

**Thickness:**
$50—2.87 mm

**Designers:**
Augustus Saint-Gaudens
(obverse), Miley Busiek
(reverse)

## $10 American Gold Eagle (1/4 oz.), Proof

*Mintage: 62,674*

| 1990-P | Grade | Purchased From | Date |
|--------|-------|----------------|------|
|        |       |                |      |

Bullion value at time of purchase: _____

## $25 American Gold Eagle (1/2 oz.), Proof

*Mintage: 51,636*

| 1990-P | Grade | Purchased From | Date |
|--------|-------|----------------|------|
|        |       |                |      |

Bullion value at time of purchase: _____

## $50 American Gold Eagle (1 oz.), Proof

*Mintage: 62,401*

| 1990-W | Grade | Purchased From | Date |
|--------|-------|----------------|------|
|        |       |                |      |

Bullion value at time of purchase: _____

## Proof Set, Gold, 1990

$5, $10, $25, and $50 American Gold Eagle
(1/10 oz. to 1 oz.), Proof

| 1990 | Grade | Purchased From | Date |
|------|-------|----------------|------|
|      |       |                |      |

Bullion value at time of purchase: _____

# 1991

**Historical context:** The American economy seemed to be strengthening in 1991 as output increased throughout the third quarter. Yet the rise in production was so slight that some feared it was not a recovery at all, but an economy stuck in slow growth. General Motors Corporation reported a record $4.5 billion loss and announced it would close 12 of its 21 plants over the coming years. Employment took a sharp downturn in November. Industrial production fell during the same time, suggesting that earlier optimism (that the recession was over) was premature. The stock market picked up at the end of 1991, however, bringing a measure of hope for the following year.

After Iraq's invasion of Kuwait, the United Nations set a deadline for President Saddam Hussein to order withdrawal. When it expired on January 16, 1991, with no response from Iraqi forces, the Persian Gulf War officially began and Iraq was promptly bombed by U.S. and British aircraft. In less than four days Iraq's poorly supplied military was overwhelmed and Kuwait was liberated, ending Operation Desert Storm. At the end of December 1991, the Soviet Union broke apart into what the individual Soviet republics called a "Commonwealth of Independent States." Mikhail Gorbachev, whose radical reforms had promoted the dissolution, stepped down from his position as president of the Soviet Union.

The American Numismatic Association's 100th anniversary was celebrated at its annual convention, held in 1991 in the city of Chicago. To promote interest and attract new collectors, ANA staff members released into circulation a pair of rare cents, creating a city-wide scavenger hunt that would reward the finder with a coin worth more than $300. The U.S. Mint issued commemorative coins in 1991 celebrating the golden anniversary of Mount Rushmore. Each coin featured the presidents on that famous American landmark: Washington, Jefferson, Roosevelt, and Lincoln.

Gold's bullion value dipped more than $20 overall for the year, compared to its 1990 average.

**Coin commentary:** The sixth year of the American Gold Eagle program—and the fifth year of full-year sales—saw decreases in the mintages of all four bullion-strike denominations. Demand for the Proof coins, too, was lower, except for the $25 half-ounce Proof, whose mintage increased slightly (by just under 1,500 pieces). The $25 half-ounce bullion strike, meanwhile, broke the previous year's record low for the entire program, with a mintage of just 24,100 coins.

Proofs of 1991 were struck at two Mint facilities: West Point for the largest ($50, one-ounce) denomination, with a W mintmark; and Philadelphia for the three fractional coins, with a P mintmark.

1991 was the final year of the American Gold Eagle's use of Roman numerals. Starting in 1992 the year date would be featured in Arabic numbers.

The 1991 $25 half-ounce American Gold Eagle was ranked no. 48 among the 100 Greatest U.S. Modern Coins, in the book of the same name. Coauthors Scott Schechter and Jeff Garrett note that the largest (one-ounce) and smallest (tenth-ounce) coins are the most popular in the American Gold Eagle series, and that "in many years, 10 times more one-ounce coins were struck than 1/2-ounce or 1/4-ounce coins." They point out that, beyond interested collectors, the main purchasers of the fractional gold coins are small investors—and in the early 1990s small investors weren't buying a lot of gold. Only 24,100 of the half-ounce 1991 American Gold Eagles were sold, most of them likely to coin collectors seeking to maintain a complete set. "Not only is this the lowest mintage figure for a 1/2-ounce bullion-issue gold eagle," Schechter and Garrett observe, "it's the lowest figure for *any* bullion-issue gold eagle. As a result, today it is, by a good margin, the most valuable 1/2-ounce gold eagle, eclipsing even the Proof and Uncirculated (with mintmark) collector issues."

# Bullion Strikes, Gold, 1991

**$5 American Gold Eagle (1/10 oz.), bullion strike**    *Mintage: 165,200*

| 1991 | Grade | Purchased From | Date |
|------|-------|----------------|------|
|      |       |                |      |

Bullion value at time of purchase: _____

**$10 American Gold Eagle (1/4 oz.), bullion strike**    *Mintage: 36,100*

| 1991 | Grade | Purchased From | Date |
|------|-------|----------------|------|
|      |       |                |      |

Bullion value at time of purchase: _____

**1991 average spot prices:**
silver, $4.06; gold, $363.29;
platinum, $371.09

**Total 1991 American Gold Eagle mintage (in ounces):**
280,695 (bullion);
96,717 (Proof)

**American Gold Eagles**
Date: MCMXCI (1991)
Mints: West Point Mint (bullion strikes [no mintmark] and $50 Proofs [W mintmark]); Philadephia Mint ($5, $10, and $25 Proofs [P mintmark])

**Composition:**
.9167 gold, .03 silver, .0533 copper
Edge: Reeded
**Weight:**
$5—0.109 oz. (3.393 grams; 1/10 oz. actual gold weight)
$10—0.273 oz. (8.483 grams; 1/4 oz. actual gold weight)
$25—0.545 oz. (16.966 grams; 1/2 oz. actual gold weight)
$50—1.091 oz. (33.931 grams; 1 oz. actual gold weight)

**Diameter:**
$5—16.5 mm
$10—22 mm
$25—27 mm
$50—32.7 mm
**Thickness:**
$50—2.87 mm
**Designers:**
Augustus Saint-Gaudens (obverse), Miley Busiek (reverse)

## $25 American Gold Eagle (1/2 oz.), bullion strike — *Mintage: 24,100*

| 1991 | Grade | Purchased From | Date |
|---|---|---|---|
|  |  |  |  |

Bullion value at time of purchase: _____

## $50 American Gold Eagle (1 oz.), bullion strike — *Mintage: 243,100*

| 1991 | Grade | Purchased From | Date |
|---|---|---|---|
|  |  |  |  |

Bullion value at time of purchase: _____

# Proof Strikes, Gold, 1991

## $5 American Gold Eagle (1/10 oz.), Proof — *Mintage: 70,334*

| 1991-P | Grade | Purchased From | Date |
|---|---|---|---|
|  |  |  |  |

Bullion value at time of purchase: _____

## $10 American Gold Eagle (1/4 oz.), Proof — *Mintage: 50,839*

| 1991-P | Grade | Purchased From | Date |
|---|---|---|---|
|  |  |  |  |

Bullion value at time of purchase: _____

## $25 American Gold Eagle (1/2 oz.), Proof — *Mintage: 53,125*

| 1991-P | Grade | Purchased From | Date |
|---|---|---|---|
|  |  |  |  |

Bullion value at time of purchase: _____

## $50 American Gold Eagle (1 oz.), Proof — *Mintage: 50,411*

| 1991-W | Grade | Purchased From | Date |
|---|---|---|---|
|  |  |  |  |

Bullion value at time of purchase: _____

# Proof Set, Gold, 1991

**$5, $10, $25, and $50 American Gold Eagle (1/10 oz. to 1 oz.), Proof**

| 1991 | Uncertified | PF-69 | PF-70 |
|---|---|---|---|
| Value* | $3,220 | $3,390 | $5,050 |

* Based on bullion value of $1,400 per ounce.

# 1992

**Historical context:** The early-1990s recession was still gripping the American economy as 1992 entered mid-year. Unemployment neared 8 percent that June, with 10 million people jobless. IBM lost $5 billion in the year, leading the company to cut 25,000 employees from its roster. Finally GDP climbed 5.7 percent during the fourth quarter, encouraging businesses to assume the recession was over and invest in their inventories accordingly. However, the recovery would slip soon after and send the economy back into the doldrums for the beginning of 1993.

On February 7, 1992, Western Europe united after hundreds of years of conflict, with signature of the Maastricht Treaty of European Union. Twelve nations would join by the time the treaty came into effect a year later, and by 2002 a common currency, the euro, would be adopted by many member nations (though some, such as Great Britain, would choose to retain their original currency).

In the fall of 1992 the American Numismatic Association made a daily two-and-a-half-minute radio program available to share history and information about coins and paper money, targeting audiences of the general public as well as active collectors. The ANA provided the program for free to more than 300 national-public-radio stations and more than 80 business-radio-network stations.

Silver and gold both continued to decline in 1992, as they had in 1991, with gold losing another $20 an ounce to average just under $345 per ounce for the year.

**Coin commentary:** A notable design change came to the American Gold Eagle coinage in 1992, with the dates switched from Roman numeral format to today's more familiar Arabic numbers. Originally the year dates were in Roman numerals to recreate the style of the Saint-Gaudens double eagle, after which the obverse of the American Gold Eagle was modeled.

Mintages increased in 1992 compared to 1991 for all four denominations of bullion-strike American Gold Eagles (most dramatically for the $25 half-ounce, which more than doubled in mintage after a record-low year in 1991). Meanwhile, the situation was reversed for the 1992 Proof coins: all four sizes saw their mintages go down slightly from 1991. (As with other recent years' offerings, the Proof coins were sold directly by the U.S. Mint to collectors, individually and in four-coin sets. The one-ounce coins were struck at West Point with a W mintmark. The three smaller denominations were struck at the Philadelphia Mint, with a P mintmark.)

## Bullion Strikes, Gold, 1992

$5 American Gold Eagle (1/10 oz.), bullion strike          *Mintage: 209,300*

| 1992 | Grade | Purchased From | Date |
|------|-------|----------------|------|
|      |       |                |      |

Bullion value at time of purchase: _____

**1992 average spot prices:**
silver, $3.95; gold, $344.97;
platinum, $360.92

**Total 1992 American Gold
Eagle mintage (in ounces):**
338,019 (bullion);
83,369 (Proof)

**American Gold Eagles**
Date:   1992
Mints:  West Point Mint (bullion
strikes [no mintmark] and
$50 Proofs [W mintmark]);
Philadephia Mint ($5,
$10, and $25 Proofs
[P mintmark])
**Composition:**
.9167 gold, .03 silver,
.0533 copper
Edge:   Reeded
**Weight:**
$5—0.109 oz.
(3.393 grams; 1/10 oz.
actual gold weight)
$10—0.273 oz.
(8.483 grams; 1/4 oz.
actual gold weight)
$25—0.545 oz.
(16.966 grams; 1/2 oz.
actual gold weight)
$50—1.091 oz.
(33.931 grams; 1 oz.
actual gold weight)
**Diameter:**
$5—16.5 mm
$10—22 mm
$25—27 mm
$50—32.7 mm
**Thickness:**
$50—2.87 mm
**Designers:**
Augustus Saint-Gaudens
(obverse), Miley Busiek
(reverse)

**$10 American Gold Eagle (1/4 oz.), bullion strike**   *Mintage: 59,546*

| 1992 | Grade | Purchased From | Date |
|---|---|---|---|
|  |  |  |  |

Bullion value at time of purchase: _____

**$25 American Gold Eagle (1/2 oz.), bullion strike**   *Mintage: 54,404*

| 1992 | Grade | Purchased From | Date |
|---|---|---|---|
|  |  |  |  |

Bullion value at time of purchase: _____

**$50 American Gold Eagle (1 oz.), bullion strike**   *Mintage: 275,000*

| 1992 | Grade | Purchased From | Date |
|---|---|---|---|
|  |  |  |  |

Bullion value at time of purchase: _____

## Proof Strikes, Gold, 1992

**$5 American Gold Eagle (1/10 oz.), Proof**   *Mintage: 64,874*

| 1992-P | Grade | Purchased From | Date |
|---|---|---|---|
|  |  |  |  |

Bullion value at time of purchase: _____

**$10 American Gold Eagle (1/4 oz.), Proof**   *Mintage: 46,269*

| 1992-P | Grade | Purchased From | Date |
|---|---|---|---|
|  |  |  |  |

Bullion value at time of purchase: _____

**$25 American Gold Eagle (1/2 oz.), Proof**   *Mintage: 40,976*

| 1992-P | Grade | Purchased From | Date |
|---|---|---|---|
|  |  |  |  |

Bullion value at time of purchase: _____

**$50 American Gold Eagle (1 oz.), Proof**   *Mintage: 44,826*

| 1992-W | Grade | Purchased From | Date |
|---|---|---|---|
|  |  |  |  |

Bullion value at time of purchase: _____

## Proof Set, Gold, 1992

**$5, $10, $25, and $50 American Gold Eagle
(1/10 oz. to 1 oz.), Proof**

| 1992 | Grade | Purchased From | Date |
|---|---|---|---|
|  |  |  |  |

Bullion value at time of purchase: _____

# 1993

**Historical context:** The U.S. economy in 1993 saw a sudden decline from the end of 1992 and struggled through the middle of the year. Recession in Europe and Japan continued to negatively affect the American economy. Exports decreased heavily in June and July. Newly elected president Bill Clinton started an economic strategy that included budget cuts that would help the economy slowly make its way out of the recession.

Six people were killed and 1,000 injured when a bomb exploded in the parking garage of the World Trade Center in New York City in February. Four men would eventually be arrested for the attack, each receiving a prison sentence of 240 years.

At the White House, representatives from Israel and Palestine—nations involved in a decades-long bloody feud—met to sign a peace accord declaring an end to their conflict and an equal right to the land between the Jordan River and the Mediterranean Sea.

May of 1993 saw the joining of a panel to choose the designs for commemorative coins celebrating the 50th anniversary of World War II. Six designs were selected from 430 contest entries: one each for the obverse and reverse of a $5 gold piece, a silver dollar, and a copper-nickel half dollar. Themes such as the Allied victory and the Battle of Normandy were legislated by Congress for the gold and silver coins, respectively.

Just before its annual convention, in Baltimore, the American Numismatic Association once again placed rare coins into circulation—this time five of them, including a 1909-S V.D.B. cent worth more than $400—to drum up publicity for the hobby.

Silver and gold, after years in the doldrums, both averaged upward in 1993, with gold some $15 per ounce higher than 1992.

**Coin commentary:** Increasing interest in precious metals brought higher mintages for the bullion-strike American Gold Eagles of 1993. The one-ounce $50 denomination rose from 1992 production of 275,000 to 480,000-plus in 1993. The fractional coins saw proportionally smaller jumps, but they did increase, as well. This year the American Gold Eagle was the world leader in gold-bullion coin sales.

Collector interest in the U.S. Mint's annually issued Proof coins, meanwhile, stayed relatively stable, deviating up or down from just a few dozen to a few thousand coins, depending on the denomination, compared to the previous year. The Mint established sales limits for the year's Proofs, but demand never approached those mintage caps.

As was customary by now, the Mint offered the 1993 Proof American Gold Eagles individually and in a four-coin set. One-ounce Proofs were struck at the West Point Mint, with a W mintmark, and the smaller fractional-ounce Proofs were struck at the Philadelphia Mint, with a P mintmark.

**1993 Philadelphia Mint Bicentennial Set (mintage: 12,689).**

**1993 average spot prices:**
silver, $4.31; gold, $360.91; platinum, $374.14

**Total 1993 American Gold Eagle mintage (in ounces):**
555,891 (bullion);
73,759 (Proof)

**American Gold Eagles**

**Date:** 1993

**Mints:** West Point Mint (bullion strikes [no mintmark] and $50 Proofs [W mintmark]); Philadephia Mint ($5, $10, and $25 Proofs [P mintmark])

**Composition:**
.9167 gold, .03 silver, .0533 copper

**Edge:** Reeded

**Weight:**
$5—0.109 oz. (3.393 grams; 1/10 oz. actual gold weight)
$10—0.273 oz. (8.483 grams; 1/4 oz. actual gold weight)
$25—0.545 oz. (16.966 grams; 1/2 oz. actual gold weight)
$50—1.091 oz. (33.931 grams; 1 oz. actual gold weight)

**Diameter:**
$5—16.5 mm
$10—22 mm
$25—27 mm
$50—32.7 mm

**Thickness:**
$50—2.87 mm

**Designers:**
Augustus Saint-Gaudens (obverse), Miley Busiek (reverse)

The fractional sizes were also included in a special package this year: the 1993 Philadelphia Mint Bicentennial Set. This celebrated the 200th anniversary of the U.S. Mint's first official regular coinage made for general circulation. It included three denominations of 1993 American Gold Eagles (the $5 tenth-ounce, the $10 quarter-ounce, and the $25 half-ounce), plus a 1993 American Silver Eagle, and a .76-ounce, .900 fine silver commemorative medal recreating the famous John Ward Dunsmore painting of Martha Washington inspecting the first U.S. coins. (For more information on Dunsmore's painting, see *The Secret History of the First U.S. Mint*, by Joel J. Orosz and Leonard Augsburger). The coins and the silver medal were all issued in Proof format, appropriately struck at the Philadelphia Mint, and the set was packaged in a green velvet box with a certificate of authenticity. Its issue price was $499. Collectors and investors bought 12,689 of the sets.

## Bullion Strikes, Gold, 1993

**$5 American Gold Eagle (1/10 oz.), bullion strike**          *Mintage: 210,709*

| 1993 | Grade | Purchased From | Date |
|------|-------|----------------|------|
|      |       |                |      |

Bullion value at time of purchase: _____

**$10 American Gold Eagle (1/4 oz.), bullion strike**          *Mintage: 71,864*

| 1993 | Grade | Purchased From | Date |
|------|-------|----------------|------|
|      |       |                |      |

Bullion value at time of purchase: _____

**$25 American Gold Eagle (1/2 oz.), bullion strike**          *Mintage: 73,324*

| 1993 | Grade | Purchased From | Date |
|------|-------|----------------|------|
|      |       |                |      |

Bullion value at time of purchase: _____

**$50 American Gold Eagle (1 oz.), bullion strike**          *Mintage: 480,192*

| 1993 | Grade | Purchased From | Date |
|------|-------|----------------|------|
|      |       |                |      |

Bullion value at time of purchase: _____

## Proof Strikes, Gold, 1993

**$5 American Gold Eagle (1/10 oz.), Proof**          *Mintage: 58,649*

| 1993-P | Grade | Purchased From | Date |
|--------|-------|----------------|------|
|        |       |                |      |

Bullion value at time of purchase: _____

$10 American Gold Eagle (1/4 oz.), Proof      *Mintage: 46,464*

| 1993-P | Grade | Purchased From | Date |
|--------|-------|----------------|------|
|        |       |                |      |

Bullion value at time of purchase: _____

$25 American Gold Eagle (1/2 oz.), Proof      *Mintage: 43,819*

| 1993-P | Grade | Purchased From | Date |
|--------|-------|----------------|------|
|        |       |                |      |

Bullion value at time of purchase: _____

$50 American Gold Eagle (1 oz.), Proof      *Mintage: 34,369*

| 1993-W | Grade | Purchased From | Date |
|--------|-------|----------------|------|
|        |       |                |      |

Bullion value at time of purchase: _____

## Proof Set, Gold, 1993

$5, $10, $25, and $50 American Gold Eagle
(1/10 oz. to 1 oz.), Proof

| 1993 | Grade | Purchased From | Date |
|------|-------|----------------|------|
|      |       |                |      |

Bullion value at time of purchase: _____

## Proof Set, Bicentennial, 1993

$5, $10, $25, and $50 American Gold Eagle (1/10 oz.
to 1 oz.), American Silver Eagle, and medal, Proof

| 1993 | Grade | Purchased From | Date |
|------|-------|----------------|------|
|      |       |                |      |

Bullion value at time of purchase: _____

# 1994

**Historical context:** After a rocky few years, the American economy turned around throughout 1994. The economic growth rate climbed to 3 percent while two million new jobs eased unemployment. The nation's exports, which had been declining for several years, were bolstered. Surprisingly, even after drastic losses in important companies like IBM and General Motors, America stood at the top of the computer and communication technology industries, ahead of other powerful countries (like Japan) that were still mired in recession. Pessimism and doomsday opinions that had haunted America since the beginning of the decade began to be pushed aside for a new and bold outlook on the nation's economic power.

The North American Free Trade Agreement—a contract between the United States, Canada, and Mexico—went into effect on January 1, 1994. It created the world's largest free-trade area, linking 450 million people and producing $17 trillion worth of goods and services, according to the president's Office of the United States Trade Representative.

During the 1994 midterm congressional elections, the Republican Party won control of both the House of Representatives and the Senate for the first time in 40 years. Representative Newt Gingrich of Georgia, coauthor of the Republicans' conservative-platform Contract With America, became speaker of the House.

More than 22 million South Africans cast their votes for Nelson Mandela in that nation's first-ever multiracial parliamentary elections. Mandela, who had fought against apartheid and spent almost three decades in jail, was inaugurated as the first black president of South Africa on May 10, 1994.

In 1994 citizens around the world proposed the creation of Peace coins for the year 2000—collectibles to mark the upcoming millennium and promote world peace. The idea was developed by a committee of the American Numismatic Association and was further discussed at the World Mint Directors Conference. Kenneth Bressett, longtime editor of the *Guide Book of United States Coins* (the "Red Book") and president of the ANA from 1993 to 1995, was influential in the Peace coin movement.

Gold's spot value was on the rise; the precious metal's average price for the year climbed more than 6 percent over that of 1993.

**Coin commentary:** The previous year's jump in bullion-strike mintage for the one-ounce American Gold Eagle proved to be an anomaly, as 1994 demand scaled back down to the 221,000 level—more akin to the 275,000 of 1992 than to the 480,000 of 1993. Demand for the fractional coins was far more steady, with the $25 half-ounce dropping by about 11,000 coins (15 percent), the $10 quarter-ounce rising by 786 coins (1 percent), and the $5 tenth-ounce dropping by just over 4,000 coins (2 percent).

Collector interest in Proofs, meanwhile, rose slightly across the board, in particular for the one-ounce $50 denomination. The Proof coins were offered individually and in a four-coin set, as in previous years.

Up until 1994, the manufacture of Proof American Gold Eagles had been divided between the West Point Mint (for the one-ounce coins) and the Philadelphia Mint (for the three smaller coins). In 1994 production of all Proof American Gold Eagles was moved to West Point. (This would be a permanent change in the bullion program.) As a result, all 1994 Proofs bear that facility's distinctive W mintmark.

## Bullion Strikes, Gold, 1994

**$5 American Gold Eagle (1/10 oz.), bullion strike**      *Mintage: 206,380*

| 1994 | Grade | Purchased From | Date |
|------|-------|----------------|------|
|      |       |                |      |

Bullion value at time of purchase: _____

**$10 American Gold Eagle (1/4 oz.), bullion strike**      *Mintage: 72,650*

| 1994 | Grade | Purchased From | Date |
|------|-------|----------------|------|
|      |       |                |      |

Bullion value at time of purchase: _____

**$25 American Gold Eagle (1/2 oz.), bullion strike**     *Mintage: 62,400*

| 1994 | Grade | Purchased From | Date |
|------|-------|----------------|------|
|      |       |                |      |

Bullion value at time of purchase: _____

**$50 American Gold Eagle (1 oz.), bullion strike**     *Mintage: 221,663*

| 1994 | Grade | Purchased From | Date |
|------|-------|----------------|------|
|      |       |                |      |

Bullion value at time of purchase: _____

# Proof Strikes, Gold, 1994

**$5 American Gold Eagle (1/10 oz.), Proof**     *Mintage: 62,849*

| 1994-W | Grade | Purchased From | Date |
|--------|-------|----------------|------|
|        |       |                |      |

Bullion value at time of purchase: _____

**$10 American Gold Eagle (1/4 oz.), Proof**     *Mintage: 48,172*

| 1994-W | Grade | Purchased From | Date |
|--------|-------|----------------|------|
|        |       |                |      |

Bullion value at time of purchase: _____

**$25 American Gold Eagle (1/2 oz.), Proof**     *Mintage: 44,584*

| 1994-W | Grade | Purchased From | Date |
|--------|-------|----------------|------|
|        |       |                |      |

Bullion value at time of purchase: _____

**$50 American Gold Eagle (1 oz.), Proof**     *Mintage: 46,674*

| 1994-W | Grade | Purchased From | Date |
|--------|-------|----------------|------|
|        |       |                |      |

Bullion value at time of purchase: _____

# Proof Set, Gold, 1994

**$5, $10, $25, and $50 American Gold Eagle (1/10 oz. to 1 oz.), Proof**

| 1994-W | Grade | Purchased From | Date |
|--------|-------|----------------|------|
|        |       |                |      |

Bullion value at time of purchase: _____

---

**1994 average spot prices:**
silver, $5.29; gold, $385.42; platinum, $404.95

**Total 1994 American Gold Eagle mintage (in ounces):**
291,664 (bullion);
87,294 (Proof)

**American Gold Eagles**
**Date:** 1994
**Mints:** West Point Mint (bullion strikes [no mintmark] and Proofs [W mintmark])
**Composition:**
.9167 gold, .03 silver, .0533 copper
**Edge:** Reeded
**Weight:**
$5—0.109 oz. (3.393 grams; 1/10 oz. actual gold weight)
$10—0.273 oz. (8.483 grams; 1/4 oz. actual gold weight)
$25—0.545 oz. (16.966 grams; 1/2 oz. actual gold weight)
$50—1.091 oz. (33.931 grams; 1 oz. actual gold weight)
**Diameter:**
$5—16.5 mm
$10—22 mm
$25—27 mm
$50—32.7 mm
**Thickness:**
$50—2.87 mm
**Designers:**
Augustus Saint-Gaudens (obverse), Miley Busiek (reverse)

# 1995

**Historical context:** The American economy expanded in 1995 with a decent amount of growth and low inflation rates. Employment continued to increase overall, though in different sectors there were wins and losses.

South of the border, the Mexican economy hit a crisis-inducing low, and President Bill Clinton used executive power to push through a $20 billion loan for the struggling country. This marked the first time the United States used its Exchange Stabilization Fund to aid a foreign currency.

On October 3, after nearly a year of trial, celebrity O.J. Simpson was acquitted of two brutal murders (of his wife and a friend) that had shocked the nation. On the international scene, in March a series of sarin-gas attacks killed 12 and injured more than 5,000 people in Tokyo's subway system. The attacks were conducted by a doomsday cult whose leader was found and arrested.

In 1995 the American Numismatic Association named NGC its official third-party coin-grading service. The U.S. Mint introduced one of its largest and most complex commemorative coin programs ever—that of the XXVI Olympiad (held in Atlanta, Georgia). More than 30 coins were minted in various formats and denominations, honoring sports such as track and field, tennis, and rowing, as well as the Olympics themselves.

The bullion market saw normal minor jumps and dives during the year but overall was stable. Over the course of 1995 precious-metal spot prices averaged out very close to their 1994 levels, with gold varying only a few cents.

**Coin commentary:** The two smaller denominations of American Gold Eagle saw slight rises in bullion-strike mintage in 1995, while demand for the two larger denominations dropped about 10 percent.

Collectors purchased the year's Proof American Gold Eagles (available individually and in four-coin sets) in quantities very close to those of 1994, up or down by just a few percentage points depending on the denomination.

In addition to the by-then-standard four-coin Proof set of American Gold Eagles, the U.S. Mint produced a special five-coin set in 1995 to mark the 10th anniversary of its American Eagle bullion program. The Mint established a sales limit of 45,000 sets, and collectors ultimately purchased 30,125. The anniversary set included all four denominations of the 1995 American Gold Eagle—the $5 tenth-ounce coin, the $10 quarter-ounce, the $25 half-ounce, and the $50 one-ounce—in Proof format. Each was struck at the West Point Mint and featured that facility's W mintmark. The fifth coin in the set, the 1995-W Proof American Silver Eagle, would become famous as the "King of the Silver Eagles," because it was available *only* in this special set. The rarity of the 1995-W American Silver Eagle drives the value of the 10th-anniversary set up to its current high level—several times its original issue price of $999.

For more on the 1995-W American Silver Eagle, consult *American Silver Eagles: A Guide to the U.S. Bullion Coin Program* (Mercanti) and *The 100 Greatest U.S. Modern Coins* (Schechter and Garrett).

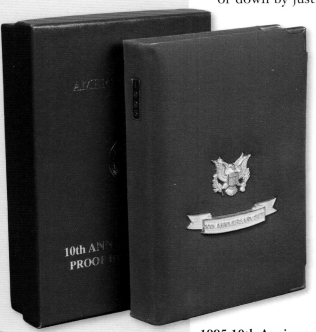

**1995 10th Anniversary Five-Coin Proof Set (mintage: 30,125).**

# Bullion Strikes, Gold, 1995

**$5 American Gold Eagle (1/10 oz.), bullion strike**     *Mintage: 223,025*

| 1995 | Grade | Purchased From | Date |
|------|-------|----------------|------|
|      |       |                |      |

Bullion value at time of purchase: _____

**$10 American Gold Eagle (1/4 oz.), bullion strike**     *Mintage: 83,752*

| 1995 | Grade | Purchased From | Date |
|------|-------|----------------|------|
|      |       |                |      |

Bullion value at time of purchase: _____

**$25 American Gold Eagle (1/2 oz.), bullion strike**     *Mintage: 53,474*

| 1995 | Grade | Purchased From | Date |
|------|-------|----------------|------|
|      |       |                |      |

Bullion value at time of purchase: _____

**$50 American Gold Eagle (1 oz.), bullion strike**     *Mintage: 200,636*

| 1995 | Grade | Purchased From | Date |
|------|-------|----------------|------|
|      |       |                |      |

Bullion value at time of purchase: _____

# Proof Strikes, Gold, 1995

**$5 American Gold Eagle (1/10 oz.), Proof**     *Mintage: 62,667*

| 1995-W | Grade | Purchased From | Date |
|--------|-------|----------------|------|
|        |       |                |      |

Bullion value at time of purchase: _____

**$10 American Gold Eagle (1/4 oz.), Proof**     *Mintage: 47,526*

| 1995-W | Grade | Purchased From | Date |
|--------|-------|----------------|------|
|        |       |                |      |

Bullion value at time of purchase: _____

**$25 American Gold Eagle (1/2 oz.), Proof**     *Mintage: 45,388*

| 1995-W | Grade | Purchased From | Date |
|--------|-------|----------------|------|
|        |       |                |      |

Bullion value at time of purchase: _____

---

**1995 average spot prices:** silver, $5.19; gold, $385.50; platinum, $424.38

**Total 1995 American Gold Eagle mintage (in ounces):** 270,614 (bullion); 87,210 (Proof)

**American Gold Eagles**

**Date:** 1995

**Mints:** West Point Mint (bullion strikes [no mintmark] and Proofs [W mintmark])

**Composition:** .9167 gold, .03 silver, .0533 copper

**Edge:** Reeded

**Weight:**
$5—0.109 oz. (3.393 grams; 1/10 oz. actual gold weight)
$10—0.273 oz. (8.483 grams; 1/4 oz. actual gold weight)
$25—0.545 oz. (16.966 grams; 1/2 oz. actual gold weight)
$50—1.091 oz. (33.931 grams; 1 oz. actual gold weight)

**Diameter:**
$5—16.5 mm
$10—22 mm
$25—27 mm
$50—32.7 mm

**Thickness:**
$50—2.87 mm

**Designers:** Augustus Saint-Gaudens (obverse), Miley Busiek (reverse)

**$50 American Gold Eagle (1 oz.), Proof** *Mintage: 46,368*

| 1995-W | Grade | Purchased From | Date |
|--------|-------|----------------|------|
|        |       |                |      |

Bullion value at time of purchase: _____

## Proof Set, Gold, 1995
**$5, $10, $25, and $50 American Gold Eagle
(1/10 oz. to 1 oz.), Proof**

| 1995-W | Grade | Purchased From | Date |
|--------|-------|----------------|------|
|        |       |                |      |

Bullion value at time of purchase: _____

## Proof Set, 10th Anniversary, 1995
**$5, $10, $25, and $50 American Gold Eagle
(1/10 oz. to 1 oz.), and American Silver Eagle, Proof**

| 1995-W | Grade | Purchased From | Date |
|--------|-------|----------------|------|
|        |       |                |      |

Bullion value at time of purchase: _____

# 1996

**Historical context:** The U.S. economy in 1996 experienced a decent amount of growth, as well as low inflation. Unemployment hit a historic low with 2.5 million jobs added to the rolls—a 2.1 percent increase over the previous year. Nonfarm payroll employment continued to increase as it had in 1995, averaging an additional 209,100 jobs every month. Industrial production picked up again as well, increasing 4.7 percent, a significant improvement over the previous year.

In 1996 Dolly the sheep, the first mammal to be cloned from an adult cell, was born at the Roslin Institute in Scotland, causing controversy—one side arguing for the benefits in medicine that cloning technology could achieve, and the other side denouncing it as unethical, especially considering the possibility of human cloning.

Sales of the U.S. Mint's commemorative 1995–1996 Olympic coins continued this year. The Mint also rolled out two new commemorative-coin programs. One was for a silver dollar honoring national community service; the other was for a silver dollar and a gold $5 piece honoring the 150th anniversary of the Smithsonian Institution.

Compared to its 1995 price, gold held stable in 1996, averaging out the year at $389.09 (up about $4). It continued to trend slightly lower than platinum's spot value.

**Coin commentary:** The three larger denominations of American Gold Eagles each saw a drop in mintage between 1995 and 1996. Demand for the smallest coin, however, spiked upward by an impressive 80 percent: sales of the tenth-ounce American Gold Eagle jumped from 223,025 to 401,964.

Proofs, too, saw slower sales. After the excitement of the 10th anniversary of the U.S. bullion program (1995), collectors purchased fewer of the Mint's Proof American Gold Eagles in 1996, with mintages dropping by about 10 percent in the tenth-ounce and about 25 percent across the three larger sizes. As with the Proof coins of 1994 and 1995, all were produced at the West Point Mint, and bear the distinctive W mintmark. They were available for sale directly to collectors from the U.S. Mint, individually and in four-coin sets.

Proof mintages were capped at 55,000 individual one-ounce coins (issue-priced at $589); 50,000 half-ounce ($299); 55,000 quarter-ounce ($159); and 70,000 tenth-ounce ($75); with no limit to the number of four-coin sets ($1,025).

# Bullion Strikes, Gold, 1996

**$5 American Gold Eagle (1/10 oz.), bullion strike**      *Mintage: 401,964*

| 1996 | Grade | Purchased From | Date |
|------|-------|----------------|------|
|      |       |                |      |

Bullion value at time of purchase: _____

**$10 American Gold Eagle (1/4 oz.), bullion strike**      *Mintage: 60,318*

| 1996 | Grade | Purchased From | Date |
|------|-------|----------------|------|
|      |       |                |      |

Bullion value at time of purchase: _____

**$25 American Gold Eagle (1/2 oz.), bullion strike**      *Mintage: 39,287*

| 1996 | Grade | Purchased From | Date |
|------|-------|----------------|------|
|      |       |                |      |

Bullion value at time of purchase: _____

**$50 American Gold Eagle (1 oz.), bullion strike**      *Mintage: 189,148*

| 1996 | Grade | Purchased From | Date |
|------|-------|----------------|------|
|      |       |                |      |

Bullion value at time of purchase: _____

# Proof Strikes, Gold, 1996

**$5 American Gold Eagle (1/10 oz.), Proof**      *Mintage: 57,047*

| 1996-W | Grade | Purchased From | Date |
|--------|-------|----------------|------|
|        |       |                |      |

Bullion value at time of purchase: _____

**1996 average spot prices:** silver, $5.20; gold, $389.09; platinum, $397.12

**Total 1996 American Gold Eagle mintage (in ounces):** 264,067 (bullion); 68,941 (Proof)

**American Gold Eagles**

**Date:** 1996

**Mints:** West Point Mint (bullion strikes [no mintmark] and Proofs [W mintmark])

**Composition:** .9167 gold, .03 silver, .0533 copper

**Edge:** Reeded

**Weight:**
$5—0.109 oz. (3.393 grams; 1/10 oz. actual gold weight)
$10—0.273 oz. (8.483 grams; 1/4 oz. actual gold weight)
$25—0.545 oz. (16.966 grams; 1/2 oz. actual gold weight)
$50—1.091 oz. (33.931 grams; 1 oz. actual gold weight)

**Diameter:**
$5—16.5 mm
$10—22 mm
$25—27 mm
$50—32.7 mm

**Thickness:**
$50—2.87 mm

**Designers:** Augustus Saint-Gaudens (obverse), Miley Busiek (reverse)

**$10 American Gold Eagle (1/4 oz.), Proof**       *Mintage: 38,219*

| 1996-W | Grade | Purchased From | Date |
|--------|-------|----------------|------|
|        |       |                |      |

Bullion value at time of purchase: _____

**$25 American Gold Eagle (1/2 oz.), Proof**       *Mintage: 35,058*

| 1996-W | Grade | Purchased From | Date |
|--------|-------|----------------|------|
|        |       |                |      |

Bullion value at time of purchase: _____

**$50 American Gold Eagle (1 oz.), Proof**       *Mintage: 36,153*

| 1996-W | Grade | Purchased From | Date |
|--------|-------|----------------|------|
|        |       |                |      |

Bullion value at time of purchase: _____

## Proof Set, Gold, 1996

**$5, $10, $25, and $50 American Gold Eagle
(1/10 oz. to 1 oz.), Proof**

| 1996-W | Grade | Purchased From | Date |
|--------|-------|----------------|------|
|        |       |                |      |

Bullion value at time of purchase: _____

# 1997

**Historical context:** The economy of the United States was on the rise in 1997 when a confidence-shaking international crisis struck. In the middle of the year the economies of Thailand, Indonesia, and South Korea collapsed, setting off a regional chain reaction of "financial contagion." Much of Asia saw its stock and currency markets plummet and private debt rise. Despite the severity of the crisis, America's economy was strong enough to avoid disaster. Against this backdrop, the long-scheduled return of Hong Kong from British to Chinese control came about in a ceremony overseen by Britain's prime minister, the Prince of Wales, the Chinese president, and the U.S. secretary of State. (Britain had governed Hong Kong since the early 1840s.)

On August 31, 1997, the car accident and death of Princess Diana of Wales made international headlines, prompting grief in Great Britain, the rest of Europe, and America.

On the numismatic scene, in December one of the most successful and popular coinage programs in U.S. history was signed into law. The 50 State Quarters® Program would distribute a unique quarter in honor of each state (five per year) between 1999 and 2008. Before long millions of Americans would be collecting the coins from their pocket change. Silver dollars and two $5 gold pieces were issued in 1997 to commemorate baseball great and humanitarian Jackie Robinson, President Franklin Roosevelt, the U.S. Botanic Garden, and the National Law Enforcement Officers Memorial.

The bullion markets dipped in 1997, with gold in particular weakening compared to 1996 spot prices—down from an average of $389.09 per ounce to $332.39. At the end of the year it was hovering just above $290.

**Coin commentary:** Although sales of *Proof* American Gold Eagles lagged in 1997, the year brought a huge upswing in demand for the coins as bullion. Measured in ounces, sales nearly tripled compared to 1996. Much of this increase was in demand for the $50 one-ounce coin: its mintage rose from 189,148 in 1996 to 664,508 in 1997. That June the U.S. Mint announced that, according to a World Gold Council survey, the American Gold Eagle was the best-selling gold investment coin in the world during the year's first quarter. Though it had always been the perennial market leader in North America, the Eagle had not held the number one position globally since 1993. This position was reaffirmed in the second quarter. "The Eagle has retained its world number one status," said Mint Director Philip N. Diehl, "garnering an impressive 43 percent of the world market share, up from 38 percent in the first quarter. Year-to-date figures reveal that worldwide bullion sales are up 31 percent over the same period last year, and that the Eagle has increased its share steadily."

As always, the Proof gold coins were available individually and in four-coin sets. The Mint lowered the mintage limits of individual Proof American Gold Eagles in 1997, and set a cap on the number of four-coin Proof sets. Proof-mintage maximums were reduced to 45,000 individual one-ounce coins (down from 55,000); 38,000 half-ounce (down from 50,000); 45,000 quarter-ounce (down from 55,000); and 45,000 tenth-ounce (down from 70,000). The number of four-coin sets was capped at 30,000. Issue prices remained the same as in 1996. "We're lowering the Proof Eagle mintages in response to our customers' interest in secondary market prices of our products," Mint Director Philip N. Diehl stated in an April 11, 1996, press release announcing the changes. "We recognize that our customers expect that our products retain a significant portion of their purchase price in the after-market. We believe lowering mintages will help us achieve that goal. This is part of a new philosophy we're pursuing in 1997 as an extension of our tradition of offering limited-edition products—such as the recent Botanic Garden Coinage & Currency Set. We believe that these lower mintage limits will make our products consistently more appealing to the collector. You can expect to see future issues structured in a similar way—to raise the value of all our products, for all collectors."

This strategy seemed to pay off, with the tenth-ounce Proof American Gold Eagle selling out in the first nine weeks of availability. During that same period more than 50 percent of the four-coin set and half-ounce mintage limits were sold.

From 1986 to 1996, the U.S. Mint's American Eagle lineup included the one-ounce American Silver Eagle and the four sizes of American Gold Eagles, in various formats and packaging options. In 1997 platinum was added to the roster for the first time. Production of the American Platinum Eagle was split between the Philadelphia Mint (for bullion strikes) and the West Point Mint (for Proofs). Both formats featured the same designs: a close view of the Statue of Liberty's head and crown, by John M. Mercanti, and a soaring bald eagle in front of the rising sun (described as a "setting" sun in some early Mint marketing materials), by Thomas D. Rogers Sr. The largest platinum coin, the

The initials of John Mercanti, the U.S. Mint sculptor-engraver who designed the Statue of Liberty obverse, are above Liberty's upraised shoulder.

one-ounce, has the highest face value of any U.S. coin: $100. The fractional pieces were denominated $50 (half-ounce), $25 (quarter-ounce), and $10 (tenth-ounce).

The Mint announced the new platinum coins on January 6, 1997. "The Platinum Eagle represents a historic expansion of the Mint's bullion coin program," said Mint Director Diehl. "As the first platinum coin ever issued by the United States Mint, this new coin enhances and completes the family of Eagles. Joining the silver and gold versions of the U.S. Eagle coins, the platinum Eagle will have a strong appeal to collectors and investors alike."

The Mint charged its Authorized Purchasers a premium of 3 percent over bullion value for the one-ounce American Platinum Eagle; 5 percent for the half-ounce; 7 percent for the quarter-ounce; and 9 percent for the tenth-ounce.

As with the gold coins, platinum Proofs were available for sale individually or in four-coin packages. The Mint put an official limit to the quantities available; the tenth-ounce and one-ounce Proof coins sold out, as did the four-coin platinum set.

The Mint director welcomed members of the press to the West Point Mint on May 1 for the ceremonial striking of the first Proof American Platinum Eagles. "The arrival of the Platinum Eagle has been one of the most anticipated stories on the numismatic horizon during 1997," noted Mint Director Diehl. "Today's production strikes presage an auspicious debut on June 6, when numismatists will have four beautiful new coins, and two new multi-coin sets to collect. We believe the beauty and value of this historic coin ensure that it will be the world's preeminent platinum coin from this day forward."

1997 Impressions of Liberty set (mintage: 5,000).

The second multi-coin set that Diehl was referring to was the Impressions of Liberty set, produced at the Philadelphia Mint to celebrate the debut of platinum in the American Eagle program. The set, limited to 5,000, contained one each of the Proof one-ounce Eagles in silver, gold, and platinum, packaged in a hardwood box with a numbered certificate personally signed by Diehl. The issue price was $1,499, and the set sold out within weeks of its June 6 debut.

"The great response to this new coinage removes any doubt about numismatic platinum coinage," Diehl said on June 27, after the Impressions of Liberty set sold out, "and augurs well for the launch of the bullion platinum Eagle this fall."

Interest in the platinum bullion-strike coinage was considerable, but muted compared to the skyrocketing American Gold Eagles. For example, after the platinum coins went on sale September 23, collectors and investors availed themselves of the smallest denomination (the $10 tenth-ounce) to the tune of some 70,250 coins, compared to the smallest American Gold Eagle (the $5 tenth-ounce) at 528,515. Still, these sales outpaced Mint predictions, surpassing 85,000 ounces by November 12, and 105,000 ounces by December 15.

The four-coin set was priced at $1,350 and limited to 8,000 sets. The Impressions of Liberty set was priced at $1,499, and limited to 5,000. Prices for the individual Proof Platinum American Eagles were $695 for the one-ounce (limited to 8,000 individually sold coins, not counting those sold in sets); $395 for the half-ounce (limited to 10,000 individually sold coins); $199 for the quarter-ounce (limited to 15,000 individual coins); and $99 for the tenth-ounce (limited to 30,000 individual coins).

The 1997 $100 American Platinum Eagle was ranked "Most Popular" by *World Coin News* in its "Coin of the Year" competition.

# Bullion Strikes, Gold, 1997

**$5 American Gold Eagle (1/10 oz.), bullion strike**   *Mintage: 528,515*

| 1997 | Grade | Purchased From | Date |
|------|-------|----------------|------|
|      |       |                |      |

Bullion value at time of purchase: _____

**$10 American Gold Eagle (1/4 oz.), bullion strike**   *Mintage: 108,805*

| 1997 | Grade | Purchased From | Date |
|------|-------|----------------|------|
|      |       |                |      |

Bullion value at time of purchase: _____

**$25 American Gold Eagle (1/2 oz.), bullion strike**   *Mintage: 79,605*

| 1997 | Grade | Purchased From | Date |
|------|-------|----------------|------|
|      |       |                |      |

Bullion value at time of purchase: _____

Sculptor-engraver Thomas D. Rogers Sr.'s initials, TDR, appear below the horizon near the bottom of the reverse.

**$50 American Gold Eagle (1 oz.), bullion strike**   *Mintage: 664,508*

| 1997 | Grade | Purchased From | Date |
|------|-------|----------------|------|
|      |       |                |      |

Bullion value at time of purchase: _____

# Proof Strikes, Gold, 1997

**$5 American Gold Eagle (1/10 oz.), Proof**   *Mintage: 34,977*

| 1997-W | Grade | Purchased From | Date |
|--------|-------|----------------|------|
|        |       |                |      |

Bullion value at time of purchase: _____

**1997 average spot prices:**
silver, $4.91; gold, $332.39;
platinum, $395.23

**Total 1997 American Gold Eagle mintage (in ounces):**
784,363 (bullion);
57,120 (Proof)

**American Gold Eagles**
Date: 1997
Mints: West Point Mint (bullion strikes [no mintmark] and Proofs [W mintmark])
Composition:
.9167 gold, .03 silver, .0533 copper
Edge: Reeded
Weight:
$5—0.109 oz. (3.393 grams; 1/10 oz. actual gold weight)
$10—0.273 oz. (8.483 grams; 1/4 oz. actual gold weight)
$25—0.545 oz. (16.966 grams; 1/2 oz. actual gold weight)
$50—1.091 oz. (33.931 grams; 1 oz. actual gold weight)
Diameter:
$5—16.5 mm
$10—22 mm
$25—27 mm
$50—32.7 mm
Thickness:
$50—2.87 mm
Designers:
Augustus Saint-Gaudens (obverse), Miley Busiek (reverse)

## $10 American Gold Eagle (1/4 oz.), Proof

*Mintage: 29,805*

| 1997-W | Grade | Purchased From | Date |
|--------|-------|----------------|------|
|        |       |                |      |

Bullion value at time of purchase: _____

## $25 American Gold Eagle (1/2 oz.), Proof

*Mintage: 26,344*

| 1997-W | Grade | Purchased From | Date |
|--------|-------|----------------|------|
|        |       |                |      |

Bullion value at time of purchase: _____

## $50 American Gold Eagle (1 oz.), Proof

*Mintage: 32,999*

| 1997-W | Grade | Purchased From | Date |
|--------|-------|----------------|------|
|        |       |                |      |

Bullion value at time of purchase: _____

# Proof Set, Gold, 1997

**$5, $10, $25, and $50 American Gold Eagle (1/10 oz. to 1 oz.), Proof**

| 1997-W | Grade | Purchased From | Date |
|--------|-------|----------------|------|
|        |       |                |      |

Bullion value at time of purchase: _____

# Proof Set, Impressions of Liberty, 1997

**$1 American Silver Eagle, $50 American Gold Eagle, and $100 American Platinum Eagle, 1 oz., Proof**

| 1997 | Grade | Purchased From | Date |
|------|-------|----------------|------|
|      |       |                |      |

Bullion value at time of purchase: _____

# Bullion Strikes, Platinum, 1997

**$10 American Platinum Eagle (1/10 oz.), bullion strike** *Mintage: 70,250*

| 1997 | Grade | Purchased From | Date |
|------|-------|----------------|------|
|      |       |                |      |

Bullion value at time of purchase: _____

**$25 American Platinum Eagle (1/4 oz.), bullion strike** *Mintage: 27,100*

| 1997 | Grade | Purchased From | Date |
|------|-------|----------------|------|
|      |       |                |      |

Bullion value at time of purchase: _____

**$50 American Platinum Eagle (1/2 oz.), bullion strike** *Mintage: 20,500*

| 1997 | Grade | Purchased From | Date |
|------|-------|----------------|------|
|      |       |                |      |

Bullion value at time of purchase: _____

**$100 American Platinum Eagle (1 oz.), bullion strike** *Mintage: 56,000*

| 1997 | Grade | Purchased From | Date |
|------|-------|----------------|------|
|      |       |                |      |

Bullion value at time of purchase: _____

# Proof Strikes, Platinum, 1997

**$10 American Platinum Eagle (1/10 oz.), Proof** *Mintage: 36,993*

| 1997-W | Grade | Purchased From | Date |
|--------|-------|----------------|------|
|        |       |                |      |

Bullion value at time of purchase: _____

**$25 American Platinum Eagle (1/4 oz.), Proof** *Mintage: 18,628*

| 1997-W | Grade | Purchased From | Date |
|--------|-------|----------------|------|
|        |       |                |      |

Bullion value at time of purchase: _____

**$50 American Platinum Eagle (1/2 oz.), Proof** *Mintage: 15,431*

| 1997-W | Grade | Purchased From | Date |
|--------|-------|----------------|------|
|        |       |                |      |

Bullion value at time of purchase: _____

**$100 American Platinum Eagle (1 oz.), Proof** *Mintage: 20,851*

| 1997-W | Grade | Purchased From | Date |
|--------|-------|----------------|------|
|        |       |                |      |

Bullion value at time of purchase: _____

# Proof Set, Platinum, 1997

**$10, $25, $50, and $100 American Platinum Eagle
(1/10 oz. to 1 oz.), Proof**

| 1997-W | Grade | Purchased From | Date |
|--------|-------|----------------|------|
|        |       |                |      |

Bullion value at time of purchase: _____

# Proof Set, Impressions of Liberty, 1997

**$1 American Silver Eagle, $50 American Gold Eagle,
and $100 American Platinum Eagle, 1 oz., Proof**

| 1997 | Grade | Purchased From | Date |
|------|-------|----------------|------|
|      |       |                |      |

Bullion value at time of purchase: _____

**American Platinum Eagles**

**Date:** 1997

**Mints:** Philadelphia Mint (bullion strikes [no mintmark]); West Point Mint (Proofs [W mintmark])

**Composition:**
.9995 platinum

**Edge:** Reeded

**Weight:**
$10—0.1001 oz. (3.112 grams; 1/10 oz. actual platinum weight)
$25—0.2501 oz. (7.780 grams; 1/4 oz. actual platinum weight)
$50—0.5003 oz. (15.560 grams; 1/2 oz. actual platinum weight)
$100—1.0005 oz. (31.120 grams; 1 oz. actual platinum weight)

**Diameter:**
$10—16.5 mm
$25—22 mm
$50—27 mm
$100—32.7 mm

**Thickness:**
$100—2.39 mm

**Designers:**
John M. Mercanti (obverse), Thomas D. Rogers Sr. (reverse)

# 1998

**Historical context:** 1998 was a mixed bag for the American economy, with low unemployment and almost zero inflation balanced by volatile asset markets, high trade deficits, and other instability. The end of the year saw weekly up-and-down changes—a gain of 40 percent in the Dow Jones (to a high of 9,300) would be followed by a 24 percent loss only a month later. Nevertheless, consumers were unalarmed by the volatile conditions, and the market grew steadily into 1999.

National headlines were dominated by President Bill Clinton's denial (and later admission) of an inappropriate relationship with former White House intern Monica Lewinsky. The president was impeached on December 19 on grounds of perjury and obstruction of justice, but would be acquitted five weeks later.

In American numismatics, the design-selection process for the upcoming U.S. "golden dollar" was under way. In a session convened by the Dollar Coin Design Advisory Committee, 17 presentations from members of the public were brought to the table. The DCDAC also considered numerous mail, phone, and email messages submitted by the public with opinions on what design should adorn the dollar coin. In June the committee recommended to the U.S. Mint that the design should be representative of Sacagawea, the young Native American woman who served as companion and guide to the famous explorers Lewis and Clark.

The Mint released a commemorative silver dollar in 1998 to honor African American patriots who fought and died in the Revolutionary War. One side of the coin featured a portrait of Crispus Attucks, the first American to be killed by British Redcoats in the Boston Massacre of 1770 (conceptualized by U.S. Mint sculptor-engraver John Mercanti, as no portraits exist of Attucks from his lifetime).

Bullion prices were relatively stable in 1998, even as demand for American Eagle coins increased over the previous year. Silver's average for the year rose about 10 percent, gold fell about the same percentage, and platinum dropped about 6 percent.

**Coin commentary:** American Eagle gold-bullion sales more than doubled in 1998 compared to the previous year, with the $50 one-ounce and $5 tenth-ounce coins finally beating the mintage records set at the program's debut in 1986. American interest in precious metals was ramping up in anticipation of Y2K (conventional wisdom foresaw a systemic, nationwide computer failure when electronic clocks struck midnight on January 1, 2000). This interest extended to silver (about 550,000 more American Silver Eagle bullion coins were sold in 1998 than in 1997), and also platinum (in that series only the smallest, tenth-ounce, coin went down in mintage, and the one-ounce more than doubled). Regarding platinum, on March 20, 1998, the Mint announced that it had already reached—in just six months of sales—its entire one-year sales target of 100,000 ounces of the precious metal.

Meanwhile, collector interest in *Proof* gold and platinum languished, with most mintages dipping slightly, and a few dropping 25 to 50 percent. This was despite the Mint reducing maximum Proof mintages in an effort to entice collectors with perceived rarity, and even lowering issue prices to their 1990

levels. ("We looked at the substantial fall in gold prices in recent months," said Director Philip N. Diehl in a press release, "and concluded that we needed to share these lower costs with our customers.") The only exception for the year was the Proof $5 tenth-ounce American Gold Eagle, which rose in sales a bit more than 10 percent. The Mint offered Proof coins individually and in four-coin sets of each precious metal.

1998 was the first year of a new series of reverse designs for the Proof platinum coinage. The series was "Vistas of Liberty," showing eagles flying through various American landscapes. "This year's Proof Platinum Eagle marks the first time in history the Mint has embarked on a five-year design series for a coin," Mint Director Philip N. Diehl said on May 18, 1998. "The Vistas of Liberty designs will profile the unique character and charisma of our nation's diverse landscapes, capturing the spirit and strength of America and its people." The 1998 reverse, "Eagle Over New England," was by John M. Mercanti, the Mint sculptor-engraver who had also designed the coin's Statue of Liberty obverse. It was featured on all four denominations of the year's Proof American Platinum Eagles.

The Proof American Platinum Eagle had a special design feature: incuse sculpting, wherein certain design elements were below the surface plane of the coin. The incused parts were the inscription E PLURIBUS UNUM on the border of the obverse, and the inscriptions for fineness (.9995 PLATINUM 1 OZ.) and the denomination ($100) on the reverse.

The tenth-ounce Proof American Platinum Eagle was announced sold out on July 24, and the quarter-ounce on August 13.

# Bullion Strikes, Gold, 1998

**$5 American Gold Eagle (1/10 oz.), bullion strike**   *Mintage: 1,344,520*

| 1998 | Grade | Purchased From | Date |
|------|-------|----------------|------|
|      |       |                |      |

Bullion value at time of purchase: _____

**$10 American Gold Eagle (1/4 oz.), bullion strike**   *Mintage: 309,829*

| 1998 | Grade | Purchased From | Date |
|------|-------|----------------|------|
|      |       |                |      |

Bullion value at time of purchase: _____

**$25 American Gold Eagle (1/2 oz.), bullion strike**   *Mintage: 169,029*

| 1998 | Grade | Purchased From | Date |
|------|-------|----------------|------|
|      |       |                |      |

Bullion value at time of purchase: _____

**$50 American Gold Eagle (1 oz.), bullion strike**   *Mintage: 1,468,530*

| 1998 | Grade | Purchased From | Date |
|------|-------|----------------|------|
|      |       |                |      |

Bullion value at time of purchase: _____

**1998 average spot prices:**
silver, $5.55; gold, $295.24; platinum, $372.15

**Total 1998 American Gold Eagle mintage (in ounces):**
1,764,954 (bullion);
49,888 (Proof)

**American Gold Eagles**
**Date:**  1998
**Mints:**  West Point Mint (bullion strikes [no mintmark] and Proofs [W mintmark])
**Composition:**
.9167 gold, .03 silver, .0533 copper
**Edge:**  Reeded
**Weight:**
$5—0.109 oz.
(3.393 grams; 1/10 oz. actual gold weight)
$10—0.273 oz.
(8.483 grams; 1/4 oz. actual gold weight)
$25—0.545 oz.
(16.966 grams; 1/2 oz. actual gold weight)
$50—1.091 oz.
(33.931 grams; 1 oz. actual gold weight)
**Diameter:**
$5—16.5 mm
$10—22 mm
$25—27 mm
$50—32.7 mm
**Thickness:**
$50—2.87 mm
**Designers:**
Augustus Saint-Gaudens (obverse), Miley Busiek (reverse)

## American Platinum Eagles
**Date:** 1998
**Mints:** Philadelphia Mint (bullion strikes [no mintmark]); West Point Mint (Proofs [W mintmark])
**Composition:** .9995 platinum
**Edge:** Reeded
**Weight:**
$10—0.1001 oz. (3.112 grams; 1/10 oz. actual platinum weight)
$25—0.2501 oz. (7.780 grams; 1/4 oz. actual platinum weight)
$50—0.5003 oz. (15.560 grams; 1/2 oz. actual platinum weight)
$100—1.0005 oz. (31.120 grams; 1 oz. actual platinum weight)
**Diameter:**
$10—16.5 mm
$25—22 mm
$50—27 mm
$100—32.7 mm
**Thickness:**
$100—2.39 mm
**Designers:** John M. Mercanti (obverse, and Proof reverse), Thomas D. Rogers Sr. (bullion-strike reverse)

# Proof Strikes, Gold, 1998
### $5 American Gold Eagle (1/10 oz.), Proof     *Mintage: 39,395*

| 1998-W | Grade | Purchased From | Date |
|---|---|---|---|
| | | | |

Bullion value at time of purchase: _____

### $10 American Gold Eagle (1/4 oz.), Proof     *Mintage: 29,503*

| 1998-W | Grade | Purchased From | Date |
|---|---|---|---|
| | | | |

Bullion value at time of purchase: _____

### $25 American Gold Eagle (1/2 oz.), Proof     *Mintage: 25,374*

| 1998-W | Grade | Purchased From | Date |
|---|---|---|---|
| | | | |

Bullion value at time of purchase: _____

### $50 American Gold Eagle (1 oz.), Proof     *Mintage: 25,886*

| 1998-W | Grade | Purchased From | Date |
|---|---|---|---|
| | | | |

Bullion value at time of purchase: _____

# Proof Set, Gold, 1998
### $5, $10, $25, and $50 American Gold Eagle (1/10 oz. to 1 oz.), Proof

| 1998-W | Grade | Purchased From | Date |
|---|---|---|---|
| | | | |

Bullion value at time of purchase: _____

# Bullion Strikes, Platinum, 1998
### $10 American Platinum Eagle (1/10 oz.), bullion strike  *Mintage: 39,525*

| 1998 | Raw coin, or certified MS-68 or lower | MS-69 | MS-70 |
|---|---|---|---|
| Value* | $175 | $200 | $1,450 |

* Based on bullion value of $1,500 per ounce.

### $25 American Platinum Eagle (1/4 oz.), bullion strike  *Mintage: 38,887*

| 1998 | Grade | Purchased From | Date |
|---|---|---|---|
| | | | |

Bullion value at time of purchase: _____

**$50 American Platinum Eagle (1/2 oz.), bullion strike**   *Mintage: 32,415*

| 1998 | Grade | Purchased From | Date |
|------|-------|----------------|------|
|      |       |                |      |

Bullion value at time of purchase: _____

**$100 American Platinum Eagle (1 oz.), bullion strike**   *Mintage: 133,002*

| 1998 | Grade | Purchased From | Date |
|------|-------|----------------|------|
|      |       |                |      |

Bullion value at time of purchase: _____

# Proof Strikes, Platinum, 1998

**$10 American Platinum Eagle (1/10 oz.), Proof**   *Mintage: 19,847*

| 1998-W | Grade | Purchased From | Date |
|--------|-------|----------------|------|
|        |       |                |      |

Bullion value at time of purchase: _____

**$25 American Platinum Eagle (1/4 oz.), Proof**   *Mintage: 14,873*

| 1998-W | Grade | Purchased From | Date |
|--------|-------|----------------|------|
|        |       |                |      |

Bullion value at time of purchase: _____

**$50 American Platinum Eagle (1/2 oz.), Proof**   *Mintage: 13,836*

| 1998-W | Grade | Purchased From | Date |
|--------|-------|----------------|------|
|        |       |                |      |

Bullion value at time of purchase: _____

**$100 American Platinum Eagle (1 oz.), Proof**   *Mintage: 14,912*

| 1998-W | Grade | Purchased From | Date |
|--------|-------|----------------|------|
|        |       |                |      |

Bullion value at time of purchase: _____

# Proof Set, Platinum, 1998

**$10, $25, $50, and $100 American Platinum Eagle
(1/10 oz. to 1 oz.), Proof**

| 1998-W | Grade | Purchased From | Date |
|--------|-------|----------------|------|
|        |       |                |      |

Bullion value at time of purchase: _____

# 1999

**Historical context:** The American economy in 1999 defied expectations, given the lingering shadow of Asia's financial crisis. Confirmation that the economy was safe from Asian collapses arrived in the beginning of the year, when growth of 5.9 percent was announced. Gasoline prices hit their lowest in almost a decade and continued to fall; interest rates were pushed down along with them. Inflation steadied at an almost nonexistent rate throughout the year, and unemployment also remained low. For the first time in its 28-year history, the NASDAQ composite index closed above 4,000, an incredible 84.3 percent increase over the year.

The American Numismatic Association's 108th convention, held in Chicago, was the stage for a heated "Great Debate" over the authenticity of a group of gold bars. Some numismatists held them to be authentic, historical pieces (including from 18th-century Mexico and 19th-century San Francisco) while others claimed they were cleverly crafted fakes.

In July, 12 special Proof Sacagawea dollars flew aboard the space shuttle *Columbia* in an orbit around the Earth—the first such flight commanded by a woman, Colonel Eileen Collins. The coins, minted in 22-karat gold, would go into storage at Fort Knox and eventually be displayed at the ANA World's Fair of Money in Milwaukee (almost 10 years later, in 2007).

The U.S. Mint on April 19, 1999, announced that it had surpassed 10 million ounces in sales since the program was launched on October 20, 1986. "Investors worldwide are attracted to the inherent value of the American Eagle because of the U.S. government guarantee of weight and volume," said Mint Director Philip N. Diehl. "We have worked closely with our distributors and blank suppliers to make the Eagle the world market leader. Four years ago, the Gold Eagle owned 18 percent of the world bullion market. Today it has a market share of 60 percent while silver and platinum Eagles hold shares approaching 80 percent of their markets."

Averaged across the year, spot prices in the bullion market were mixed but fairly stable for 1999. Silver's average dropped slightly (by about 30 cents per ounce) compared to 1998, gold fell by $15, and platinum rose $5.

**Coin commentary:** 1999 brought a new record-high production for bullion-strike American Gold Eagles. Mintages for the $50 one-ounce coin and the $5 tenth-ounce coin were particularly large—especially the tenth-ounce, which saw a mintage more than twice that of 1998 (which had been a record-setting year itself). The combined annual sales quantity of more than 2 million ounces of gold remains unsurpassed today. Much of the demand for precious metal was driven by worries of social and infrastructural collapse come midnight, January 1, 2000—"Y2K," when online systems were feared to crash from a global electronic-clock glitch.

Sales of Proof American Gold Eagles, like those of bullion strikes, also increased in 1999, with the coins once again available for purchase individually and in four-piece sets. The Mint announced in April that it was reducing the total program mintage for Proofs. "As the last Proof Eagles to be issued in the 1900s, we anticipate very high demand for these coins," said Mint Director

Philip N. Diehl. "We've reduced the mintage of one-ounce Proof Gold Eagles to only 8,000, and the total mintage for the program is reduced from 1998 levels as well." To celebrate the historical significance of the gold and silver Proofs, and to thank its customers for their loyalty, the Mint offered a specially commissioned Art Nouveau–style poster of the Augustus Saint-Gaudens "Striding Liberty" design free to those who placed orders for $150 or more by June 15. Mint promotional literature described the poster's artist: "Renowned illustrator Oren Sherman has created a stunning Art Nouveau interpretation of the most cherished and enduring gold coin design on U.S. coinage, which originally graced the 1907 twenty dollar gold piece. A nationally acclaimed artist and illustrator working in Boston's Fenway Studios, Sherman's award-winning poster designs have depicted the Tall Ships, the Kentucky Derby, the Brooklyn Bridge Centennial, the Ringling Brothers Barnum & Bailey Circus, and numerous magazine covers, theatre productions, and movies."

Proof gold sales were strong out of the gate, with the Mint announcing after six weeks that more than 50 percent of the maximum mintage had already been purchased. That announcement was made June 14; by July 26 the Mint announced the 67 percent mark had been reached—with total sales up 16 percent benchmarked against the previous year.

Platinum bullion strikes held steady in the middle sizes (quarter-ounce and half-ounce), while the tenth-ounce increased in mintage and the one-ounce, which had skyrocketed in 1998, fell back to its 1997 level.

The "Vistas of Liberty" design series continued with the 1999 American Platinum Eagle Proofs, which went on sale July 23—available until December 31, or until a sellout, whichever came first. This year's motif, featured on the reverse of all four platinum coins, was "Eagle Above Southeastern Wetlands," by Mint sculptor-engraver John Mercanti. Collector demand dropped slightly compared to the series' inaugural year of 1998. As with their gold counterparts, the American Platinum Eagle Proofs were available for purchase by collectors directly from the U.S. Mint, individually or in four-coin sets.

Holiday shoppers could purchase an American Platinum Eagle pendant and chain in the Mint's annual holiday catalog. This popular item was announced sold out on November 12. Other gift items included watches and jewelry featuring the silver, gold, and platinum bullion coins.

Collectors discovered an unusual die variety among the $10 (quarter-ounce) and $5 (tenth-ounce) American Gold Eagles of 1999. A small quantity of bullion-strike coins were inadvertently produced with the W mintmark typically intended for their Proof counterparts. (Usually the bullion strikes, although produced at West Point, bear no mintmark.) In *100 Greatest U.S. Modern Coins*, researchers Scott Schechter and Jeff Garrett opine that a few coinage dies intended for making Proofs weren't brightly polished, as they normally would be to make the brilliant collector-format coins. They were then accidentally put to use making regular bullion strikes, each of which of course had the W mintmark from the unpolished die, creating an anomaly. Schechter and Garrett attribute the mistake to "the enormous number of gold bullion coins struck in 1999," noting that most years only 70,000 to 80,000 quarter-ounce coins would have been struck, but 1999 saw more than 560,000, and the tenth-

**1999-W $10 made from unpolished Proof dies (shown enlarged).**

**1999-W $5 made from unpolished Proof dies (shown enlarged).**

**1999 average spot prices:**
silver, $5.22; gold, $279.91;
platinum, $377.93

**Total 1999 American Gold
Eagle mintage (in ounces):**
2,052,624 (bullion);
60,088 (Proof)

**American Gold Eagles**
**Date:** 1999
**Mints:** West Point Mint (bullion
strikes [no mintmark] and
Proofs [W mintmark])
**Composition:**
.9167 gold, .03 silver,
.0533 copper
**Edge:** Reeded
**Weight:**
$5—0.109 oz.
(3.393 grams; 1/10 oz.
actual gold weight)
$10—0.273 oz.
(8.483 grams; 1/4 oz.
actual gold weight)
$25—0.545 oz.
(16.966 grams; 1/2 oz.
actual gold weight)
$50—1.091 oz.
(33.931 grams; 1 oz.
actual gold weight)
**Diameter:**
$5—16.5 mm
$10—22 mm
$25—27 mm
$50—32.7 mm
**Thickness:**
$50—2.87 mm
**Designers:**
Augustus Saint-Gaudens
(obverse), Miley Busiek
(reverse)

ounce mintage skyrocketed into the millions. "The die-production facilities and the quality-control processes were so overworked," they write, "that it's easy to understand how such an error may have been created."

An estimated 6,000 of the $10 quarter-ounce coins were struck with this die error, and 14,500 of the $5 tenth-ounce coins. These estimates are based on the average production life of American Platinum Eagle coinage dies. Some 3,000 of the quarter-ounce coins have already been discovered, and 6,000 of the tenth-ounce, leaving many waiting to be found by keen-eyed collectors. For their rarity, historical significance, and remarkable back story, these coins were ranked no. 25 (quarter-ounce) and no. 31 (tenth-ounce) among the 100 Greatest U.S. Modern Coins (in the book of the same name).

# Bullion Strikes, Gold, 1999

**$5 American Gold Eagle (1/10 oz.), bullion strike**    *Mintage: 2,750,338*

| 1999 | Grade | Purchased From | Date |
|------|-------|----------------|------|
|      |       |                |      |

Bullion value at time of purchase: _____

**$5 (1/10 oz.), bullion strike, from unpolished Proof dies** *Mintage: ~14,500*

| 1999-W | Grade | Purchased From | Date |
|--------|-------|----------------|------|
|        |       |                |      |

Bullion value at time of purchase: _____

**$10 American Gold Eagle (1/4 oz.), bullion strike**    *Mintage: 564,232*

| 1999 | Grade | Purchased From | Date |
|------|-------|----------------|------|
|      |       |                |      |

Bullion value at time of purchase: _____

**$10 (1/4 oz.), bullion strike, from unpolished Proof dies**    *Mintage: ~6,000*

| 1999-W | Grade | Purchased From | Date |
|--------|-------|----------------|------|
|        |       |                |      |

Bullion value at time of purchase: _____

**$25 American Gold Eagle (1/2 oz.), bullion strike**    *Mintage: 263,013*

| 1999 | Grade | Purchased From | Date |
|------|-------|----------------|------|
|      |       |                |      |

Bullion value at time of purchase: _____

**$50 American Gold Eagle (1 oz.), bullion strike**    *Mintage: 1,505,026*

| 1999 | Grade | Purchased From | Date |
|------|-------|----------------|------|
|      |       |                |      |

Bullion value at time of purchase: _____

# Proof Strikes, Gold, 1999

## $5 American Gold Eagle (1/10 oz.), Proof

*Mintage: 48,428*

| 1999-W | Grade | Purchased From | Date |
|--------|-------|----------------|------|
|        |       |                |      |

Bullion value at time of purchase: _____

## $10 American Gold Eagle (1/4 oz.), Proof

*Mintage: 34,417*

| 1999-W | Grade | Purchased From | Date |
|--------|-------|----------------|------|
|        |       |                |      |

Bullion value at time of purchase: _____

## $25 American Gold Eagle (1/2 oz.), Proof

*Mintage: 30,427*

| 1999-W | Grade | Purchased From | Date |
|--------|-------|----------------|------|
|        |       |                |      |

Bullion value at time of purchase: _____

## $50 American Gold Eagle (1 oz.), Proof

*Mintage: 31,427*

| 1999-W | Grade | Purchased From | Date |
|--------|-------|----------------|------|
|        |       |                |      |

Bullion value at time of purchase: _____

# Proof Set, Gold, 1999

## $5, $10, $25, and $50 American Gold Eagle (1/10 oz. to 1 oz.), Proof

| 1999-W | Grade | Purchased From | Date |
|--------|-------|----------------|------|
|        |       |                |      |

Bullion value at time of purchase: _____

# Bullion Strikes, Platinum, 1999

## $10 American Platinum Eagle (1/10 oz.), bullion strike *Mintage: 55,955*

| 1999 | Grade | Purchased From | Date |
|------|-------|----------------|------|
|      |       |                |      |

Bullion value at time of purchase: _____

## $25 American Platinum Eagle (1/4 oz.), bullion strike *Mintage: 39,734*

| 1999 | Grade | Purchased From | Date |
|------|-------|----------------|------|
|      |       |                |      |

Bullion value at time of purchase: _____

**American Platinum Eagles**

**Date:** 1999
**Mints:** Philadelphia Mint (bullion strikes [no mintmark]); West Point Mint (Proofs [W mintmark])
**Composition:** .9995 platinum
**Edge:** Reeded
**Weight:**
  $10—0.1001 oz. (3.112 grams; 1/10 oz. actual platinum weight)
  $25—0.2501 oz. (7.780 grams; 1/4 oz. actual platinum weight)
  $50—0.5003 oz. (15.560 grams; 1/2 oz. actual platinum weight)
  $100—1.0005 oz. (31.120 grams; 1 oz. actual platinum weight)
**Diameter:**
  $10—16.5 mm
  $25—22 mm
  $50—27 mm
  $100—32.7 mm
**Thickness:**
  $100—2.39 mm
**Designers:** John M. Mercanti (obverse, and Proof reverse), Thomas D. Rogers Sr. (bullion-strike reverse)

**$50 American Platinum Eagle (1/2 oz.), bullion strike**   *Mintage: 32,309*

| 1999 | Grade | Purchased From | Date |
|---|---|---|---|
|  |  |  |  |

Bullion value at time of purchase: _____

**$100 American Platinum Eagle (1 oz.), bullion strike**   *Mintage: 56,707*

| 1999 | Grade | Purchased From | Date |
|---|---|---|---|
|  |  |  |  |

Bullion value at time of purchase: _____

## Proof Strikes, Platinum, 1999

**$10 American Platinum Eagle (1/10 oz.), Proof**   *Mintage: 19,133*

| 1999-W | Grade | Purchased From | Date |
|---|---|---|---|
|  |  |  |  |

Bullion value at time of purchase: _____

**$25 American Platinum Eagle (1/4 oz.), Proof**   *Mintage: 13,507*

| 1999-W | Grade | Purchased From | Date |
|---|---|---|---|
|  |  |  |  |

Bullion value at time of purchase: _____

**$50 American Platinum Eagle (1/2 oz.), Proof**   *Mintage: 11,103*

| 1999-W | Grade | Purchased From | Date |
|---|---|---|---|
|  |  |  |  |

Bullion value at time of purchase: _____

**$100 American Platinum Eagle (1 oz.), Proof**   *Mintage: 12,363*

| 1999-W | Grade | Purchased From | Date |
|---|---|---|---|
|  |  |  |  |

Bullion value at time of purchase: _____

## Proof Set, Platinum, 1999

**$10, $25, $50, and $100 American Platinum Eagle
(1/10 oz. to 1 oz.), Proof**

| 1999-W | Grade | Purchased From | Date |
|---|---|---|---|
|  |  |  |  |

Bullion value at time of purchase: _____

# 2000

**Historical context:** In September of 2000, in a controversial move that was both praised and disputed, Congress granted China permanent normal trade relations status with the United States. Much of the debate centered on human rights and the treatment of Chinese citizens by their government. Supporters of the trade agreement argued that wealth and resources brought by trade would not remain solely in the hands of the Chinese government but would help the people of China as well. Opponents countered that, despite years of trade relations already approved by Congress, political freedom in China was still nonexistent.

The U.S. economy was strong overall, with low unemployment.

George W. Bush became the 43rd president of the United States after a hard fight in the 2000 elections. It would take five weeks for the vote to become official due to disputed ballots in Florida, pushing Bush's victory over Democratic candidate Al Gore into the first week of the following year.

February of 2000 saw the recovery of the unique Proof 1866 "No Motto" Liberty Seated quarter dollar, stolen at gunpoint from the collection of Willis H. du Pont in 1967. The coin, authenticated by the American Numismatic Association, was later loaned by the du Pont family for display at the ANA's Colorado Springs museum.

Among the commemoratives issued by the U.S. Mint in 2000 was a unique innovation: a bimetallic (platinum encircled by gold) $10 coin celebrating the bicentennial of the Library of Congress. The coin was designed by John Mercanti (obverse) and Thomas D. Rogers Sr. (reverse), the same team who crafted the American Platinum Eagle.

On the bullion markets in 2000, silver and gold averaged very close (within a few cents) to their averages for 1999. Platinum, in the meantime, jumped more than $150 per ounce, averaging well above $500 for the year.

**Coin commentary:** 2000 brought significantly decreased mintages across the spectrum of the gold and platinum bullion series.

Compared to the record highs of 1999, the American Gold Eagle's drop in 2000 appears dramatic (nearly a 75 percent plunge), but some historical context is needed. The year's total weight of 562,119 gold ounces sold was actually higher than any other year from 1988 to 1996 (before the 1997–1999 boom, encouraged by Y2K anxiety), and it would not be exceeded until 2008.

Proof American Gold Eagles, meanwhile, saw slightly higher sales for the year, in all four denominations. The Mint announced the start of Proof gold sales on May 9. "The 2000 American Eagle gold and silver Proof coins are the perfect collector's item to commemorate the year 2000," said Acting Director John P. Mitchell.

Platinum bullion-strike sales dropped most notably for the $100 one-ounce coin; the 10,003 sold in 2000 were a shadow of 1999's mintage of nearly 57,000—perhaps not surprising, given platinum's rising price (more than a 40 percent increase averaged over the year).

The third reverse design of the platinum Proof "Vistas of Liberty" series was "Eagle Above America's Heartland," by Alfred Maletsky. Proof sales of the 2000 American Platinum Eagle were close to those of 1999 in the two

**2000 average spot prices:**
silver, $4.95; gold, $280.10;
platinum, $544.03

**Total 2000 American Gold
Eagle mintage (in ounces):**
562,119 (bullion);
63,027 (Proof)

**American Gold Eagles**
Date:   2000
Mints:  West Point Mint (bullion
        strikes [no mintmark] and
        Proofs [W mintmark])
**Composition:**
        .9167 gold, .03 silver,
        .0533 copper
Edge:   Reeded
**Weight:**
        $5—0.109 oz.
        (3.393 grams; 1/10 oz.
        actual gold weight)
        $10—0.273 oz.
        (8.483 grams; 1/4 oz.
        actual gold weight)
        $25—0.545 oz.
        (16.966 grams; 1/2 oz.
        actual gold weight)
        $50—1.091 oz.
        (33.931 grams; 1 oz.
        actual gold weight)
**Diameter:**
        $5—16.5 mm
        $10—22 mm
        $25—27 mm
        $50—32.7 mm
**Thickness:**
        $50—2.87 mm
**Designers:**
        Augustus Saint-Gaudens
        (obverse), Miley Busiek
        (reverse)

larger denominations, varying by fewer than 100 coins in the half-ounce and one-ounce categories. The two smaller sizes saw their mintages drop more significantly, by 11 percent (quarter-ounce) and 18 percent (tenth-ounce). (The Proof coins were available, as in recent years, individually or in a four-coin set, and all featured the year's Vistas of Liberty design.)

The U.S. Mint's holiday catalog for 2000 included bullion-related gift items such as a tenth-ounce platinum "eagle star pendant," and tuxedo stud sets made from the tenth-ounce gold and tenth-ounce platinum Eagles.

## Bullion Strikes, Gold, 2000

**$5 American Gold Eagle (1/10 oz.), bullion strike**      *Mintage: 569,153*

| 2000 | Grade | Purchased From | Date |
|------|-------|----------------|------|
|      |       |                |      |

Bullion value at time of purchase: _____

**$10 American Gold Eagle (1/4 oz.), bullion strike**      *Mintage: 128,964*

| 2000 | Grade | Purchased From | Date |
|------|-------|----------------|------|
|      |       |                |      |

Bullion value at time of purchase: _____

**$25 American Gold Eagle (1/2 oz.), bullion strike**      *Mintage: 79,287*

| 2000 | Grade | Purchased From | Date |
|------|-------|----------------|------|
|      |       |                |      |

Bullion value at time of purchase: _____

**$50 American Gold Eagle (1 oz.), bullion strike**      *Mintage: 433,319*

| 2000 | Grade | Purchased From | Date |
|------|-------|----------------|------|
|      |       |                |      |

Bullion value at time of purchase: _____

## Proof Strikes, Gold, 2000

**$5 American Gold Eagle (1/10 oz.), Proof**      *Mintage: 49,971*

| 2000-W | Grade | Purchased From | Date |
|--------|-------|----------------|------|
|        |       |                |      |

Bullion value at time of purchase: _____

**$10 American Gold Eagle (1/4 oz.), Proof**      *Mintage: 36,036*

| 2000-W | Grade | Purchased From | Date |
|--------|-------|----------------|------|
|        |       |                |      |

Bullion value at time of purchase: _____

## Proof Set, Gold, 2001

**$5, $10, $25, and $50 American Gold Eagle
(1/10 oz. to 1 oz.), Proof**

| 2001-W | Grade | Purchased From | Date |
|--------|-------|----------------|------|
|        |       |                |      |

Bullion value at time of purchase: _____

## Bullion Strikes, Platinum, 2001

**$10 American Platinum Eagle (1/10 oz.), bullion strike**  *Mintage: 52,017*

| 2001 | Grade | Purchased From | Date |
|------|-------|----------------|------|
|      |       |                |      |

Bullion value at time of purchase: _____

**$25 American Platinum Eagle (1/4 oz.), bullion strike**  *Mintage: 21,815*

| 2001 | Grade | Purchased From | Date |
|------|-------|----------------|------|
|      |       |                |      |

Bullion value at time of purchase: _____

**$50 American Platinum Eagle (1/2 oz.), bullion strike**  *Mintage: 12,815*

| 2001 | Grade | Purchased From | Date |
|------|-------|----------------|------|
|      |       |                |      |

Bullion value at time of purchase: _____

**$100 American Platinum Eagle (1 oz.), bullion strike**  *Mintage: 14,070*

| 2001 | Grade | Purchased From | Date |
|------|-------|----------------|------|
|      |       |                |      |

Bullion value at time of purchase: _____

## Proof Strikes, Platinum, 2001

**$10 American Platinum Eagle (1/10 oz.), Proof**  *Mintage: 12,174*

| 2001-W | Grade | Purchased From | Date |
|--------|-------|----------------|------|
|        |       |                |      |

Bullion value at time of purchase: _____

**$25 American Platinum Eagle (1/4 oz.), Proof**  *Mintage: 8,847*

| 2001-W | Grade | Purchased From | Date |
|--------|-------|----------------|------|
|        |       |                |      |

Bullion value at time of purchase: _____

**American Platinum Eagles**

**Date:** 2001

**Mints:** Philadelphia Mint (bullion strikes [no mintmark]); West Point Mint (Proofs [W mintmark])

**Composition:**
.9995 platinum

**Edge:** Reeded

**Weight:**
$10—0.1001 oz. (3.112 grams; 1/10 oz. actual platinum weight)
$25—0.2501 oz. (7.780 grams; 1/4 oz. actual platinum weight)
$50—0.5003 oz. (15.560 grams; 1/2 oz. actual platinum weight)
$100—1.0005 oz. (31.120 grams; 1 oz. actual platinum weight)

**Diameter:**
$10—16.5 mm
$25—22 mm
$50—27 mm
$100—32.7 mm

**Thickness:**
$100—2.39 mm

**Designers:**
John M. Mercanti (obverse), Thomas D. Rogers Sr. (bullion-strike reverse, Proof reverse)

**$50 American Platinum Eagle (1/2 oz.), Proof**     *Mintage: 8,254*

| 2001-W | Grade | Purchased From | Date |
|--------|-------|----------------|------|
|        |       |                |      |

Bullion value at time of purchase: _____

**$100 American Platinum Eagle (1 oz.), Proof**     *Mintage: 8,969*

| 2001-W | Grade | Purchased From | Date |
|--------|-------|----------------|------|
|        |       |                |      |

Bullion value at time of purchase: _____

## Proof Set, Platinum, 2001

**$10, $25, $50, and $100 American Platinum Eagle
(1/10 oz. to 1 oz.), Proof**

| 2001-W | Grade | Purchased From | Date |
|--------|-------|----------------|------|
|        |       |                |      |

Bullion value at time of purchase: _____

# 2002

**Historical context:** After the financial scare following the attacks of September 11, 2001, it appeared to analysts and the American public alike that the U.S. economy was down for the count. Yet in January of 2002 there was a dramatic recovery and, despite fears of an early bust, the economy continued to grow throughout the fall. Employment levels and consumer confidence remained uncertain throughout the year, but the United States staved off the kind of collapse that had hit many other countries in the 1990s.

Numerous corporate scandals were revealed during the year. Previously well respected companies such as Enron, Johnson & Johnson, Citigroup, and Kmart, among others, came under fire. CEOs were taken to task for bad business practices. By July Congress was passing legislation to control the factors that had allowed the corruption to grow rampant.

To combat terrorism and reduce the nation's vulnerability to attack, Congress passed the Homeland Security Act in November 2002, establishing the new federal Department of Homeland Security. The United Nations Security Council unanimously adopted Resolution 1441, giving Iraq's Saddam Hussein a final chance to comply with UN disarmament demands.

Numismatics made national headlines in July 2002 when a 1933 double eagle ($20 gold coin) once owned by Egypt's King Farouk (and one of only a handful known to have survived government melting during the Great Depression) was sold for a record-setting $7,590,000—the highest auction price ever for a single coin. To that price was added $20 as the Treasury Department officially monetized the coin, making it legal to own and sell—all other 1933 double eagles being deemed government property and off-limits for private ownership.

Precious-metal prices rose in 2002, compared average-to-average to 2001. The rise of silver and platinum was modest: less than 25 cents per ounce and

$10 per ounce, respectively. Gold's yearly average rose by nearly $40 per ounce over 2001.

**Coin commentary:** Gold investors and collectors were bullish on the bullion-strike American Gold Eagle of 2002—or at least the two larger denominations. The $50 one-ounce and $25 half-ounce coins saw increased mintages, about 50 percent higher than the previous year's. Demand for the quarter-ounce and tenth-ounce coins fell from 2001, but not enough to erase the increase in half-ounce and one-ounce coinage. Overall the year's total volume of bullion-strike sales was 40 percent higher than 2001.

Proof sales were stronger for the year, as well, with collectors buying about 3,000 more of each American Gold Eagle denomination than they did in 2001. As usual, the coins were offered by the Mint individually and in a four-coin package. Proof sales started June 5. Taking advantage of the hot numismatic news of the day, Mint Director Henrietta Holsman Fore made a historical connection in a May 22 statement: "Proof Gold Eagles bear the same obverse design as the historic 1933 gold double eagle, which will be placed on auction by the United States Mint on July 30, 2002, in New York City."

The American Gold Eagle Proof one-ounce coin had an issue price of $570 (8,000 individual coins available / maximum mintage, 33,000); the half-ounce coin sold for $285 (7,000 individual / 32,000 maximum); the quarter-ounce coin for $150 (11,000 individual / 36,000 maximum); the one-tenth ounce coin for $70 (25,000 individual / 50,000 maximum); and the four-coin set for $999 (25,000 sets available).

Mintages rose for the quarter-ounce and half-ounce and American Platinum Eagles this year, and fell for the tenth-ounce and one-ounce bullion coins. Proof platinum coins, which went on sale August 5, saw modest increases—fewer than a thousand additional coins per denomination, compared to 2001. This was the fifth and final year of the Mint's "Vistas of Liberty" reverse-design series, capped off with Alfred Maletsky's "Eagle Fishing in America's Northwest" tableau. The Proof platinum coins were available from the Mint directly to collectors, individually or in four-coin sets.

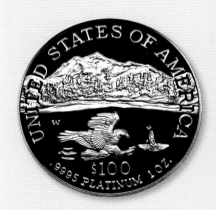

In late November 2002 the U.S. Mint launched a new $2.5 million holiday advertising campaign that featured, among other products, the silver, gold, and platinum American Eagle Proof coins—"core products that the public has a long-standing tradition of purchasing as holiday gifts," as a November 25 press release put it. The ads, under the "Genuine United States Mint" title, began appearing in periodicals (including *USA Today, Newsweek, TV Guide,* and *People* magazine) and airing nationally on cable and network television on November 29. They ran through December 20. "This is the ideal time of year to reach out to new customers," said Mint Director Fore. "We want to let the public know that the 'United States Mint' brand stands for the highest-quality products that can be shared by generations of Americans. Our customers should expect nothing less from their official national mint." The ad campaign was meant to reintroduce products to Americans who had memories of coin collecting from childhood, and introduce a new generation to the hobby. Its ads focused on gift giving, coin collecting as a family tradition, American history, and U.S. Mint products as cultural icons.

2002 average spot prices:
silver, $4.61; gold, $311.33;
platinum, $539.11

**Total 2002 American Gold
Eagle mintage (in ounces):**
295,552 (bullion);
52,219 (Proof)

**American Gold Eagles**
Date: 2002
Mints: West Point Mint (bullion
strikes [no mintmark] and
Proofs [W mintmark])
**Composition:**
.9167 gold, .03 silver,
.0533 copper
Edge: Reeded
**Weight:**
$5—0.109 oz.
(3.393 grams; 1/10 oz.
actual gold weight)
$10—0.273 oz.
(8.483 grams; 1/4 oz.
actual gold weight)
$25—0.545 oz.
(16.966 grams; 1/2 oz.
actual gold weight)
$50—1.091 oz.
(33.931 grams; 1 oz.
actual gold weight)
**Diameter:**
$5—16.5 mm
$10—22 mm
$25—27 mm
$50—32.7 mm
**Thickness:**
$50—2.87 mm
**Designers:**
Augustus Saint-Gaudens
(obverse), Miley Busiek
(reverse)

# Bullion Strikes, Gold, 2002

**$5 American Gold Eagle (1/10 oz.), bullion strike**   *Mintage: 230,027*

| 2002 | Grade | Purchased From | Date |
|------|-------|----------------|------|
|      |       |                |      |

Bullion value at time of purchase: _____

**$10 American Gold Eagle (1/4 oz.), bullion strike**   *Mintage: 62,027*

| 2002 | Grade | Purchased From | Date |
|------|-------|----------------|------|
|      |       |                |      |

Bullion value at time of purchase: _____

**$25 American Gold Eagle (1/2 oz.), bullion strike**   *Mintage: 70,027*

| 2002 | Grade | Purchased From | Date |
|------|-------|----------------|------|
|      |       |                |      |

Bullion value at time of purchase: _____

**$50 American Gold Eagle (1 oz.), bullion strike**   *Mintage: 222,029*

| 2002 | Grade | Purchased From | Date |
|------|-------|----------------|------|
|      |       |                |      |

Bullion value at time of purchase: _____

# Proof Strikes, Gold, 2002

**$5 American Gold Eagle (1/10 oz.), Proof**   *Mintage: 40,864*

| 2002-W | Grade | Purchased From | Date |
|--------|-------|----------------|------|
|        |       |                |      |

Bullion value at time of purchase: _____

**$10 American Gold Eagle (1/4 oz.), Proof**   *Mintage: 29,242*

| 2002-W | Grade | Purchased From | Date |
|--------|-------|----------------|------|
|        |       |                |      |

Bullion value at time of purchase: _____

**$25 American Gold Eagle (1/2 oz.), Proof**   *Mintage: 26,646*

| 2002-W | Grade | Purchased From | Date |
|--------|-------|----------------|------|
|        |       |                |      |

Bullion value at time of purchase: _____

**$50 American Gold Eagle (1 oz.), Proof**     *Mintage: 27,499*

| 2002-W | Grade | Purchased From | Date |
|--------|-------|----------------|------|
|        |       |                |      |

Bullion value at time of purchase: _____

# Proof Set, Gold, 2002
**$5, $10, $25, and $50 American Gold Eagle (1/10 oz. to 1 oz.), Proof**

| 2002-W | Grade | Purchased From | Date |
|--------|-------|----------------|------|
|        |       |                |      |

Bullion value at time of purchase: _____

# Bullion Strikes, Platinum, 2002
**$10 American Platinum Eagle (1/10 oz.), bullion strike**  *Mintage: 23,005*

| 2002 | Grade | Purchased From | Date |
|------|-------|----------------|------|
|      |       |                |      |

Bullion value at time of purchase: _____

**$25 American Platinum Eagle (1/4 oz.), bullion strike**  *Mintage: 27,405*

| 2002 | Grade | Purchased From | Date |
|------|-------|----------------|------|
|      |       |                |      |

Bullion value at time of purchase: _____

**$50 American Platinum Eagle (1/2 oz.), bullion strike**  *Mintage: 24,005*

| 2002 | Grade | Purchased From | Date |
|------|-------|----------------|------|
|      |       |                |      |

Bullion value at time of purchase: _____

**$100 American Platinum Eagle (1 oz.), bullion strike**  *Mintage: 11,502*

| 2002 | Grade | Purchased From | Date |
|------|-------|----------------|------|
|      |       |                |      |

Bullion value at time of purchase: _____

# Proof Strikes, Platinum, 2002
**$10 American Platinum Eagle (1/10 oz.), Proof**     *Mintage: 12,365*

| 2002-W | Grade | Purchased From | Date |
|--------|-------|----------------|------|
|        |       |                |      |

Bullion value at time of purchase: _____

---

**American Platinum Eagles**

**Date:** 2002
**Mints:** Philadelphia Mint (bullion strikes [no mintmark]); West Point Mint (Proofs [W mintmark])
**Composition:** .9995 platinum
**Edge:** Reeded
**Weight:**
    $10—0.1001 oz. (3.112 grams; 1/10 oz. actual platinum weight)
    $25—0.2501 oz. (7.780 grams; 1/4 oz. actual platinum weight)
    $50—0.5003 oz. (15.560 grams; 1/2 oz. actual platinum weight)
    $100—1.0005 oz. (31.120 grams; 1 oz. actual platinum weight)
**Diameter:**
    $10—16.5 mm
    $25—22 mm
    $50—27 mm
    $100—32.7 mm
**Thickness:**
    $100—2.39 mm
**Designers:**
    John M. Mercanti (obverse), Thomas D. Rogers Sr. (bullion-strike reverse), Alfred Maletsky (Proof reverse)

### $25 American Platinum Eagle (1/4 oz.), Proof — *Mintage: 9,282*

| 2002-W | Grade | Purchased From | Date |
|--------|-------|----------------|------|
|        |       |                |      |

Bullion value at time of purchase: _____

### $50 American Platinum Eagle (1/2 oz.), Proof — *Mintage: 8,772*

| 2002-W | Grade | Purchased From | Date |
|--------|-------|----------------|------|
|        |       |                |      |

Bullion value at time of purchase: _____

### $100 American Platinum Eagle (1 oz.), Proof — *Mintage: 9,834*

| 2002-W | Grade | Purchased From | Date |
|--------|-------|----------------|------|
|        |       |                |      |

Bullion value at time of purchase: _____

## Proof Set, Platinum, 2002

$10, $25, $50, and $100 American Platinum Eagle
(1/10 oz. to 1 oz.), Proof

| 2002-W | Grade | Purchased From | Date |
|--------|-------|----------------|------|
|        |       |                |      |

Bullion value at time of purchase: _____

# 2003

**Historical context:** Despite an economy that continued strong throughout 2003, with increased household income and high growth percentages, Americans were still uneasy. The dollar was suffering abroad, falling by over 15 percent in many major foreign currencies. Job production was at a low compared to the numbers achieved before the 2001 recession and it continued to go down throughout the year, accompanied by a rising unemployment rate. Knowing the numbers, economists were confident that the nation's resilience would carry over into 2004, but for the everyday American the outlook was more worrisome.

Internationally, the war on terror was taken to Iraq in March 2003, when forces from Great Britain and the United States attacked following Saddam Hussein's refusal to disarm according to United Nations regulations. A secondary objective was to free the Iraqi people from what had been a brutal regime. Hussein went into hiding soon after the attack, which lasted until May. He would be captured that December.

In the numismatic arena, the spring National Money Show of the American Numismatic Association was held in Charlotte, North Carolina, attracting thousands of coin dealers and collectors to the Queen City. The association's even larger summer show, the World's Fair of Money, would convene in Baltimore that August.

As they had the year before, 1933 double eagles made national headlines in 2003 when 10 of the coins were found in a safe-deposit box by the descendants of Philadelphia jeweler Israel Switt. What appeared to be a multi-million-dollar lucky find quickly turned into a lawsuit, however, when the federal government seized the coins, declaring that they belonged to the people of the United States and not to the family that found them. The $20 gold coins, dating back to the Great Depression, were never officially monetized and released by the Treasury Department. All but two, which were sent to the Smithsonian Institution, were supposed to have been melted down.

Precious metals continued on the rise in 2003. The spot price of silver bullion neared $6 per ounce in the fourth quarter and averaged at just under $5 for the year. Gold surged as well, with its annual average up by more than $50, and platinum was even stronger, its average jumping more than $150 per ounce compared to 2002.

**Coin commentary:** Demand for American Gold Eagles mirrored the bullion value of gold in 2003—both were on the rise. Gold sales (in terms of total ounces) experienced a healthy 69 percent increase over 2002. Most of the bump was in a 194,000-ounce increase in the sale of $50 one-ounce coins.

Given the year's trending-upward spot price of gold, the U.S. Mint increased the issue price of the Proof versions of American Gold Eagles in 2003. The tenth-ounce was set at $85 (with a sale limit of 25,000 individual coins, and production limit of 46,000 including sales from sets); the quarter-ounce at $165 (limit 10,000, maximum mintage of 31,000); the half-ounce at $315 (limit 8,000, maximum mintage of 29,000); and the one-ounce at $630 (limit 8,000, maximum mintage of 29,000). The year's four-coin Proof gold set was priced at $1,098, with a limit of 21,000 sets. Proof American Gold Eagle sales started on May 13, and, as was the case with their bullion counterparts, sales generally increased in 2003 over the previous year. The Mint announced that on July 6 the individual one-ounce Proof had sold out, after just seven weeks of sales. "As a result," said its July 24 press release, "one-ounce 2003-dated American Eagle Gold Proof Coins are now available only as part of the United States Mint's American Eagle Gold Proof Four-Coin Set." By November 24, the four-coin Proof set itself was 95 percent sold out, and the fractional gold Proofs were between 70 and 90 percent sold out, depending on the size.

While buyer interest in gold rose along with gold prices, the increasing market value for platinum (and the Mint's increased issue prices) seemed to have the opposite effect on collectors and investors. American Platinum Eagle sales fell across the board, in every denomination and both formats (bullion-strike and Proof).

The 2003 Proof platinum coins went on sale September 17. The Mint offered them directly to the public, individually and in four-coin packages. "For the first time in three years," the Mint announced, "the price of the American Eagle platinum Proof coins will be adjusted to compensate for increasing platinum prices, which affect the overall production costs of the program. The newly adjusted prices for the American Eagle platinum Proof coins will be $1,073 per one-ounce coin, $587 per half-ounce coin, $329 per quarter-ounce coin, $170 per tenth-ounce coin, and $1,995 for the four-coin set. All American Eagle platinum Proof coins are presented in luxurious velvet packaging, and are accompanied by a certificate of authenticity."

**2003 average spot prices:**
silver, $4.87; gold, $364.80;
platinum, $691.31

**Total 2003 American Gold
Eagle mintage (in ounces):**
498,557 (bullion);
54,055 (Proof)

**American Gold Eagles**
Date: 2003
Mints: West Point Mint (bullion
strikes [no mintmark] and
Proofs [W mintmark])
**Composition:**
.9167 gold, .03 silver,
.0533 copper
Edge: Reeded
**Weight:**
$5—0.109 oz.
(3.393 grams; 1/10 oz.
actual gold weight)
$10—0.273 oz.
(8.483 grams; 1/4 oz.
actual gold weight)
$25—0.545 oz.
(16.966 grams; 1/2 oz.
actual gold weight)
$50—1.091 oz.
(33.931 grams; 1 oz.
actual gold weight)
**Diameter:**
$5—16.5 mm
$10—22 mm
$25—27 mm
$50—32.7 mm
**Thickness:**
$50—2.87 mm
**Designers:**
Augustus Saint-Gaudens
(obverse), Miley Busiek
(reverse)

The year's Proof reverse design was a bald eagle in front of an American flag, by Alfred Maletsky. This design marked the first time in history that the American bald eagle and Old Glory appeared together on a U.S. coin.

## Bullion Strikes, Gold, 2003

**$5 American Gold Eagle (1/10 oz.), bullion strike** *Mintage: 245,029*

| 2003 | Grade | Purchased From | Date |
|---|---|---|---|
| | | | |

Bullion value at time of purchase: _____

**$10 American Gold Eagle (1/4 oz.), bullion strike** *Mintage: 74,029*

| 2003 | Grade | Purchased From | Date |
|---|---|---|---|
| | | | |

Bullion value at time of purchase: _____

**$25 American Gold Eagle (1/2 oz.), bullion strike** *Mintage: 79,029*

| 2003 | Grade | Purchased From | Date |
|---|---|---|---|
| | | | |

Bullion value at time of purchase: _____

**$50 American Gold Eagle (1 oz.), bullion strike** *Mintage: 416,032*

| 2003 | Grade | Purchased From | Date |
|---|---|---|---|
| | | | |

Bullion value at time of purchase: _____

## Proof Strikes, Gold, 2003

**$5 American Gold Eagle (1/10 oz.), Proof** *Mintage: 40,027*

| 2003-W | Grade | Purchased From | Date |
|---|---|---|---|
| | | | |

Bullion value at time of purchase: _____

**$10 American Gold Eagle (1/4 oz.), Proof** *Mintage: 30,292*

| 2003-W | Grade | Purchased From | Date |
|---|---|---|---|
| | | | |

Bullion value at time of purchase: _____

**$25 American Gold Eagle (1/2 oz.), Proof** *Mintage: 28,270*

| 2003-W | Grade | Purchased From | Date |
|---|---|---|---|
| | | | |

Bullion value at time of purchase: _____

## $50 American Gold Eagle (1 oz.), Proof          *Mintage: 28,344*

| 2003-W | Grade | Purchased From | Date |
|--------|-------|----------------|------|
|        |       |                |      |

Bullion value at time of purchase: _____

# Proof Set, Gold, 2003

**$5, $10, $25, and $50 American Gold Eagle
(1/10 oz. to 1 oz.), Proof**

| 2003-W | Grade | Purchased From | Date |
|--------|-------|----------------|------|
|        |       |                |      |

Bullion value at time of purchase: _____

# Bullion Strikes, Platinum, 2003

**$10 American Platinum Eagle (1/10 oz.), bullion strike** *Mintage: 22,007*

| 2003 | Grade | Purchased From | Date |
|------|-------|----------------|------|
|      |       |                |      |

Bullion value at time of purchase: _____

**$25 American Platinum Eagle (1/4 oz.), bullion strike** *Mintage: 25,207*

| 2003 | Grade | Purchased From | Date |
|------|-------|----------------|------|
|      |       |                |      |

Bullion value at time of purchase: _____

**$50 American Platinum Eagle (1/2 oz.), bullion strike** *Mintage: 17,409*

| 2003 | Grade | Purchased From | Date |
|------|-------|----------------|------|
|      |       |                |      |

Bullion value at time of purchase: _____

**$100 American Platinum Eagle (1 oz.), bullion strike** *Mintage: 8,007*

| 2003 | Grade | Purchased From | Date |
|------|-------|----------------|------|
|      |       |                |      |

Bullion value at time of purchase: _____

# Proof Strikes, Platinum, 2003

**$10 American Platinum Eagle (1/10 oz.), Proof** *Mintage: 9,534*

| 2003-W | Grade | Purchased From | Date |
|--------|-------|----------------|------|
|        |       |                |      |

Bullion value at time of purchase: _____

---

**American Platinum Eagles**

**Date:** 2003
**Mints:** Philadelphia Mint (bullion strikes [no mintmark]); West Point Mint (Proofs [W mintmark])
**Composition:** .9995 platinum
**Edge:** Reeded
**Weight:**
   $10—0.1001 oz. (3.112 grams; 1/10 oz. actual platinum weight)
   $25—0.2501 oz. (7.780 grams; 1/4 oz. actual platinum weight)
   $50—0.5003 oz. (15.560 grams; 1/2 oz. actual platinum weight)
   $100—1.0005 oz. (31.120 grams; 1 oz. actual platinum weight)
**Diameter:**
   $10—16.5 mm
   $25—22 mm
   $50—27 mm
   $100—32.7 mm
**Thickness:**
   $100—2.39 mm
**Designers:**
   John M. Mercanti (obverse), Thomas D. Rogers Sr. (bullion-strike reverse), Alfred Maletsky (Proof reverse)

### $25 American Platinum Eagle (1/4 oz.), Proof    *Mintage: 7,044*

| 2003-W | Grade | Purchased From | Date |
|--------|-------|----------------|------|
|        |       |                |      |

Bullion value at time of purchase: _____

### $50 American Platinum Eagle (1/2 oz.), Proof    *Mintage: 7,131*

| 2003-W | Grade | Purchased From | Date |
|--------|-------|----------------|------|
|        |       |                |      |

Bullion value at time of purchase: _____

### $100 American Platinum Eagle (1 oz.), Proof    *Mintage: 8,246*

| 2003-W | Grade | Purchased From | Date |
|--------|-------|----------------|------|
|        |       |                |      |

Bullion value at time of purchase: _____

## Proof Set, Platinum, 2003

**$10, $25, $50, and $100 American Platinum Eagle (1/10 oz. to 1 oz.), Proof**

| 2003-W | Grade | Purchased From | Date |
|--------|-------|----------------|------|
|        |       |                |      |

Bullion value at time of purchase: _____

# 2004

**Historical context:** The end of 2003 and the beginning of 2004 inspired confidence in the American people once again, if only a hesitating confidence. Despite the caution bred by the past several years of uncertainty, the U.S. economy looked promising. However, in 2004 it did not perform quite as well as was hoped. Unemployment had been falling since mid-2003 after a record peak, and from the beginning of the year job creation had been hitting highs not seen in the past two years by a large margin. The labor market began creating worry, however, as job creation slowed drastically in June. A month later, deceleration was a real fear.

In September thousands of people were killed in the disastrous landing of Hurricane Jeanne on Haiti; the storm followed directly after Hurricane Ivan. Some 250,000 people were left homeless from flash floods and related damage.

In U.S. numismatics, in late 2004 collectors discovered there was something unusual about the Wisconsin state quarters produced at the Denver Mint: three versions, whether purposefully or accidentally, were released into circulation. The differences between the quarters are slight enough to be easily missed. However, numismatists observed that two of the varieties have extra lines in the ear of corn in the reverse design, resembling extra leaves. The "Extra Leaf High" and "Extra Leaf Low" varieties would soon command hundreds of dollars in the marketplace.

Bullion spot prices continued their remarkable ascent in 2004. Silver's average for the year climbed more than $1.75 per ounce over 2003. Gold was up nearly $45, and platinum increased more than $150.

**Coin commentary:** Gold bullion sales increased in 2004 as the price of the metal went up in the market. The rise wasn't dramatic—some 10,000 ounces more than were sold in 2003—but it was the highest total since the year 2000. (This would be the last of a three-year uptick in gold bullion sales, followed by several years of decline, and then the explosive escalation of 2008.)

The annually issued American Gold Eagle Proof coins went on sale May 24. The U.S. Mint announced that, for the second consecutive year (and only the second time since 1998), it would raise Proof gold coin prices to compensate for the rising gold prices that were affecting overall production costs for the program. At the same time, mintage limits would be adjusted for 2004. The four-coin Proof package was limited to 25,000 sets. The one-ounce gold Proof was limited to 9,000 individual coins (total mintage limit, 34,000); the half-ounce, 8,000 coins (33,000 limit); the quarter-ounce, 11,000 coins (36,000 limit); and the tenth-ounce, 25,000 coins (50,000 limit).

Each of the Proof American Gold Eagle denominations saw a decline in sales this year, with the Proof program selling about 1,500 ounces less, in total, than in 2003.

The American Platinum Eagle's bullion coinage saw notably smaller mintages in 2004, with production dropping by about 30 percent. Platinum Proofs, too, plummeted in mintage—this after their issue prices were increased by about 25 percent to adjust for rising bullion prices. The year's Proof platinum mintages were record lows for the series.

The reverse of the 2004 Proof American Platinum Eagle coins (all four denominations) features a design by artist Donna Weaver, based on Daniel Chester French's sculpture "America" (located at the U.S. Customs House in New York City).

# Bullion Strikes, Gold, 2004

**$5 American Gold Eagle (1/10 oz.), bullion strike**     *Mintage: 250,016*

| 2004 | Grade | Purchased From | Date |
|------|-------|----------------|------|
|      |       |                |      |

Bullion value at time of purchase: _____

**$10 American Gold Eagle (1/4 oz.), bullion strike**     *Mintage: 72,014*

| 2004 | Grade | Purchased From | Date |
|------|-------|----------------|------|
|      |       |                |      |

Bullion value at time of purchase: _____

**$25 American Gold Eagle (1/2 oz.), bullion strike**     *Mintage: 98,040*

| 2004 | Grade | Purchased From | Date |
|------|-------|----------------|------|
|      |       |                |      |

Bullion value at time of purchase: _____

## 2004 average spot prices:
silver, $6.66; gold, $409.72; platinum, $845.31

**Total 2004 American Gold Eagle mintage (in ounces):**
509,044 (bullion); 52,603 (Proof)

**American Gold Eagles**
Date: 2004
Mints: West Point Mint (bullion strikes [no mintmark] and Proofs [W mintmark])
**Composition:**
.9167 gold, .03 silver, .0533 copper
Edge: Reeded
**Weight:**
$5—0.109 oz. (3.393 grams; 1/10 oz. actual gold weight)
$10—0.273 oz. (8.483 grams; 1/4 oz. actual gold weight)
$25—0.545 oz. (16.966 grams; 1/2 oz. actual gold weight)
$50—1.091 oz. (33.931 grams; 1 oz. actual gold weight)
**Diameter:**
$5—16.5 mm
$10—22 mm
$25—27 mm
$50—32.7 mm
**Thickness:**
$50—2.87 mm
**Designers:**
Augustus Saint-Gaudens (obverse), Miley Busiek (reverse)

**$50 American Gold Eagle (1 oz.), bullion strike**   *Mintage: 417,019*

| 2004 | Grade | Purchased From | Date |
| --- | --- | --- | --- |
|  |  |  |  |

Bullion value at time of purchase: _____

# Proof Strikes, Gold, 2004
**$5 American Gold Eagle (1/10 oz.), Proof**   *Mintage: 35,131*

| 2004-W | Grade | Purchased From | Date |
| --- | --- | --- | --- |
|  |  |  |  |

Bullion value at time of purchase: _____

**$10 American Gold Eagle (1/4 oz.), Proof**   *Mintage: 28,839*

| 2004-W | Grade | Purchased From | Date |
| --- | --- | --- | --- |
|  |  |  |  |

Bullion value at time of purchase: _____

**$25 American Gold Eagle (1/2 oz.), Proof**   *Mintage: 27,330*

| 2004-W | Grade | Purchased From | Date |
| --- | --- | --- | --- |
|  |  |  |  |

Bullion value at time of purchase: _____

**$50 American Gold Eagle (1 oz.), Proof**   *Mintage: 28,215*

| 2004-W | Grade | Purchased From | Date |
| --- | --- | --- | --- |
|  |  |  |  |

Bullion value at time of purchase: _____

# Proof Set, Gold, 2004
**$5, $10, $25, and $50 American Gold Eagle (1/10 oz. to 1 oz.), Proof**

| 2004-W | Grade | Purchased From | Date |
| --- | --- | --- | --- |
|  |  |  |  |

Bullion value at time of purchase: _____

# Bullion Strikes, Platinum, 2004
**$10 American Platinum Eagle (1/10 oz.), bullion strike**   *Mintage: 15,010*

| 2004 | Grade | Purchased From | Date |
| --- | --- | --- | --- |
|  |  |  |  |

Bullion value at time of purchase: _____

**$25 American Platinum Eagle (1/4 oz.), bullion strike**   *Mintage: 18,010*

| 2004 | Grade | Purchased From | Date |
| --- | --- | --- | --- |
|  |  |  |  |

Bullion value at time of purchase: _____

**$50 American Platinum Eagle (1/2 oz.), bullion strike**  *Mintage: 13,236*

| 2004 | Grade | Purchased From | Date |
|------|-------|----------------|------|
|      |       |                |      |

Bullion value at time of purchase: _____

**$100 American Platinum Eagle (1 oz.), bullion strike**  *Mintage: 7,009*

| 2004 | Grade | Purchased From | Date |
|------|-------|----------------|------|
|      |       |                |      |

Bullion value at time of purchase: _____

# Proof Strikes, Platinum, 2004

**$10 American Platinum Eagle (1/10 oz.), Proof**  *Mintage: 7,161*

| 2004-W | Grade | Purchased From | Date |
|--------|-------|----------------|------|
|        |       |                |      |

Bullion value at time of purchase: _____

**$25 American Platinum Eagle (1/4 oz.), Proof**  *Mintage: 5,193*

| 2004-W | Grade | Purchased From | Date |
|--------|-------|----------------|------|
|        |       |                |      |

Bullion value at time of purchase: _____

**$50 American Platinum Eagle (1/2 oz.), Proof**  *Mintage: 5,063*

| 2004-W | Grade | Purchased From | Date |
|--------|-------|----------------|------|
|        |       |                |      |

Bullion value at time of purchase: _____

**$100 American Platinum Eagle (1 oz.), Proof**  *Mintage: 6,007*

| 2004-W | Grade | Purchased From | Date |
|--------|-------|----------------|------|
|        |       |                |      |

Bullion value at time of purchase: _____

# Proof Set, Platinum, 2004

**$10, $25, $50, and $100 American Platinum Eagle (1/10 oz. to 1 oz.), Proof**

| 2004-W | Grade | Purchased From | Date |
|--------|-------|----------------|------|
|        |       |                |      |

Bullion value at time of purchase: _____

---

**American Platinum Eagles**

**Date:**  2004

**Mints:**  Philadelphia Mint (bullion strikes [no mintmark]); West Point Mint (Proofs [W mintmark])

**Composition:**
.9995 platinum

**Edge:**  Reeded

**Weight:**
$10—0.1001 oz. (3.112 grams; 1/10 oz. actual platinum weight)
$25—0.2501 oz. (7.780 grams; 1/4 oz. actual platinum weight)
$50—0.5003 oz. (15.560 grams; 1/2 oz. actual platinum weight)
$100—1.0005 oz. (31.120 grams; 1 oz. actual platinum weight)

**Diameter:**
$10—16.5 mm
$25—22 mm
$50—27 mm
$100—32.7 mm

**Thickness:**
$100—2.39 mm

**Designers:**
John M. Mercanti (obverse), Thomas D. Rogers Sr. (bullion-strike reverse), Donna Weaver (Proof reverse)

# 2005

**Historical context:** The 2005 U.S. economy was in good health before the year's hurricane season hit with catastrophic power. The Gulf Coast was confronted by multiple storms, including the devastating Hurricane Katrina, and many Americans feared that economic damage would be felt immediately, as it was after the 9/11 terror attacks. However, it wasn't until the end of the year that the economy began to truly suffer. Economic growth weakened to its lowest rate in three years. Consumer spending fell, and in response businesses slowed their investments.

In London, three subways were attacked in suicide bombings during peak hours on July 7, killing 56 people and injuring 700 more. An hour after the bombs in the underground went off, a double-decker bus was similarly attacked. Al-Qaeda would claim the attacks in September.

In American numismatics, longtime coin dealer Steven L. Contursi paid $8.5 million for one of the most famous coin sets in the world, known as the King of Siam set. The collection of U.S. Proof coins, including an extremely rare 1804-dated silver dollar, had been delivered as a gift of the United States to the king of Siam, Rama III, in 1836.

In December 2005 the American Numismatic Association officially named its museum after Edward C. Rochette, a former ANA president, executive director, and editor of *The Numismatist*. Rochette had also been influential in developing the association's Summer Seminars, still held annually at ANA headquarters in Colorado Springs.

Silver, gold, and platinum spot prices all continued their rise in 2005. Silver enjoyed an increase of more than $2 per ounce (comparing its year average to 2004). Gold rose $40, breaking the $500 per ounce barrier at the end of the year and averaging just under $450 per ounce for the year. Platinum was up as well, with its average price rising $50 per ounce.

**Coin commentary:** Sales for bullion-strike American Gold Eagles dropped about 13 percent in 2005 compared to the previous year. This was a reduction from 509,044 to 444,575 total ounces sold. Most of the decline (60,464 ounces) was from slower sales of the $50 one-ounce coin. Mintage of the $25 half-ounce declined by about 18 percent, but this denomination hadn't broken the 100,000-coin mark since 1999, and only accounted for some 49,000 ounces in 2004. The $10 quarter-ounce mintage for 2005 was almost identical to that of 2004—actually up by a single coin. And while demand for the $5 tenth-ounce increased by 50,000 coins, this only moved the year's needle by 500 ounces of gold. Counting only *bullion* (not including Proofs), the U.S. Mint's gold sales were at the start of a three-year downward slope.

Proof American Gold Eagles, meanwhile, were beginning a three-year rise in sales. Each denomination saw increased mintages in 2005 compared to 2004. Undoubtedly some of the credit goes to the Mint's earlier-than-usual release date: the Proof coins were available for purchase starting January 13—four months earlier than in 2004. A Mint press release described this as "part of the United States Mint's commitment to make many of its 2005 products available earlier in the year, at the request of its customers." The Mint raised the issue prices and adjusted the mintage limits for the 2005 Proofs. The four-coin gold Proof set sold for $1,260 (with a production limit of 26,000 sets). The one-ounce Proof sold for $720 (limited to 10,000 individual coins, and 36,000 total, including those sold in sets). The half-ounce was priced at $360 (limit 9,000 individual coins; 35,000 total). The quarter-ounce was released at $190 (limit 12,000 individual coins; 38,000 total). The tenth-ounce had an issue price of $95 (limit 26,000 individual coins; 52,000 total). The Proof American Gold Eagles neared their mintage limits but didn't sell out this year.

The Mint's platinum coinage followed a path similar to gold's in 2005: bullion strikes languished (setting new record lows) while Proofs saw increased demand—not surprising, given the rising price of platinum in the second half of the year. As it did with its gold Proof coins, the Mint released this year's platinum Proofs early, on April 7, 2005 (five months earlier than 2004's launch date). The year's new reverse design for Proof American Platinum Eagles was by Donna Weaver: a bald eagle with outstretched wings, guarding a cornucopia of American riches—wheat, grapes, and other agricultural bounty. The four-coin platinum Proof set sold for $2,495 (with production limited to 10,000 sets). The one-ounce Proof sold for $1,345 (limited to 4,000 individual coins, and 14,000 total, including those sold in sets). The half-ounce was priced at $735 (limit 3,000 individual coins; 13,000 total). The quarter-ounce was released at $410 (limit 5,000 individual coins; 15,000 total). The tenth-ounce had an issue price of $210 (limit 10,000 individual coins; 20,000 total). Demand was higher than in 2004, but still the Proof American Platinum Eagles came nowhere near selling out.

## Bullion Strikes, Gold, 2005

**$5 American Gold Eagle (1/10 oz.), bullion strike**  *Mintage: 300,034*

| 2005 | Grade | Purchased From | Date |
|------|-------|----------------|------|
|      |       |                |      |

Bullion value at time of purchase: _____

**$10 American Gold Eagle (1/4 oz.), bullion strike**  *Mintage: 72,015*

| 2005 | Grade | Purchased From | Date |
|------|-------|----------------|------|
|      |       |                |      |

Bullion value at time of purchase: _____

**$25 American Gold Eagle (1/2 oz.), bullion strike**  *Mintage: 80,023*

| 2005 | Grade | Purchased From | Date |
|------|-------|----------------|------|
|      |       |                |      |

Bullion value at time of purchase: _____

**2005 average spot prices:** silver, $8.82; gold, $446.00; platinum, $896.87

**Total 2005 American Gold Eagle mintage (in ounces):** 444,575 (bullion); 66,630 (Proof)

**American Gold Eagles**
**Date:** 2005
**Mints:** West Point Mint (bullion strikes [no mintmark] and Proofs [W mintmark])
**Composition:** .9167 gold, .03 silver, .0533 copper
**Edge:** Reeded
**Weight:**
  $5—0.109 oz. (3.393 grams; 1/10 oz. actual gold weight)
  $10—0.273 oz. (8.483 grams; 1/4 oz. actual gold weight)
  $25—0.545 oz. (16.966 grams; 1/2 oz. actual gold weight)
  $50—1.091 oz. (33.931 grams; 1 oz. actual gold weight)
**Diameter:**
  $5—16.5 mm
  $10—22 mm
  $25—27 mm
  $50—32.7 mm
**Thickness:**
  $50—2.87 mm
**Designers:**
  Augustus Saint-Gaudens (obverse), Miley Busiek (reverse)

## American Platinum Eagles

**Date:** 2005

**Mints:** Philadelphia Mint (bullion strikes [no mintmark]); West Point Mint (Proofs [W mintmark])

**Composition:**
.9995 platinum

**Edge:** Reeded

**Weight:**
$10—0.1001 oz.
(3.112 grams; 1/10 oz. actual platinum weight)
$25—0.2501 oz.
(7.780 grams; 1/4 oz. actual platinum weight)
$50—0.5003 oz.
(15.560 grams; 1/2 oz. actual platinum weight)
$100—1.0005 oz.
(31.120 grams; 1 oz. actual platinum weight)

**Diameter:**
$10—16.5 mm
$25—22 mm
$50—27 mm
$100—32.7 mm

**Thickness:**
$100—2.39 mm

**Designers:**
John M. Mercanti (obverse), Thomas D. Rogers Sr. (bullion-strike reverse), Donna Weaver (Proof reverse)

### $50 American Gold Eagle (1 oz.), bullion strike — *Mintage: 356,555*

| 2005 | Grade | Purchased From | Date |
|---|---|---|---|
|  |  |  |  |

Bullion value at time of purchase: _____

## Proof Strikes, Gold, 2005

### $5 American Gold Eagle (1/10 oz.), Proof — *Mintage: 49,265*

| 2005-W | Grade | Purchased From | Date |
|---|---|---|---|
|  |  |  |  |

Bullion value at time of purchase: _____

### $10 American Gold Eagle (1/4 oz.), Proof — *Mintage: 37,207*

| 2005-W | Grade | Purchased From | Date |
|---|---|---|---|
|  |  |  |  |

Bullion value at time of purchase: _____

### $25 American Gold Eagle (1/2 oz.), Proof — *Mintage: 34,311*

| 2005-W | Grade | Purchased From | Date |
|---|---|---|---|
|  |  |  |  |

Bullion value at time of purchase: _____

### $50 American Gold Eagle (1 oz.), Proof — *Mintage: 35,246*

| 2005-W | Grade | Purchased From | Date |
|---|---|---|---|
|  |  |  |  |

Bullion value at time of purchase: _____

## Proof Set, Gold, 2005

$5, $10, $25, and $50 American Gold Eagle (1/10 oz. to 1 oz.), Proof

| 2005-W | Uncertified | PF-69 | PF-70 |
|---|---|---|---|
| Value* | $3,180 | $3,325 | $4,050 |

* Based on bullion value of $1,400 per ounce.

## Bullion Strikes, Platinum, 2005

### $10 American Platinum Eagle (1/10 oz.), bullion strike *Mintage: 14,013*

| 2005 | Grade | Purchased From | Date |
|---|---|---|---|
|  |  |  |  |

Bullion value at time of purchase: _____

### $25 American Platinum Eagle (1/4 oz.), bullion strike *Mintage: 12,013*

| 2005 | Grade | Purchased From | Date |
|---|---|---|---|
|  |  |  |  |

Bullion value at time of purchase: _____

**$50 American Platinum Eagle (1/2 oz.), bullion strike**    *Mintage: 9,013*

| 2005 | Grade | Purchased From | Date |
|------|-------|----------------|------|
|      |       |                |      |

Bullion value at time of purchase: _____

**$100 American Platinum Eagle (1 oz.), bullion strike**    *Mintage: 6,310*

| 2005 | Grade | Purchased From | Date |
|------|-------|----------------|------|
|      |       |                |      |

Bullion value at time of purchase: _____

# Proof Strikes, Platinum, 2005

**$10 American Platinum Eagle (1/10 oz.), Proof**    *Mintage: 8,104*

| 2005-W | Grade | Purchased From | Date |
|--------|-------|----------------|------|
|        |       |                |      |

Bullion value at time of purchase: _____

**$25 American Platinum Eagle (1/4 oz.), Proof**    *Mintage: 6,592*

| 2005-W | Grade | Purchased From | Date |
|--------|-------|----------------|------|
|        |       |                |      |

Bullion value at time of purchase: _____

**$50 American Platinum Eagle (1/2 oz.), Proof**    *Mintage: 5,942*

| 2005-W | Grade | Purchased From | Date |
|--------|-------|----------------|------|
|        |       |                |      |

Bullion value at time of purchase: _____

**$100 American Platinum Eagle (1 oz.), Proof**    *Mintage: 6,602*

| 2005-W | Grade | Purchased From | Date |
|--------|-------|----------------|------|
|        |       |                |      |

Bullion value at time of purchase: _____

# Proof Set, Platinum, 2005

**$10, $25, $50, and $100 American Platinum Eagle
(1/10 oz. to 1 oz.), Proof**

| 2005-W | Grade | Purchased From | Date |
|--------|-------|----------------|------|
|        |       |                |      |

Bullion value at time of purchase: _____

# 2006

**Historical context:** The U.S. housing bubble deflated in 2006, taking with it any economic or job growth that was left over from previous years. Hit with high interest rates (on the rise due to a growing federal deficit) and rising oil prices, families throughout America struggled. The labor market shrank and wages accounted for a record-low share of national income. Debt for the average consumer rose. Imports surpassed exports by a wide margin—the second time such a high had been achieved since the Great Depression (the first had been in 2005).

On the international scene, in October 2006 North Korea announced its first nuclear weapons test, an underground explosion that was heralded by the communist state as a "great leap forward." Despite strong international pressure to cease nuclear testing, North Korea claimed that it needed the technology to ward off American military aggression. Asian stock markets plunged in the wake of the international condemnation.

In American numismatics, there was a new face at the U.S. Mint in 2006: Edmund C. Moy was confirmed by the Senate on July 26 and Treasury Secretary Henry Paulson swore him into the post of director on September 5. "As director of the United States Mint," a press release announced, "Moy will oversee an agency that is the world's largest manufacturer of coins, medals, and coin-related products. Since Congress created it in 1792, the United States Mint has grown into a highly efficient enterprise with 1,900 employees and operations in five states and the District of Columbia."

Another new face at the Mint in 2006: Thomas Jefferson, when the latest nickel rolled into circulation. Designer Jamie Franki intended a sense of optimism in the slight smile that enlightened his coinage portrait of the nation's third president.

It was in 2006 that John M. Mercanti became head of the U.S. Mint department in charge of design (supervisor of design and master tooling development specialist), a position he would hold until his retirement in late 2010. "The Mint had lost its way on design, and made it subservient to the manufacturing process," Ed Moy recalls of the period predating his directorship. "I believed that we needed a leader to start an artistic revival of our coin designs." Later, in 2009, Moy would officially resurrect the title of *chief engraver* (the historically presidentially appointed and Senate-confirmed position had been eliminated in 1996 under Mint reform legislation) and bestow it upon Mercanti—"to recognize his service functioning as the chief engraver," Moy says, "and to highlight the importance of artistic excellence and design." Bullion-coin collectors were already well acquainted with Mercanti as the designer of the American Silver Eagle reverse, the American Platinum Eagle obverse, and two reverse designs for the platinum Proof coins.

Silver bullion was up $2.72 per ounce averaged over the year. Gold's average spot price increased from $446 to $606—an impressive $160 jump. Platinum, too, continued its trend with a $245 leap, breaking the barrier of $1,000 per ounce and averaging more than $1,100 for the year.

**Coin commentary:** 2006 marked the 20th anniversary of the U.S. bullion coin program. The celebrations included new coinage formats (the "Uncirculated" or "Burnished" finish, available in the silver, gold, and platinum coins; and the Reverse Proof finish, available in silver and gold), plus three new coin sets. (The two-piece 20th Anniversary Gold and Silver Coin Set and the three-piece 20th Anniversary Gold Coin Set are described below. The three-piece 20th Anniversary Silver Coin Set, which contained no gold or platinum, is discussed in detail in *American Silver Eagles*, by John M. Mercanti.)

Among the program's bullion-strike coins, gold sales continued on the downward slope that had started in 2005. Buyers claimed some 130,000 fewer ounces of gold, in total, for 2006; this trend would continue for one more year before an upswing. The biggest slowdown was in sales of the $50 one-ounce coin, with nearly 120,000 fewer sold. Some of this decline was undoubtedly caused by the Mint's introduction this year of the .9999 fine American Buffalo gold bullion coins (which had a mintage of more than 337,000 one-ounce bullion strikes, and nearly 250,000 Proofs).

Proof American Gold Eagles, meanwhile, continued the upward ride that had started the previous year. Collectors and investors bought nearly 12,000 more ounces in total of the brilliantly struck collectibles. The coins were available individually or in four-coin sets; in addition, the one-ounce Proof was included in the three-coin 20th Anniversary Gold Coin Set (see below), issued to celebrate the milestone year in the American Eagle bullion program.

A new coinage format debuted for the American Gold Eagles this year: the Reverse Proof, featuring a brilliant mirrored surface for the raised devices and lettering, surrounded by frosted fields (the opposite of a normal Proof coin). The new format was available on the 2006 American Silver Eagle, and in the gold series it was available only on the $50 one-ounce coin, as part of the year's three-piece 20th Anniversary Gold Coin Set. The 2006-W $50 American Gold Eagle Reverse Proof is ranked no. 6 among the 100 Greatest U.S. Modern Coins, in the book of the same title by Scott Schechter and Jeff Garrett. "The announcement of the Reverse Proof gold eagle was made nine days before the coin went on sale," they write, "and it was immediately clear that it would be something special. It was the only coin of its kind in the American Gold Eagle series. . . . Further, its mintage was limited to

**2006-W, Reverse Proof.**

**2006-W American Eagle 20th Anniversary Gold & Silver Coin Set (mintage: 20,000).**

**2006-W, Burnished.**

just 10,000 coins—far below what was then the lowest Proof one-ounce Gold Eagle mintage, the 24,555 pieces of the 2001 issue. As expected, the coin was a quick and complete sellout (accounting for returns, the net mintage is now reported as 9,996). Prices doubled in the secondary market."

Overall demand for the American Platinum Eagle bullion strikes trended slightly downward in 2006, although the $50 half-ounce saw an uptick of about 7 percent. The resulting rarity of the 2006 one-ounce ($100) American Platinum Eagle—only 6,000 coins—gained it a ranking of no. 33 among the 100 Greatest U.S. Modern Coins.

The platinum bullion coins' Proof sisters, meanwhile, saw increased mintages across the spectrum, from tenth-ounce to one-ounce. Mintage limits were maintained at their 2005 levels, but the Mint raised the Proof coins' prices as platinum's bullion value increased over the year. As usual, the Proofs were available directly from the Mint, sold individually or in a four-coin set.

2006 brought the first Proof platinum reverse design in a new three-year series of motifs honoring "The Foundations of American Democracy" and the three branches of government. A rendition of the Legislative Muse was flanked by two eagles symbolizing the strength and wisdom that guard the law-making process. Corinthian columns, emblematic of the U.S. Senate and the House of Representatives, completed the scene. This design, by U.S. Mint Artistic Infusion Program master designer Joel Iskowitz, was inspired by the marble statue "The Car of History" by Carlo Franzoni, in the National Statuary Hall, Washington, D.C. Iskowitz's design was executed for coinage by Mint sculptor-engraver Don Everhart. (The Proof platinum reverses in 2007 and 2008 would commemorate the executive branch and the judicial branch.)

Another new format of coinage finish was introduced to the American Eagle program in 2006, in all three metals (silver, gold, and platinum). The new coins, called *Uncirculated* by the Mint (to distinguish them from Proofs and regular bullion strikes), were struck on specially burnished planchets. The surface finish of the Burnished coins is nearly indistinguishable from that of regular bullion strikes, but the W mintmark (for West Point) easily identifies their special status. The coins were introduced in the Mint's 2006 holiday catalog and went on sale September 28. "The diverse product offerings in our 2006 Holiday Collection are certain to please collectors, American history lovers, and others who are looking for fine quality gifts," said Mint Director Edmund Moy.

The Burnished gold coins were available in all four denominations. In the three fractional sizes collectors bought about half as many Burnished gold coins as they did Proofs in 2006, while sales of the $50 one-ounce coins were more evenly matched between the two formats (45,053 Burnished and 47,092 Proof). Among the platinum series, sales of the 2006 Burnished coins were the lowest in the history of the entire American Eagle bullion program. Mintages averaged about 3,000 coins for each of the four Burnished platinum denominations, which featured the same "Legislative" reverse design as the Proof American Platinum Eagles.

American Gold Eagles were included in two of the three coinage sets issued in 2006 to mark the 20th anniversary of the U.S. bullion program. The "American Eagle 20th Anniversary Gold & Silver Coin Set" was packaged with an informative booklet exploring the global history of gold and silver coinage. The set included the 2006 one-ounce American Silver Eagle and a 2006 one-ounce American Gold Eagle (both coins struck at West Point in the new Burnished or "Uncirculated" format). Production was capped at 20,000 sets, with an issue price of $850 and a limit of 10 sets per household. It was a sellout within a few months. The three-piece "20th Anniversary Gold Coin Set" went on sale August 30, 2006, priced at $2,610, limited to 10 sets per household, and with production cap of 10,000. Collectors were intrigued by the new Reverse Proof one-ounce American Gold Eagle included in the three-coin ensemble (the other two coins were Burnished and Proof one-ounces). This set sold out in about a month.

## Bullion Strikes, Gold, 2006

**$5 American Gold Eagle (1/10 oz.), bullion strike**  *Mintage: 285,006*

| 2006 | Grade | Purchased From | Date |
|------|-------|----------------|------|
|      |       |                |      |

Bullion value at time of purchase: _____

**$10 American Gold Eagle (1/4 oz.), bullion strike**  *Mintage: 60,004*

| 2006 | Grade | Purchased From | Date |
|------|-------|----------------|------|
|      |       |                |      |

Bullion value at time of purchase: _____

**$25 American Gold Eagle (1/2 oz.), bullion strike**  *Mintage: 66,005*

| 2006 | Grade | Purchased From | Date |
|------|-------|----------------|------|
|      |       |                |      |

Bullion value at time of purchase: _____

**$50 American Gold Eagle (1 oz.), bullion strike**  *Mintage: 237,510*

| 2006 | Grade | Purchased From | Date |
|------|-------|----------------|------|
|      |       |                |      |

Bullion value at time of purchase: _____

## Burnished, Gold, 2006

**$5 American Gold Eagle (1/10 oz.), Burnished**  *Mintage: 20,643*

| 2006-W | Grade | Purchased From | Date |
|--------|-------|----------------|------|
|        |       |                |      |

Bullion value at time of purchase: _____

**$10 American Gold Eagle (1/4 oz.), Burnished**  *Mintage: 15,188*

| 2006-W | Grade | Purchased From | Date |
|--------|-------|----------------|------|
|        |       |                |      |

Bullion value at time of purchase: _____

---

**2006 average spot prices:**
silver, $8.82; gold, $606.00; platinum, $1,142.31

**Total 2006 American Gold Eagle mintage (in ounces):**
314,014 (bullion);
78,012 (Proof)

**American Gold Eagles**

**Date:** 2006

**Mints:** West Point Mint (bullion strikes [no mintmark]; Proofs, Reverse Proofs, and Burnished [W mintmark])

**Composition:**
.9167 gold, .03 silver, .0533 copper

**Edge:** Reeded

**Weight:**
$5—0.109 oz. (3.393 grams; 1/10 oz. actual gold weight)
$10—0.273 oz. (8.483 grams; 1/4 oz. actual gold weight)
$25—0.545 oz. (16.966 grams; 1/2 oz. actual gold weight)
$50—1.091 oz. (33.931 grams; 1 oz. actual gold weight)

**Diameter:**
$5—16.5 mm
$10—22 mm
$25—27 mm
$50—32.7 mm

**Thickness:**
$50—2.87 mm

**Designers:**
Augustus Saint-Gaudens (obverse), Miley Busiek (reverse)

## American Platinum Eagles

**Date:** 2006

**Mints:** Philadelphia Mint (bullion strikes [no mintmark]); West Point Mint (Proofs and Burnished [W mintmark])

**Composition:**
.9995 platinum

**Edge:** Reeded

**Weight:**
$10—0.1001 oz.
(3.112 grams; 1/10 oz. actual platinum weight)
$25—0.2501 oz.
(7.780 grams; 1/4 oz. actual platinum weight)
$50—0.5003 oz.
(15.560 grams; 1/2 oz. actual platinum weight)
$100—1.0005 oz.
(31.120 grams; 1 oz. actual platinum weight)

**Diameter:**
$10—16.5 mm
$25—22 mm
$50—27 mm
$100—32.7 mm

**Thickness:**
$100—2.39 mm

**Designers:**
John M. Mercanti (obverse), Thomas D. Rogers Sr. (bullion-strike reverse), Joel Iskowitz (Proof and Burnished reverse)

---

### $25 American Gold Eagle (1/2 oz.), Burnished

*Mintage: 15,164*

| 2006-W | Grade | Purchased From | Date |
|---|---|---|---|
|  |  |  |  |

Bullion value at time of purchase: _____

### $50 American Gold Eagle (1 oz.), Burnished

*Mintage: 45,053*

| 2006-W | Grade | Purchased From | Date |
|---|---|---|---|
|  |  |  |  |

Bullion value at time of purchase: _____

## Burnished Set, Gold, 2006

**$5, $10, $25, and $50 American Gold Eagle (1/10 oz. to 1 oz.), Burnished**

| 2006-W | Grade | Purchased From | Date |
|---|---|---|---|
|  |  |  |  |

Bullion value at time of purchase: _____

## Proof Strikes, Gold, 2006

### $5 American Gold Eagle (1/10 oz.), Proof

*Mintage: 47,277*

| 2006-W | Grade | Purchased From | Date |
|---|---|---|---|
|  |  |  |  |

Bullion value at time of purchase: _____

### $10 American Gold Eagle (1/4 oz.), Proof

*Mintage: 36,127*

| 2006-W | Grade | Purchased From | Date |
|---|---|---|---|
|  |  |  |  |

Bullion value at time of purchase: _____

### $25 American Gold Eagle (1/2 oz.), Proof

*Mintage: 34,322*

| 2006-W | Grade | Purchased From | Date |
|---|---|---|---|
|  |  |  |  |

Bullion value at time of purchase: _____

### $50 American Gold Eagle (1 oz.), Proof

*Mintage: 47,092*

| 2006-W | Grade | Purchased From | Date |
|---|---|---|---|
|  |  |  |  |

Bullion value at time of purchase: _____

# Reverse Proof, Gold, 2006

$50 American Gold Eagle (1 oz.), Proof          *Mintage: 9,996*

| 2006-W | Grade | Purchased From | Date |
|--------|-------|----------------|------|
|        |       |                |      |

Bullion value at time of purchase: _____

# Proof Set, Gold, 2006

$5, $10, $25, and $50 American Gold Eagle
(1/10 oz. to 1 oz.), Proof

| 2006-W | Grade | Purchased From | Date |
|--------|-------|----------------|------|
|        |       |                |      |

Bullion value at time of purchase: _____

# Bullion Strikes, Platinum, 2006

$10 American Platinum Eagle (1/10 oz.), bullion strike  *Mintage: 11,001*

| 2006 | Grade | Purchased From | Date |
|------|-------|----------------|------|
|      |       |                |      |

Bullion value at time of purchase: _____

$25 American Platinum Eagle (1/4 oz.), bullion strike    *Mintage: 12,001*

| 2006 | Grade | Purchased From | Date |
|------|-------|----------------|------|
|      |       |                |      |

Bullion value at time of purchase: _____

$50 American Platinum Eagle (1/2 oz.), bullion strike    *Mintage: 9,602*

| 2006 | Grade | Purchased From | Date |
|------|-------|----------------|------|
|      |       |                |      |

Bullion value at time of purchase: _____

$100 American Platinum Eagle (1 oz.), bullion strike    *Mintage: 6,000*

| 2006 | Grade | Purchased From | Date |
|------|-------|----------------|------|
|      |       |                |      |

Bullion value at time of purchase: _____

# Burnished, Platinum, 2006

$10 American Platinum Eagle (1/10 oz.), Burnished    *Mintage: 3,544*

| 2006-W | Grade | Purchased From | Date |
|--------|-------|----------------|------|
|        |       |                |      |

Bullion value at time of purchase: _____

### $25 American Platinum Eagle (1/4 oz.), Burnished

*Mintage: 2,676*

| 2006-W | Grade | Purchased From | Date |
|--------|-------|----------------|------|
|        |       |                |      |

Bullion value at time of purchase: _____

### $50 American Platinum Eagle (1/2 oz.), Burnished

*Mintage: 2,577*

| 2006-W | Grade | Purchased From | Date |
|--------|-------|----------------|------|
|        |       |                |      |

Bullion value at time of purchase: _____

### $100 American Platinum Eagle (1 oz.), Burnished

*Mintage: 3,068*

| 2006-W | Grade | Purchased From | Date |
|--------|-------|----------------|------|
|        |       |                |      |

Bullion value at time of purchase: _____

## Burnished Set, Platinum, 2006

$10, $25, $50, and $100 American Platinum Eagle
(1/10 oz. to 1 oz.), Burnished

| 2006-W | Grade | Purchased From | Date |
|--------|-------|----------------|------|
|        |       |                |      |

Bullion value at time of purchase: _____

## Proof Strikes, Platinum, 2006

### $10 American Platinum Eagle (1/10 oz.), Proof

*Mintage: 10,205*

| 2006-W | Grade | Purchased From | Date |
|--------|-------|----------------|------|
|        |       |                |      |

Bullion value at time of purchase: _____

### $25 American Platinum Eagle (1/4 oz.), Proof

*Mintage: 7,813*

| 2006-W | Grade | Purchased From | Date |
|--------|-------|----------------|------|
|        |       |                |      |

Bullion value at time of purchase: _____

### $50 American Platinum Eagle (1/2 oz.), Proof

*Mintage: 7,649*

| 2006-W | Grade | Purchased From | Date |
|--------|-------|----------------|------|
|        |       |                |      |

Bullion value at time of purchase: _____

$100 American Platinum Eagle (1 oz.), Proof       *Mintage: 8,363*

| 2007-W | Grade | Purchased From | Date |
|--------|-------|----------------|------|
|        |       |                |      |

Bullion value at time of purchase: _____

$100 American Platinum Eagle (1 oz.), Proof,
**Frosted FREEDOM**       *Mintage: 12*

| 2007-W | Grade | Purchased From | Date |
|--------|-------|----------------|------|
|        |       |                |      |

Bullion value at time of purchase: _____

## Proof Set, Platinum, 2007

$10, $25, $50, and $100 American Platinum Eagle
(1/10 oz. to 1 oz.), Proof

| 2007-W | Grade | Purchased From | Date |
|--------|-------|----------------|------|
|        |       |                |      |

Bullion value at time of purchase: _____

## 10th Anniversary Platinum Coin Set, 2007

Two $50 American Platinum Eagles (1/2 oz.),
**Proof and enhanced Reverse Proof**

| 2007-W | Grade | Purchased From | Date |
|--------|-------|----------------|------|
|        |       |                |      |

Bullion value at time of purchase: _____

# 2008

**Historical context:** In the first 10 months of 2008 more than a million U.S. jobs were cut, with the likelihood of 300,000 more to follow soon after. The American housing market collapsed. In February Congress passed a $170 billion tax rebate as an economic-stimulus package to aid struggling families; its effects were disappointingly short-lived. The continuing recession prompted politicians to advocate another stimulus later in the year. Economists, on the other hand, made no promises that the downturn would end any time soon, hoping for the best-case scenario of an economic bottom the next year, from which the economy could slowly climb back up.

In the midst of these challenges, one of the largest investment-fraud scandals in American history rocked Wall Street in 2008. Bernard Madoff was arrested in December for heading a Ponzi scheme that involved nearly $65 billion. His victims ran the gamut from Hollywood celebrities and the country-club set to charitable foundations, universities, and regular individual investors, some of whom lost their life savings. Madoff would be sentenced to 150 years in jail.

In November of 2008 Illinois Democratic senator Barack Obama was elected the 44th president of the United States after a hard-fought campaign against Arizona senator John McCain. November 4 brought a historic

turnout of voters, giving Obama victory in the majority of states, including some previous Republican strongholds.

In American numismatics, the U.S. Mint added tenth-ounce, quarter-ounce, and half-ounce coins to its program of American Buffalo .9999 fine gold bullion. "Planning the fractional American Buffalo coins was one of my early key tasks as director of the Mint," Edmund Moy says. "We offered the smaller denominations in Burnished and Proof collector formats, individually and in sets. The one-ounce was also available in the collectible finishes, in addition to being minted as a bullion strike."

Gold spot prices rose dramatically, ramping up from an average of $699 per ounce in 2007 to an average of $900 in 2008. The nation's weak economy turned record numbers of investors toward the precious metal, especially in the second half of the year, and demand temporarily exceeded the Mint's supply. Sales of the Mint's bullion coins were suspended in August for a two-week hiatus, and after that rationed with limits on the quantities Authorized Purchasers could buy. Platinum also rose for the year, its average of $1,573 being $270 per ounce higher than in 2007. These numbers by themselves fail to illustrate the rollercoaster ride platinum took in 2008, starting around $1,500, peaking close to $2,300 in March, and then dropping through the summer and autumn to $800–$900 by the end of the year.

**Coin commentary:** American Gold Eagle bullion sales boomed in 2008, quadrupling the previous year's 191,019 total ounces (a low record for the program) to more than 788,000 ounces. The most in-demand gold coin for the year was the $50 one-ounce, a convenient way to pack a lot of gold into a bullion purchase. Its mintage rose from 140,016 in 2007 to 710,000 in 2008. In October, in order to focus on producing the larger coins, the Mint stopped production of new half-ounce and quarter-ounce American Gold Eagles, and announced that it would also stop tenth-ounce coinage after its supply of blanks ran out. "The United States Mint has worked diligently to attempt to meet demand," it announced in a memorandum to its Authorized Purchasers, "however, blank supplies are very limited and it is necessary . . . to focus remaining bullion production primarily on American Eagle Gold One Ounce and Silver One Ounce Coins."

The Mint first offered its 2008 Proof American Gold Eagles on March 4. At that time gold's spot price happened to be at a market peak for the year—close to $1,000 per ounce—and the Proofs were priced accordingly:

| | | |
|---|---|---|
| $5 tenth-ounce: | $149.95 | (30,000 individual coins maximum) |
| $10 quarter-ounce: | $329.95 | (16,000 individual coins maximum) |
| $25 half-ounce: | $609.95 | (15,000 individual coins maximum) |
| $50 one-ounce: | $1,199.95 | (25,000 individual coins maximum) |

Gold prices dropped from March's temporary peak (averaging closer to $900 in April, $890 in May and June, then down to $830 in September . . . $806 in October . . . and bottoming at the year's lowest monthly average of $760 in November). As the bullion value dropped, the Mint's issue prices for Proof American Gold Eagles became less and less attractive to collectors—their premiums were simply too high. It was only toward the end of the year that the Mint lowered its Proof prices to adjust to the market. In response sales finally ramped up, but the intervening months of languish resulted in one of the lowest one-ounce mintages in the Proof American Gold Eagle series, and record lows for the three fractional coins. Sales were so low in 2008 that the Proof gold program would be cancelled for a year.

Sales for 2008 American Gold Eagles in the other collector-coin format, Burnished (called *Uncirculated* by the Mint), started on April 1. The Mint described their issue prices as "the relative mid-point" between regular bullion strikes and Proofs:

| | |
|---|---|
| $5 tenth-ounce: | $124.95 |
| $10 quarter-ounce: | $295.95 |
| $25 half-ounce: | $565.95 |
| $50 one-ounce: | $1,119.95 |

The Mint established no maximum mintages for the Burnished gold coins, but, as was the case with the 2008 Proofs, collectors found the issue prices too high—especially as gold's bullion value dropped after peaking in March. The result was record-low sales for three of the four Burnished gold denominations this year. The 2008 four-coin American Gold Eagle set in Burnished format is ranked no. 27 among the 100 Greatest U.S. Coins, with authors Scott Schechter and Jeff Garrett noting that "Sales were so devastatingly low that the Mint cancelled the Uncirculated bullion program entirely for 2009 and 2010." When gold's Burnished format resumed in 2011, it would be available only for the largest, one-ounce coin.

Platinum's dramatic rise and plunge over the course of 2008—up, up, up in January, February, and March, down slightly in April, back up in May, then down, down, down through December—encouraged investors to jump into the turbulent market. Mintages rose remarkably for all four denominations of American Platinum Eagle, doubling for the $50 half-ounce and tripling for the $100 one-ounce compared to 2007 . The Mint suspended platinum sales in early winter to focus on the public's even more vigorous demand for silver and gold bullion, announcing in an October 6 memo to its Authorized Purchasers: "All [platinum] denominations were depleted last week. More coins will be produced based on current blank supplies, however, once that remaining inventory is depleted, no more coins will be produced for 2008."

Proof 2008 American Platinum Eagle sales started on May 5, with the four coin sizes available individually and in a packaged set. This was the third and final year of the Mint's "Foundations of American Democracy" series, and the featured reverse design, honoring the judicial branch of government, was a Joel Iskowitz creation engraved by Charles Vickers. "Emblazoned on the reverse . . . is an allegorical image of Lady Justice, a classic symbol dating back to the Greeks and Romans," the Mint's literature noted. "Scales, suspended from a finger of her right hand, represent the delicate balance of the law. A sword in her left hand symbolizes the power of reason, which can be wielded in either direction. The bald eagle—our Nation's symbol of courage and freedom—watches over our firm foundation of democracy." Prices for the Proof platinum coins, and their production limits, were thus:

---

**2008 average spot prices:** silver, $14.99; gold, $900.00; platinum, $1,573.53

**Total 2008 American Gold Eagle mintage (in ounces):** 788,500 (bullion); 49,069 (Proof)

**American Gold Eagles**

**Date:** 2008

**Mints:** West Point Mint (bullion strikes [no mintmark]; Proofs and Burnished [W mintmark])

**Composition:** .9167 gold, .03 silver, .0533 copper

**Edge:** Reeded

**Weight:**
$5—0.109 oz. (3.393 grams; 1/10 oz. actual gold weight)
$10—0.273 oz. (8.483 grams; 1/4 oz. actual gold weight)
$25—0.545 oz. (16.966 grams; 1/2 oz. actual gold weight)
$50—1.091 oz. (33.931 grams; 1 oz. actual gold weight)

**Diameter:**
$5—16.5 mm
$10—22 mm
$25—27 mm
$50—32.7 mm

**Thickness:**
$50—2.87 mm

**Designers:**
Augustus Saint-Gaudens (obverse), Miley Busiek (reverse)

## American Platinum Eagles

**Date:** 2008

**Mints:** Philadelphia Mint (bullion strikes [no mintmark]); West Point Mint (Proofs and Burnished [W mintmark])

**Composition:**
.9995 platinum

**Edge:** Reeded

**Weight:**
$10—0.1001 oz. (3.112 grams; 1/10 oz. actual platinum weight)
$25—0.2501 oz. (7.780 grams; 1/4 oz. actual platinum weight)
$50—0.5003 oz. (15.560 grams; 1/2 oz. actual platinum weight)
$100—1.0005 oz. (31.120 grams; 1 oz. actual platinum weight)

**Diameter:**
$10—16.5 mm
$25—22 mm
$50—27 mm
$100—32.7 mm

**Thickness:**
$100—2.39 mm

**Designers:**
John M. Mercanti (obverse), Thomas D. Rogers Sr. (bullion-strike reverse), Joel Iskowitz (Proof and Burnished reverse)

| 2008-W Platinum | Issue Price | Maximum Mintage | Individual Coin Limit |
|---|---|---|---|
| Proof one-ounce | $2,299.95 | 16,000* | 6,000 |
| Proof half-ounce | $1,174.95 | 15,000* | 5,000 |
| Proof quarter-ounce | $609.95 | 15,000* | 5,000 |
| Proof tenth-ounce | $269.95 | 20,000* | 10,000 |
| Proof four-coin set | $4,119.95 | 10,000 | — |

*Including those sold in sets.

Sales of the Proof American Platinum Eagles were slow, with collectors reluctant to accept their premiums as the precious metal's bullion value dropped over the summer. The Mint suspended sales, adjusted its pricing, and then resumed offering the coins. With the cost lowered, collectors bought up the remaining inventory, but the year's slow (and at times completely stopped) sales resulted in very small mintages across all four Proof denominations. "Investors sought exposure to precious metals, causing the surge of interest in bullion," Scott Schechter and Jeff Garrett note in *100 Greatest U.S. Modern Coins.* "Collectors, meanwhile, buying coins with discretionary money, were much more sensitive to price. . . . [The] aggressive pricing on collectibles in an uncertain economy discouraged collectors from buying." In particular, the low mintage of the half-ounce platinum Proof (only 4,020 coins) gained it a spot among the 100 Greatest U.S. Modern Coins, at no. 42. "With so few to go around," Schechter and Garrett observe, "this coin is already seldom-found in the marketplace and is widely thought to be a major key issue."

Like their Proof counterparts, the 2008 Burnished platinum coins also featured the "Judicial Branch" design. And like the Proofs, the Burnished pieces saw very low mintages. The Mint put the coins on sale July 17, but then suspended their offering as platinum's bullion price continued to plummet. After a price reduction late in the year, collectors bought up the Burnished American Platinum Eagles still in inventory, but 2008 was no barnburner. In fact, the Burnished $50 half-ounce had the lowest mintage (2,253) of any U.S. coin since the Arkansas Centennial half dollar of 1939. For its rarity and key-date status, it was ranked no. 36 among the 100 Greatest U.S. Modern Coins.

Because the Proof and Burnished American Platinum Eagles sold so poorly, and because the Mint needed to focus its production capacity on silver and gold one-ounce coins, two major program changes were made after 2008. First, the Burnished format was completely canceled for the platinum coinage. Second, platinum Proofs were eliminated in all but the largest, one-ounce format.

## Bullion Strikes, Gold, 2008

**$5 American Gold Eagle (1/10 oz.), bullion strike** *Mintage: 305,000*

| 2008 | Grade | Purchased From | Date |
|---|---|---|---|
| | | | |

Bullion value at time of purchase: _____

**$10 American Gold Eagle (1/4 oz.), bullion strike**     *Mintage: 70,000*

| 2008 | Grade | Purchased From | Date |
|------|-------|----------------|------|
|      |       |                |      |

Bullion value at time of purchase: _____

**$25 American Gold Eagle (1/2 oz.), bullion strike**     *Mintage: 61,000*

| 2008 | Grade | Purchased From | Date |
|------|-------|----------------|------|
|      |       |                |      |

Bullion value at time of purchase: _____

**$50 American Gold Eagle (1 oz.), bullion strike**     *Mintage: 710,000*

| 2008 | Grade | Purchased From | Date |
|------|-------|----------------|------|
|      |       |                |      |

Bullion value at time of purchase: _____

# Burnished, Gold, 2008

**$5 American Gold Eagle (1/10 oz.), Burnished**     *Mintage: 12,657*

| 2008-W | Grade | Purchased From | Date |
|--------|-------|----------------|------|
|        |       |                |      |

Bullion value at time of purchase: _____

**$10 American Gold Eagle (1/4 oz.), Burnished**     *Mintage: 8,883*

| 2008-W | Grade | Purchased From | Date |
|--------|-------|----------------|------|
|        |       |                |      |

Bullion value at time of purchase: _____

**$25 American Gold Eagle (1/2 oz.), Burnished**     *Mintage: 15,682*

| 2008-W | Grade | Purchased From | Date |
|--------|-------|----------------|------|
|        |       |                |      |

Bullion value at time of purchase: _____

**$50 American Gold Eagle (1 oz.), Burnished**     *Mintage: 11,908*

| 2008-W | Grade | Purchased From | Date |
|--------|-------|----------------|------|
|        |       |                |      |

Bullion value at time of purchase: _____

## Burnished Set, Gold, 2008

$5, $10, $25, and $50 American Gold Eagle
(1/10 oz. to 1 oz.), Burnished

| 2008-W | Grade | Purchased From | Date |
|--------|-------|----------------|------|
|        |       |                |      |

Bullion value at time of purchase: _____

## Proof Strikes, Gold, 2008

$5 American Gold Eagle (1/10 oz.), Proof          *Mintage: 28,116*

| 2008-W | Grade | Purchased From | Date |
|--------|-------|----------------|------|
|        |       |                |      |

Bullion value at time of purchase: _____

$10 American Gold Eagle (1/4 oz.), Proof          *Mintage: 18,877*

| 2008-W | Grade | Purchased From | Date |
|--------|-------|----------------|------|
|        |       |                |      |

Bullion value at time of purchase: _____

$25 American Gold Eagle (1/2 oz.), Proof          *Mintage: 22,602*

| 2008-W | Grade | Purchased From | Date |
|--------|-------|----------------|------|
|        |       |                |      |

Bullion value at time of purchase: _____

$50 American Gold Eagle (1 oz.), Proof          *Mintage: 30,237*

| 2008-W | Grade | Purchased From | Date |
|--------|-------|----------------|------|
|        |       |                |      |

Bullion value at time of purchase: _____

## Proof Set, Gold, 2008

$5, $10, $25, and $50 American Gold Eagle
(1/10 oz. to 1 oz.), Proof

| 2008-W | Grade | Purchased From | Date |
|--------|-------|----------------|------|
|        |       |                |      |

Bullion value at time of purchase: _____

## Bullion Strikes, Platinum, 2008

$10 American Platinum Eagle (1/10 oz.), bullion strike *Mintage: 17,000*

| 2008 | Grade | Purchased From | Date |
|------|-------|----------------|------|
|      |       |                |      |

Bullion value at time of purchase: _____

**$25 American Platinum Eagle (1/4 oz.), bullion strike**   *Mintage: 22,800*

| 2008 | Grade | Purchased From | Date |
|------|-------|----------------|------|
|      |       |                |      |

Bullion value at time of purchase: _____

**$50 American Platinum Eagle (1/2 oz.), bullion strike**   *Mintage: 14,000*

| 2008 | Grade | Purchased From | Date |
|------|-------|----------------|------|
|      |       |                |      |

Bullion value at time of purchase: _____

**$100 American Platinum Eagle (1 oz.), bullion strike**   *Mintage: 21,800*

| 2008 | Grade | Purchased From | Date |
|------|-------|----------------|------|
|      |       |                |      |

Bullion value at time of purchase: _____

# Burnished, Platinum, 2008

**$10 American Platinum Eagle (1/10 oz.), Burnished**   *Mintage: 3,706*

| 2008-W | Grade | Purchased From | Date |
|--------|-------|----------------|------|
|        |       |                |      |

Bullion value at time of purchase: _____

**$25 American Platinum Eagle (1/4 oz.), Burnished**   *Mintage: 2,481*

| 2008-W | Grade | Purchased From | Date |
|--------|-------|----------------|------|
|        |       |                |      |

Bullion value at time of purchase: _____

**$50 American Platinum Eagle (1/2 oz.), Burnished**   *Mintage: 2,253*

| 2008-W | Grade | Purchased From | Date |
|--------|-------|----------------|------|
|        |       |                |      |

Bullion value at time of purchase: _____

**$100 American Platinum Eagle (1 oz.), Burnished**   *Mintage: 2,876*

| 2008-W | Grade | Purchased From | Date |
|--------|-------|----------------|------|
|        |       |                |      |

Bullion value at time of purchase: _____

## Burnished Set, Platinum, 2008

$10, $25, $50, and $100 American Platinum Eagle
(1/10 oz. to 1 oz.), Burnished

| 2008-W | Grade | Purchased From | Date |
|--------|-------|----------------|------|
|        |       |                |      |

Bullion value at time of purchase: _____

## Proof Strikes, Platinum, 2008

$10 American Platinum Eagle (1/10 oz.), Proof          *Mintage: 5,138*

| 2008-W | Grade | Purchased From | Date |
|--------|-------|----------------|------|
|        |       |                |      |

Bullion value at time of purchase: _____

$25 American Platinum Eagle (1/4 oz.), Proof          *Mintage: 4,153*

| 2008-W | Grade | Purchased From | Date |
|--------|-------|----------------|------|
|        |       |                |      |

Bullion value at time of purchase: _____

$50 American Platinum Eagle (1/2 oz.), Proof          *Mintage: 4,020*

| 2008-W | Grade | Purchased From | Date |
|--------|-------|----------------|------|
|        |       |                |      |

Bullion value at time of purchase: _____

$100 American Platinum Eagle (1 oz.), Proof          *Mintage: 4,769*

| 2008-W | Grade | Purchased From | Date |
|--------|-------|----------------|------|
|        |       |                |      |

Bullion value at time of purchase: _____

## Proof Set, Platinum, 2008

$10, $25, $50, and $100 American Platinum Eagle
(1/10 oz. to 1 oz.), Proof

| 2008-W | Grade | Purchased From | Date |
|--------|-------|----------------|------|
|        |       |                |      |

Bullion value at time of purchase: _____

# 2009

**Historical context:** In 2009, in response to the continued foundering of the American economy, the U.S. Senate passed the $787 billion American Recovery and Reinvestment Act, signed by newly elected president Barack Obama four days after it passed. The act's main objective was to create jobs—

especially, in a New Deal–style philosophy, jobs that would repair the infrastructure, modernize schools and hospitals, and promote alternative energy sources. The majority of Republicans and some fiscally conservative Democrats were unhappy with the plan, opposed to its size most of all as well as to its contents.

The American economy hit rock bottom in 2009 but by the end of the year showed some signs of improvement.

A dramatic water-landing in the Hudson River dominated headlines for a time, when a plane with 155 passengers was forced into the New York waterway after hitting a bird on takeoff. What could have been a disaster was handled so expertly by Captain Chesley Sullenberger that no deaths occurred and injuries were contained to just over a dozen individuals. "Sully" would be lauded for his heroic control of the situation.

In April 2009 the H1N1 influenza virus, also known as Swine Flu, appeared in the United States. The World Health Organization announced a pandemic state on June 11, and by the 19th the sickness was reported in all 50 states in America, as well as Puerto Rico and the Virgin Islands. At least one million cases were reported by June 25.

This year marked the bicentennial of Abraham Lincoln's birth, which the U.S. Mint commemorated with four new reverse designs for the Lincoln cent. Each represented a different stage in Abe's life—his birth and early childhood in Kentucky; his formative years in Indiana; his professional life in Illinois; and his presidency in Washington, D.C. Fred Reed's book *Abraham Lincoln: The Image of His Greatness* would win the Numismatic Literary Guild's 2009 "Book of the Year" award as the work having the greatest potential impact on numismatics.

The Smithsonian's National Museum of American History removed some of its numismatic highlights to be taken in a traveling display titled "Good as Gold—America's Double Eagles." The national tour began at the August 2009 American Numismatic Association World's Fair of Money in Los Angeles. Following this event the exhibit would visit ANA conventions in Texas, Massachusetts, California, and elsewhere, continuing on until 2011. "Good as Gold" focused on the evolution of the $20 double eagle, the largest-denomination federal coin to circulate in the United States.

The bullion markets were turbulent in 2009. Silver ranged from $10.51 to $19 per ounce, and ended up averaging 30 cents lower for the year than in 2008. Gold reached a peak of $1,215 per ounce at the end of the year, but its overall average was just $910 per ounce, about 1 percent higher than 2008. Platinum, meanwhile, dropped $170, to just over $1,203.

**Coin commentary:** In 2009 the U.S. Mint began adjusting its American Eagle gold and platinum prices on a weekly basis (as needed), as it constantly monitored the precious-metal markets. This new procedure (which applied to *numismatic* products, such as Proof and Burnished coins) was published on January 6 in the *Federal Register* and took effect January 12, 2009. In its "Notification of New Pricing Methodology for Numismatic Products Containing Platinum and Gold Coins," the Mint announced, "The new pricing methodology is based primarily on the London Fix weekly average (average of the London Fix prices covering the previous Thursday a.m. Fix through the Wednesday a.m. Fix) platinum and gold prices, which reflect the market value

**2009 average spot prices:**
silver, $14.66; gold, $910.00;
platinum, $1,203.49

**Total 2009 American Gold
Eagle mintage (in ounces):**
1,602,500 (bullion);
0 (Proof)

**American Gold Eagles**

Date:  2009
Mints:  West Point Mint (bullion
strikes [no mintmark])
Composition:
.9167 gold, .03 silver,
.0533 copper
Edge:  Reeded
Weight:
$5—0.109 oz.
(3.393 grams; 1/10 oz.
actual gold weight)
$10—0.273 oz.
(8.483 grams; 1/4 oz.
actual gold weight)
$25—0.545 oz.
(16.966 grams; 1/2 oz.
actual gold weight)
$50—1.091 oz.
(33.931 grams; 1 oz.
actual gold weight)
Diameter:
$5—16.5 mm
$10—22 mm
$25—27 mm
$50—32.7 mm
Thickness:
$50—2.87 mm
Designers:
Augustus Saint-Gaudens
(obverse), Miley Busiek
(reverse)

of the platinum and gold bullion that these products contain. As required by law, the prices of these products also must be sufficient to recover all other costs incurred by the United States Mint, such as the cost of minting, marketing, and distributing such products (including labor, materials, dies, use of machinery, and promotional and overhead expenses). This pricing methodology will allow the United States Mint to change the prices of these products as often as weekly so they better reflect the costs of platinum and gold on the open markets." Effective January 12, the Mint began selling "numismatic products containing American Eagle Gold and Platinum Coins, American Buffalo Gold Coins, First Spouse Gold Coins, and the 2009 United States Mint Ultra High Relief Double Eagle Gold Coin at prices established by using the new pricing methodology."

Other changes were afoot in the American Gold Eagle program for 2009, as the Mint continued to face sourcing challenges created by the increased international demand for gold. The Mint's rationing of purchases that started in the fall of 2008 continued into mid-June of 2009; was lifted; then ran again December 15 to the end of the year. For most of the year mintage of gold bullion strikes was limited to one-ounce coins (no fractionals), a restriction that would lift briefly at the end of the year. Proof and Burnished coins hadn't yet gone on sale by March, and that month the Mint announced it was suspending their sale—the precious metal that normally would have gone into those products was routed into regular bullion-strike production to keep up with demand. The Mint's intention was to "resume the American Eagle Gold Proof and Uncirculated Coin Programs once sufficient inventories of gold bullion blanks can be acquired to meet market demand for all three American Eagle Gold Coin products," according to a press release. "Additionally, as a result of the recent numismatic product portfolio analysis, fractional sizes of American Eagle Gold Uncirculated Coins will no longer be produced." Despite the best of intentions, the Mint would end up completely canceling Proof and Burnished American Gold Eagles for 2009; that announcement was made in October. In November the Mint sent a memorandum to its Authorized Purchasers, informing them that it had "depleted its current inventory of 2009 American Eagle 1-ounce gold bullion coins due to the continued strong demand for this product" and that "We will temporarily suspend sales of this product to build up additional inventory." The one-ounce bullion coins would go back on sale in December, finally joined by their tenth-ounce, quarter-ounce, and half-ounce counterparts. Demand was so high that mintages for the fractional coins would be in the hundreds of thousands, despite the year's very short sales period. The Mint produced 2009-dated American Gold Eagles through to the end of the year, instead of what would have been its normal practice of minting 2010-dated coins in November and December for pre-order sales to be delivered in January.

Platinum collectors and investors were kept waiting until early winter 2009 to know if the year's coins would be available at all. The Mint announced on October 6 that it would not produce any bullion-strike American Platinum Eagles in 2009. The year's platinum production would consist of only a one-ounce Proof—no fractionals. This was a dramatic scaling back of the 1997–2008 program that had included tenth-ounce, quarter-ounce, half-ounce, and one-ounce coins, in bullion-strike, Burnished, and Proof formats, with a rich

**$50 American Gold Eagle (1 oz.), Proof**   *Mintage: 60,000*

| 2010-W | Grade | Purchased From | Date |
|--------|-------|----------------|------|
|        |       |                |      |

Bullion value at time of purchase: _____

## Proof Set, Gold, 2010

**$5, $10, $25, and $50 American Gold Eagle**
**(1/10 oz. to 1 oz.), Proof**

| 2010-W | Grade | Purchased From | Date |
|--------|-------|----------------|------|
|        |       |                |      |

Bullion value at time of purchase: _____

## Proof Strikes, Platinum, 2010

**$100 American Platinum Eagle (1 oz.), Proof**   *Mintage: 10,000*

| 2010-W | Grade | Purchased From | Date |
|--------|-------|----------------|------|
|        |       |                |      |

Bullion value at time of purchase: _____

# 2011

**Historical context:** America's economic woes continued in 2011. "Occupy Wall Street," a mostly peaceful protest movement that would become a national sensation, took to the streets of New York, targeting Manhattan's financial district to protest the role of powerful financial corporations in the state of the economy.

In March 2011 an 8.9 magnitude earthquake combined with a resulting tsunami struck Japan, killing more than 100,000 people. The crisis was heightened when damage to the Fukushima Dai-ichi nuclear plant created a nuclear emergency that took weeks to entirely contain.

In May elusive al-Qaeda leader Osama bin Laden was killed by the U.S. Navy's SEAL Team Six. After taking meticulous precautions in properly identifying bin Laden, the U.S. military buried the terrorist leader at sea to prevent his grave becoming an important site for extremist sympathizers. In Libya, Muammar Gaddafi was overthrown and killed in a civil-war uprising.

An important numismatic court case was decided in July 2011. A jury unanimously found in favor of the federal government regarding the 10 rare 1933 double eagles that came to light in 2003. The jury concluded that the $20 gold coins had been obtained illegally from the U.S. Mint, and therefore still belonged to the American people as embodied by the government, and were subject to forfeiture. (This decision would be affirmed in August 2012.)

The metal markets were strong in 2011. Silver's yearly average spot value increased 75 percent over that of 2010, at $35 per ounce. Gold, too, saw a robust overall increase, its annual average shooting upward nearly $450 to $1,571. (In September its spot price spiked to more than $1,900 per ounce.) Platinum's averaged price surged forward $100 per ounce over 2010.

**Coin commentary:** The U.S. Mint began accepting orders for 2011 one-ounce bullion-strike American Gold Eagles on January 3. Authorized Purchasers were allowed to order in any quantity, with no allocation restrictions (as they had seen imposed in recent years). The tenth-ounce, quarter-ounce, and half-ounce bullion coins would go on sale the next month. Overall, by total ounces, sales for 2011 were down about 20 percent from 2010.

Demand for gold bullion had been so high in recent years that the Mint had delayed, rationed, and temporarily suspended sales several times, and even canceled the production of Proofs and Burnished coins. The latter were secondary to the Mint's congressional mandate to produce *bullion* gold coins—not limited-edition collector-format coins—sufficient to meet public demand. Late in 2010 this mandate was lifted, giving the Mint more flexibility to produce collector coins in 2011. Proof versions of all four sizes of American Gold Eagle were offered for sale starting April 21, with maximum product limits increased for some of the coins over their 2010 limits:

| 2011-W Gold | Maximum Mintage | Individual Coin Limit |
|---|---|---|
| Proof one-ounce | 70,000* | 30,000 |
| Proof half-ounce | 55,000* | 15,000 |
| Proof quarter-ounce | 56,000* | 16,000 |
| Proof tenth-ounce | 70,000* | 30,000 |
| Proof four-coin set | 40,000 | — |

\* Including those sold in sets.

The Mint's prices for the Proof coins were established, monitored, and modified as necessary, using the "New Pricing Methodology for Numismatic Products Containing Platinum and Gold Coins" announced in January 2009. Collector interest in the Proofs was lower than in 2010; the $50 one-ounce coins experienced a sellout first, and eventually the fractional sizes reached their individual-coin limits, but when sales for the program year ended on December 31 the four-coin Proof sets still hadn't sold out.

With the lifting of the old "public demand" requirement (which had forced all the Mint's planchets, manpower, and machine time to be sucked up by bullion coinage when demand was high) came the flexibility in 2011 to re-introduce the Burnished format, last seen in 2008. The Mint announced the 2011 Burnished (called *Uncirculated*) American Gold Eagles on April 28, and sales started on May 5. No order limits were established.

The American Platinum Eagle program continued in 2011 with the third annual design in its six-year "Preamble" series, honoring important principles from the U.S. Constitution. "To Insure Domestic Tranquility" was the concept embodied by Joel Iskowitz's vision of Miss Liberty, engraved for coinage by Mint sculptor-engraver Phebe Hemphill. "The design depicts the harvest goddess emerging from a field of wheat, symbolizing the vastness of our Nation and its wide diversity of views," the Mint revealed in a May 19 press release. "She bears a stalk of wheat in her left hand, as she extends her right hand to a landing dove, representing the fulfillment of tranquility in our

Nation's cohesive yet free society." The coin went on sale May 26, 2011, with a maximum mintage of 15,000 (compared to 10,000 in 2010). Orders at first were limited to five per household; this restriction was later lifted. The Mint's issue price of $2,092 per coin was adjusted downward as platinum's bullion value fell through the year; at its lowest it would be $1,692. A sellout of the coin's 15,000 mintage was announced in August 2012.

No Burnished American Platinum Eagles were released in 2011.

## Bullion Strikes, Gold, 2011

### $5 American Gold Eagle (1/10 oz.), bullion strike — *Mintage: 350,000*

| 2011 | Grade | Purchased From | Date |
|------|-------|----------------|------|
|      |       |                |      |

Bullion value at time of purchase: _____

### $10 American Gold Eagle (1/4 oz.), bullion strike — *Mintage: 80,000*

| 2011 | Grade | Purchased From | Date |
|------|-------|----------------|------|
|      |       |                |      |

Bullion value at time of purchase: _____

### $25 American Gold Eagle (1/2 oz.), bullion strike — *Mintage: 70,000*

| 2011 | Grade | Purchased From | Date |
|------|-------|----------------|------|
|      |       |                |      |

Bullion value at time of purchase: _____

### $50 American Gold Eagle (1 oz.), bullion strike — *Mintage: 857,000*

| 2011 | Grade | Purchased From | Date |
|------|-------|----------------|------|
|      |       |                |      |

Bullion value at time of purchase: _____

## Burnished, Gold, 2011

### $50 American Gold Eagle (1 oz.), Burnished — *Mintage: 8,822*

| 2011-W | Grade | Purchased From | Date |
|--------|-------|----------------|------|
|        |       |                |      |

Bullion value at time of purchase: _____

## Proof Strikes, Gold, 2011

### $5 American Gold Eagle (1/10 oz.), Proof — *Mintage: 42,873*

| 2011-W | Grade | Purchased From | Date |
|--------|-------|----------------|------|
|        |       |                |      |

Bullion value at time of purchase: _____

**2011 average spot prices:**
silver, $35.12; gold, $1,571.52;
platinum, $1,721.86

**Total 2011 American Gold Eagle mintage (in ounces):**
947,000 (bullion);
73,943 (Proof)

**American Gold Eagles**
**Date:** 2011
**Mints:** West Point Mint (bullion strikes [no mintmark]; Proofs and Burnished [W mintmark])
**Composition:** .9167 gold, .03 silver, .0533 copper
**Edge:** Reeded
**Weight:**
$5—0.109 oz. (3.393 grams; 1/10 oz. actual gold weight)
$10—0.273 oz. (8.483 grams; 1/4 oz. actual gold weight)
$25—0.545 oz. (16.966 grams; 1/2 oz. actual gold weight)
$50—1.091 oz. (33.931 grams; 1 oz. actual gold weight)
**Diameter:**
$5—16.5 mm
$10—22 mm
$25—27 mm
$50—32.7 mm
**Thickness:**
$50—2.87 mm
**Designers:**
Augustus Saint-Gaudens (obverse), Miley Busiek (reverse)

**American Platinum Eagles**
Date: 2011
Mints: West Point Mint (Proofs [W mintmark])
Composition:
.9995 platinum
Edge: Reeded
Weight:
$100—1.0005 oz.
(31.120 grams; 1 oz. actual platinum weight)
Diameter:
$100—32.7 mm
Thickness:
$100—2.39 mm
Designers:
John M. Mercanti (obverse), Joel Iskowitz (reverse)

## $10 American Gold Eagle (1/4 oz.), Proof — *Mintage: 29,254*

| 2011-W | Grade | Purchased From | Date |
|---|---|---|---|
|  |  |  |  |

Bullion value at time of purchase: _____

## $25 American Gold Eagle (1/2 oz.), Proof — *Mintage: 26,939*

| 2011-W | Grade | Purchased From | Date |
|---|---|---|---|
|  |  |  |  |

Bullion value at time of purchase: _____

## $50 American Gold Eagle (1 oz.), Proof — *Mintage: 48,873*

| 2011-W | Grade | Purchased From | Date |
|---|---|---|---|
|  |  |  |  |

Bullion value at time of purchase: _____

## Proof Set, Gold, 2011

**$5, $10, $25, and $50 American Gold Eagle (1/10 oz. to 1 oz.), Proof**

| 2011-W | Grade | Purchased From | Date |
|---|---|---|---|
|  |  |  |  |

Bullion value at time of purchase: _____

## Proof Strikes, Platinum, 2011

**$100 American Platinum Eagle (1 oz.), Proof** — *Mintage: 15,000*

| 2011-W | Grade | Purchased From | Date |
|---|---|---|---|
|  |  |  |  |

Bullion value at time of purchase: _____

# 2012

**Historical context:** Even though uncertainty continued to haunt the U.S. economy through 2012, the stock market performed relatively well, with gains surprising many observers. It was a year of extremes rather than gradual changes as the market swung up and down. By the third quarter of the year the economy was growing better than it had since 2009, tempting confidence that America was shaking off the doldrums.

Hurricane Sandy, which struck the New York coastline in October, closed the U.S. stock exchange for two days—the first time since 1888 that weather has caused such a delay. Despite the shutdown, economists were confident that the market would handle the break as a "long weekend" rather than the type of closing that occurred after the September 11 terror attacks of 2001.

In the numismatic market, a half dozen coins sold for more than $1 million apiece in various auctions across the year. The record for 2012 was a Proof

1907 Ultra High Relief $20 gold coin, auctioned in June for $2,760,000 by Stack's Bowers Galleries.

Studies from 2011 showed that U.S. coins were more expensive to mint than their face value in circulation, prompting the Obama administration to petition for a more cost-effective minting process, including cheaper metals. The Treasury had already been researching potential new metals, and no recipe had been found to warrant a change.

Silver ranged from a high of $34.14 per ounce in February 2012 to a low of $27.43 at midyear, climbing back up past $30 through the year's final four months. The cumulative average price of silver for the year was $31.15 per ounce, down $4 from 2011. Gold started strong in January and February, averaging $1,700 per ounce for those two months. It then slid down and played in the $1,500s and $1,600s through most of the summer before beginning rising in September through November, ending the year at $1,688. Gold's average for the year was $1,668.98 per ounce, almost $100 above its 2011 average. Platinum's general trends mirrored those of gold, but the metal was consistently weaker compared to 2011, with spot price averaging $1,551.48 for the year, down from $1,721.86.

**Coin commentary:** All four sizes of 2012 American Gold Eagle bullion strikes, from one-ounce down to tenth-ounce, were available to the Mint's Authorized Purchasers starting January 3. Demand for the coins declined by about 20 percent as measured by total ounces sold in 2011 and 2012. Still, it was a strong year for sales at more than 750,000 cumulative ounces (higher than most of the 1990s and 2000s).

For collectors, 2012 Proof American Gold Eagles rolled out on April 19, with all four sizes available individually as well as in a four-coin Proof set. The Mint lowered the mintage caps for each of the individual fractional-ounce coins as well as for the set.

| 2012-W Gold | Maximum Mintage | Individual Coin Limit |
|---|---|---|
| Proof one-ounce | 60,000* | 30,000 |
| Proof half-ounce | 40,000* | 10,000 |
| Proof quarter-ounce | 42,000* | 12,000 |
| Proof tenth-ounce | 55,000* | 25,000 |
| Proof four-coin set | 30,000 | — |

* Including those sold in sets.

Proof American Gold Eagle sales were moribund in 2012, with collectors buying fewer than half of the previous year's mintage in each denomination. This created record lows—mintages lower even than those of 2008, a year so lackluster that the Mint canceled Proof gold production for 2009.

The Burnished format returned in 2012 for the American Gold Eagle, again just for the $50 one-ounce size, as was the case in 2011. The coins went on sale June 28, with customer demand determining their mintage (no maximum established). Another record low awaits final official accounting from the Mint: reported sales for the Burnished 2012 American Gold Eagle are just 6,118 coins, which would be the lowest production in the entire U.S. bullion program to date.

**2012 average spot prices:**
silver, $31.15; gold, $1,668.98;
platinum, $1,551.48

**Total 2012 American Gold Eagle mintage (in ounces):**
753,000 (bullion);
35,810 (Proof)

**American Gold Eagles**

**Date:** 2012

**Mints:** West Point Mint (bullion strikes [no mintmark]; Proofs and Burnished [W mintmark])

**Composition:**
.9167 gold, .03 silver, .0533 copper

**Edge:** Reeded

**Weight:**
$5—0.109 oz.
(3.393 grams; 1/10 oz. actual gold weight)
$10—0.273 oz.
(8.483 grams; 1/4 oz. actual gold weight)
$25—0.545 oz.
(16.966 grams; 1/2 oz. actual gold weight)
$50—1.091 oz.
(33.931 grams; 1 oz. actual gold weight)

**Diameter:**
$5—16.5 mm
$10—22 mm
$25—27 mm
$50—32.7 mm

**Thickness:**
$50—2.87 mm

**Designers:**
Augustus Saint-Gaudens (obverse), Miley Busiek (reverse)

The American Platinum Eagle continued into the fourth year of its six-year "Preamble" program commemorating the core concepts of American democracy in the six principles of the Preamble to the U.S. Constitution. The Proof $100 one-ounce coins were put on sale August 9. "The 2012 coin's reverse design is emblematic of the theme 'To Provide for the Common Defence,' the fourth principle in the Preamble," noted the Mint's literature. "Designed by United States Mint Artistic Infusion Program associate designer Barbara Fox and sculpted by United States Mint sculptor-engraver Charles L. Vickers, it depicts a vigilant minuteman from the Revolutionary War, representing the protection and defense of the country during its early days. The minuteman carries a rifle and a book, which symbolizes the importance of knowledge in defending our Nation. The design also features an American Eagle privy mark from an original 'coin punch' identified at the United States Mint at Philadelphia."

The 2012 Proof American Platinum Eagle's mintage was capped at 15,000, the same as 2011's (which had eventually sold out). Sales began with a limit (later retracted) of five coins per household, and the initial issue price was $1,692. The price fluctuated as the Mint monitored and adjusted it according to the weekly precious-metal market. Collectors bought half of the maximum mintage between the debut of August 9 and the end of the year, and sales continued into 2013.

No 2012-dated bullion-strike or Burnished American Platinum Eagles were offered by the Mint.

# Bullion Strikes, Gold, 2012

**$5 American Gold Eagle (1/10 oz.), bullion strike**　　*Mintage: ~315,000*

| 2012 | Grade | Purchased From | Date |
|---|---|---|---|
|  |  |  |  |

Bullion value at time of purchase: _____

**$10 American Gold Eagle (1/4 oz.), bullion strike**　　*Mintage: ~76,000*

| 2012 | Grade | Purchased From | Date |
|---|---|---|---|
|  |  |  |  |

Bullion value at time of purchase: _____

**$25 American Gold Eagle (1/2 oz.), bullion strike**　　*Mintage: ~71,000*

| 2012 | Grade | Purchased From | Date |
|---|---|---|---|
|  |  |  |  |

Bullion value at time of purchase: _____

**$50 American Gold Eagle (1 oz.), bullion strike**　　*Mintage: ~667,000*

| 2012 | Grade | Purchased From | Date |
|---|---|---|---|
|  |  |  |  |

Bullion value at time of purchase: _____

## Burnished, Gold, 2012

**$50 American Gold Eagle (1 oz.), Burnished**    *Mintage: ~6,118*

| 2012-W | Grade | Purchased From | Date |
|--------|-------|----------------|------|
|        |       |                |      |

Bullion value at time of purchase: _____

## Proof Strikes, Gold, 2012

**$5 American Gold Eagle (1/10 oz.), Proof**    *Mintage: ~20,637*

| 2012-W | Grade | Purchased From | Date |
|--------|-------|----------------|------|
|        |       |                |      |

Bullion value at time of purchase: _____

**$10 American Gold Eagle (1/4 oz.), Proof**    *Mintage: ~13,926*

| 2012-W | Grade | Purchased From | Date |
|--------|-------|----------------|------|
|        |       |                |      |

Bullion value at time of purchase: _____

**$25 American Gold Eagle (1/2 oz.), Proof**    *Mintage: ~12,919*

| 2012-W | Grade | Purchased From | Date |
|--------|-------|----------------|------|
|        |       |                |      |

Bullion value at time of purchase: _____

**$50 American Gold Eagle (1 oz.), Proof**    *Mintage: ~23,805*

| 2012-W | Grade | Purchased From | Date |
|--------|-------|----------------|------|
|        |       |                |      |

Bullion value at time of purchase: _____

## Proof Set, Gold, 2012

**$5, $10, $25, and $50 American Gold Eagle (1/10 oz. to 1 oz.), Proof**

| 2012-W | Grade | Purchased From | Date |
|--------|-------|----------------|------|
|        |       |                |      |

Bullion value at time of purchase: _____

## Proof Strikes, Platinum, 2012

**$100 American Platinum Eagle (1 oz.), Proof**    *Mintage: ~10,000 (not final)*

| 2012-W | Grade | Purchased From | Date |
|--------|-------|----------------|------|
|        |       |                |      |

Bullion value at time of purchase: _____

---

**American Platinum Eagles**

**Date:** 2012
**Mints:** West Point Mint (Proofs [W mintmark])
**Composition:** .9995 platinum
**Edge:** Reeded
**Weight:**
$100—1.0005 oz. (31.120 grams; 1 oz. actual platinum weight)
**Diameter:**
$100—32.7 mm
**Thickness:**
$100—2.39 mm
**Designers:**
John M. Mercanti (obverse), Barbara Fox (reverse)

# 2013

**Historical context:** The American economy had been growing since 2012, slowly but surely, with household debt down, corporate profits up, and home prices starting to rise. However, a report halfway through the year of 2013 showed that the rates of improvement were not high enough to indicate a technical end of the recession. According to the UCLA Anderson Forecast, in order for the economy to return to a normal trend, strong growth would have to remain consistent for an extended period of time—as long as 15 years. Congress and the president continued to pursue legislation and policies to spur growth.

In U.S. numismatics, a new world record was set for a single coin sold at auction: an exemplary 1794 silver dollar went for $10,016,875 in January (beating the previous record by more than $2 million). Later in the year, one of five known 1913 Liberty Head nickels sold at auction for $3.1 million.

The American Numismatic Association held its spring 2013 National Money Show in New Orleans. The U.S. Mint hosted two interactive coin forums during the show, giving attendees a chance to share their ideas about U.S. coinage and learn about the Mint's coin programs and initiatives. Later in the year the ANA hosted its summer World's Fair of Money in Chicago, attracting thousands of collectors to the Rosemont convention center. Mint Deputy Director Richard A. Peterson participated in the official ribbon-cutting ceremony on August 13. One numismatic star of the show was the Mint's 2013 American Buffalo 24k gold bullion coin in Reverse Proof, debuting to celebrate the 100th anniversary of its inspiration coin, the 1913 Buffalo nickel.

The Philadelphia Mint won a top safety award for the third time in 2013. The facility was designated as a Volunteer Protection Programs (VPP) Star site—the highest honor given by the Occupational Safety and Health Administration to recognize safety in the workplace. VPP Star status "is awarded to worksites that have designed and implemented outstanding safety and health programs based on rigorous performance criteria."

Precious metals started strong early in 2013, but weakened throughout the summer and autumn. At the end of the third quarter, all of their cumulative averages were down compared to their 2012 spot prices: silver from $31.15 to $24.80 per ounce; gold from $1,669 to $1,455; platinum from $1,551 to $1,515.

**Coin commentary:** American Gold Eagle bullion was off to a good start in 2013, with the Mint beginning its annual sales to Authorized Purchasers on January 2. All four bullion-coin sizes were available, from $50 one-ounce down to $5 tenth-ounce. Demand was strong, with some 150,000 ounces purchased in the month of January—the largest monthly total in more than two years. As the spot price of gold bullion declined on the world's markets through the spring and into summer 2013, purchasing of the U.S. Mint's bullion coins increased.

The Mint announced on April 16 that it would begin accepting orders for the year's Proof American Gold Eagles on April 18. Some mintage limits were lowered for 2013:

| Date | $50 (1 oz.) | $25 (1/2 oz.) | $10 (1/4 oz.) | $5 (1/10 oz.) | Grand total (ounces) |
|---|---|---|---|---|---|
| 2008 | 710,000 | 61,000 | 70,000 | 305,000 | 788,500 |
| 2009 | 1,493,000 | 110,000 | 110,000 | 270,000 | 1,602,500 |
| 2010 | 1,125,000 | 53,000 | 74,000 | 435,000 | 1,213,500 |
| 2011 | 857,000 | 70,000 | 80,000 | 350,000 | 947,000 |
| 2012* | 667,000 | 71,000 | 76,000 | 315,000 | 753,000 |
| 2013* | 465,000 | 104,000 | 53,000 | 605,000 | 590,750 |
| Total | 16,593,538 | 2,706,746 | 3,571,508 | 12,785,757 | 20,118,364 |

* Mintages not final.

# American Gold Eagle Mintages: Burnished

| Date | $50 (1 oz.) | $25 (1/2 oz.) | $10 (1/4 oz.) | $5 (1/10 oz.) |
|---|---|---|---|---|
| 2006 | 45,053 | 15,164 | 15,188 | 20,643 |
| 2007 | 18,066 | 11,455 | 12,766 | 22,501 |
| 2008 | 11,908 | 15,682 | 8,883 | 12,657 |
| 2009 | 0 | 0 | 0 | 0 |
| 2010 | 0 | 0 | 0 | 0 |
| 2011 | 8,822 | 0 | 0 | 0 |
| 2012* | 6,118 | 0 | 0 | 0 |
| 2013* | 5,480 | 0 | 0 | 0 |
| Total | 95,447 | 42,301 | 36,837 | 55,801 |

* Mintages not final.

# American Gold Eagle Mintages: Proofs

| Date | $50 (1 oz.) | $25 (1/2 oz.) | $10 (1/4 oz.) | $5 (1/10 oz.) |
|---|---|---|---|---|
| 1986 | 446,290 | 0 | 0 | 0 |
| 1987 | 147,498 | 143,398 | 0 | 0 |
| 1988 | 87,133 | 76,528 | 98,028 | 143,881 |
| 1989 | 54,570 | 44,798 | 54,170 | 84,647 |
| 1990 | 62,401 | 51,636 | 62,674 | 99,349 |
| 1991 | 50,411 | 53,125 | 50,839 | 70,334 |
| 1992 | 44,826 | 40,976 | 46,269 | 64,874 |
| 1993 | 34,369 | 43,819 | 46,464 | 58,649 |
| 1994 | 46,674 | 44,584 | 48,172 | 62,849 |
| 1995 | 46,368 | 45,388 | 47,526 | 62,667 |
| 1996 | 36,153 | 35,058 | 38,219 | 57,047 |
| 1997 | 32,999 | 26,344 | 29,805 | 34,977 |
| 1998 | 25,886 | 25,374 | 29,503 | 39,395 |
| 1999 | 31,427 | 30,427 | 34,417 | 48,428 |
| 2000 | 33,007 | 32,028 | 36,036 | 49,971 |

| Date | $50 (1 oz.) | $25 (1/2 oz.) | $10 (1/4 oz.) | $5 (1/10 oz.) |
|---|---|---|---|---|
| 2001 | 24,555 | 23,240 | 25,613 | 37,530 |
| 2002 | 27,499 | 26,646 | 29,242 | 40,864 |
| 2003 | 28,344 | 28,270 | 30,292 | 40,027 |
| 2004 | 28,215 | 27,330 | 28,839 | 35,131 |
| 2005 | 35,246 | 34,311 | 37,207 | 49,265 |
| 2006 | 47,092 | 34,322 | 36,127 | 47,277 |
| 2007 | 51,810 | 44,025 | 46,189 | 58,553 |
| 2008 | 30,237 | 22,602 | 18,877 | 28,116 |
| 2009 | 0 | 0 | 0 | 0 |
| 2010 | 60,000 | 45,000 | 45,000 | 55,000 |
| 2011 | 48,873 | 26,939 | 29,254 | 42,873 |
| 2012* | *23,805* | *12,919* | *13,926* | *20,637* |
| 2013* | *12,995* | *2,192* | *3,024* | *9,649* |
| Total | 1,598,683 | 1,021,279 | 965,712 | 1,341,990 |

* Mintages not final.

# AMERICAN PLATINUM EAGLE MINTAGES: BULLION STRIKES

| Date | $100 (1 oz.) | $50 (1/2 oz.) | $25 (1/4 oz.) | $10 (1/10 oz.) |
|---|---|---|---|---|
| 1997 | 56,000 | 20,500 | 27,100 | 70,250 |
| 1998 | 133,002 | 32,419 | 38,887 | 39,525 |
| 1999 | 56,707 | 32,309 | 39,734 | 55,955 |
| 2000 | 10,003 | 18,892 | 20,054 | 34,027 |
| 2001 | 14,070 | 12,815 | 21,815 | 52,017 |
| 2002 | 11,502 | 24,005 | 27,405 | 23,005 |
| 2003 | 8,007 | 17,409 | 25,207 | 22,007 |
| 2004 | 7,009 | 13,236 | 18,010 | 15,010 |
| 2005 | 6,310 | 9,013 | 12,013 | 14,013 |
| 2006 | 6,000 | 9,602 | 12,001 | 11,001 |
| 2007 | 7,202 | 7,001 | 8,402 | 13,003 |
| 2008 | 21,800 | 14,000 | 22,800 | 17,000 |
| 2009 | 0 | 0 | 0 | 0 |
| 2010 | 0 | 0 | 0 | 0 |
| 2011 | 0 | 0 | 0 | 0 |
| 2012 | 0 | 0 | 0 | 0 |
| 2013 | 0 | 0 | 0 | 0 |
| Total | 337,612 | 211,201 | 273,428 | 366,813 |

# AMERICAN PLATINUM EAGLE MINTAGES: BURNISHED

| Date | $100 (1 oz.) | $50 (1/2 oz.) | $25 (1/4 oz.) | $10 (1/10 oz.) |
|---|---|---|---|---|
| 2006 | 3,068 | 2,577 | 2,676 | 3,544 |
| 2007 | 4,177 | 3,635 | 3,690 | 5,556 |
| 2008 | 2,876 | 2,253 | 2,481 | 3,706 |
| 2000 | 10,003 | 18,892 | 20,054 | 34,027 |
| 2001 | 14,070 | 12,815 | 21,815 | 52,017 |
| 2002 | 11,502 | 24,005 | 27,405 | 23,005 |
| 2003 | 8,007 | 17,409 | 25,207 | 22,007 |
| 2004 | 7,009 | 13,236 | 18,010 | 15,010 |
| 2005 | 6,310 | 9,013 | 12,013 | 14,013 |
| 2006 | 6,000 | 9,602 | 12,001 | 11,001 |
| 2007 | 7,202 | 7,001 | 8,402 | 13,003 |
| 2008 | 21,800 | 14,000 | 22,800 | 17,000 |
| 2009 | 0 | 0 | 0 | 0 |
| 2010 | 0 | 0 | 0 | 0 |
| 2011 | 0 | 0 | 0 | 0 |
| 2012 | 0 | 0 | 0 | 0 |
| 2013 | 0 | 0 | 0 | 0 |
| Total | 337,612 | 211,201 | 273,428 | 366,813 |

# AMERICAN PLATINUM EAGLE MINTAGES: PROOFS

| Date | $100 (1 oz.) | $50 (1/2 oz.) | $25 (1/4 oz.) | $10 (1/10 oz.) |
|---|---|---|---|---|
| 1997 | 20,851 | 15,431 | 18,628 | 36,993 |
| 1998 | 14,912 | 13,836 | 14,873 | 19,847 |
| 1999 | 12,363 | 11,103 | 13,507 | 19,133 |
| 2000 | 12,453 | 11,049 | 11,995 | 15,651 |
| 2001 | 8,969 | 8,254 | 8,847 | 12,174 |
| 2002 | 9,834 | 8,772 | 9,282 | 12,365 |
| 2003 | 8,246 | 7,131 | 7,044 | 9,534 |
| 2004 | 6,007 | 5,063 | 5,193 | 7,161 |
| 2005 | 6,602 | 5,942 | 6,592 | 8,104 |
| 2006 | 9,152 | 7,649 | 7,813 | 10,205 |
| 2007 | 8,363 | 25,519 | 6,017 | 8,176 |
| 2008 | 4,769 | 4,020 | 4,153 | 5,138 |
| 2009 | 9,871 | 0 | 0 | 0 |
| 2010 | 10,000 | 0 | 0 | 0 |
| 2011 | 15,000 | 0 | 0 | 0 |
| 2012 | 15,000 | 0 | 0 | 0 |
| 2013* | 4,156 | 0 | 0 | 0 |
| Total | 176,548 | 123,769 | 113,944 | 164,481 |

* Mintage not final.

# B

# U.S. Silver and Palladium Bullion Programs

Silver is another precious metal figuring highly in our modern era of U.S. bullion coin production. Once upon a time, a U.S. dime had 10 cents worth of silver in it. The silver content of early quarters, half dollars, and dollars also matched their face values. Occasionally in the 1800s, as the price of silver increased the Mint reduced the silver content of these coins. By the early 1960s, the slowly increasing international demand for silver, combined with an impending shortage of coining silver in the federal stockpile, caused a surge in price to $1.29 per ounce. Guess what happened next? Hoarding. Silver coins began disappearing from cash registers and purses and going into money jars and sock drawers. It didn't take long for the Mint to announce (in 1964) that it would no longer strike dimes and quarters in silver, and that the silver fineness of half dollars would be reduced from .900 to .400. In 1971 silver was completely removed from the half dollar.

These moves effectively stabilized federal stockpiles, and from time to time various legislators urged a sell-off of silver bullion to supplement the federal budget. Resistance from silver-mining states, which feared a resulting drop in silver prices, and from the military, which uses silver in some defense applications, kept this from happening through the 1970s.

The astonishing "silver bubble" of 1979 and 1980 (created when the Hunt brothers of Texas bought up 200 million ounces, or half the world's supply) drove the price of silver from $4 to nearly $50 per ounce in a few months' time. Suddenly silver took on the attributes of a serious investment-quality precious metal. Then came the Reagan administration's 1981 announcement that it would sell off some of the federal stockpile. The mere mention of this *intention* to sell was enough to cause an 11 percent drop in silver prices, and the sale never took place. But the point was driven home: any sales from the federal stockpile would have to be carefully controlled.

# THE LIBERTY COIN ACT OF 1985, AND THE AMERICAN SILVER EAGLE

Balance came in the form of the Liberty Coin Act of 1985, originally proposed by Senator James McClure (R–Idaho), which created the American Silver Eagle bullion-coin program. This empowered the Mint to issue silver bullion coins and sell them, one ounce at a time, to collectors and investors. Dispersing millions of ounces of silver gradually throughout the population seemed far less likely to depress silver prices than selling the same amount, in bars and bulk shipments, all at once to wholesalers. Because silver bullion coins are more afford-able than gold, they are within the price reach of a wider population of collector/investors. Since they were first launched, more than 340 mil-lion ounces of silver have gone into the production of these coins.

The Liberty Walking half dollar of 1916 to 1947; Adolph A. Weinman's obverse design would later be used on the American Silver Eagle.

Under the Liberty Coin Act, the new silver bullion coins were man-dated to have a face value of $1 and contain .999 fine silver, with a design symbolic of Liberty on the obverse, and an eagle on the reverse. They would also have a reeded edge. For the obverse, the long-admired Liberty Walking design created by sculptor Adolph Weinman for the 1916 half dollar was adopted. The reverse bears an eagle design by U.S. Mint chief engraver John M. Mercanti. Amer-ican Silver Eagles have been issued in five formats: bul-lion strike, Burnished, Proof, Reverse Proof, and Enhanced Uncirculated. Various special sets have also been made. For a full history of these wonderful coins, see John Mercanti's book, *American Silver Eagles: A Guide to the U.S. Bullion Coin Program*.

American Silver Eagle, bullion strike.

American Silver Eagle, Burnished.

American Silver Eagle, Proof.

American Silver Eagle, Reverse Proof.

American Silver Eagle, Enhanced Uncirculated.

# AMERICA THE BEAUTIFUL SILVER BULLION COINS

After the roaring success of the 50 State Quarters® Program, in which the U.S. Mint issued five new reverse designs each year for 10 years (plus the addition of the District of Columbia and five U.S. territorial quarters in 2009), it was deemed a good idea to create another new series for the quarter collector that would pick up where those programs left off. In 2010 the Mint launched the next quarter dollar design series, which will continue through 2021: the America the Beautiful™ Quarters Program. Maintaining the practice of issuing five new reverse designs per year, these quarters have the familiar 1932 John Flanagan portrait (after Houdon) of George Washington on the obverse. The reverses feature America's national parks, forests, monuments, and historic sites, one per state, district, and territory. The first five reverses, issued in 2010, depicted Hot Springs National Park, Old Faithful Geyser, El Capitan at Yosemite, the Grand Canyon, and Mount Hood.

Without a magnifying glass, these beautifully sculpted reverse scenes of are somewhat hard to appreciate in the 24.3 mm format (about 15/16 of an inch in diameter). For durability as well as stackability, the relief on these circulating coins is necessarily low.

Luckily for silver bullion-coin buyers, the Mint has created complementary pieces in pure silver to show off the designs to best advantage. There is no chance, however, that these beautiful bullion issues could be mistaken for circulating quarters. Struck on a specially designed Gräbener coinage press, they are three times bigger than a quarter dollar (76.2 mm) and have a net weight of five ounces of .999 fine silver. On these coins the American landscapes stand out in crisp detail. Around the edge of each coin is incused the fineness and weight. The America the Beautiful silver bullion coins are available in bullion strikes and Burnished ("Uncirculated") format.

**The first five America the Beautiful quarter designs, and their common obverse design (shown enlarged).**

The 2010 Yellowstone "America the Beautiful" silver bullion coin, shown at actual size, and several others at reduced size.

# PALLADIUM EAGLES: WE LOVE THEM, WE LOVE THEM NOT?

In December 2010, the 111th Congress generated excitement among the bullion-coin investment community by enacting Public Law 111-303, the "American Eagle Palladium Bullion Coin Act of 2010." The legislation authorized the U.S. Mint to produce a $25 denominated coin "of an appropriate size and thickness, as determined by the Secretary [of the Treasury], that weighs 1 troy ounce and contains .9995 fine palladium." The law spelled out what the design would be:

**The obverse of the Winged Liberty dime of 1916 to 1945, by Adolph Weinman (shown enlarged).**

DESIGN.—Coins minted and issued under this subsection shall bear designs on the obverse and reverse that are close likenesses of the work of famed American coin designer and medallic artist Adolph Alexander Weinman—

(A) the obverse shall bear a high-relief likeness of the 'Winged Liberty' design used on the obverse of the so-called 'Mercury dime.'

(B) the reverse shall bear a high-relief version of the reverse design of the 1907 American Institute of Architects medal.

Reading on, the law states:

(1) IN GENERAL.—Subject to the submission to the Secretary and the Congress of a marketing study described in paragraph (8), beginning not more than 1 year after the submission of the study to the Secretary and the Congress, the Secretary shall mint and issue the palladium coins. . . .

And paragraph (8) reads:

(8) MARKETING STUDY DEFINED.—The market study described in paragraph (1) means an analysis of the market for palladium bullion investments conducted by a reputable, independent third party that demonstrates that there would be adequate demand for palladium bullion coins produced by the United States Mint to ensure that such coins could be minted and issued at no net cost to taxpayers.

And there was the rub. The 142-page study by the New York City firm CPM Group, LLC, presented to Congress in March 2013, predicted that there *would* be a net cost to taxpayers, at least for a bullion coin. Numismatic palladium coins, the study said, might develop a following and turn a profit, but sales volume was predicted to be low. The firm's analysis was comprehensive, taking into account the sales volume of Canadian Maple Leaf palladium bullion coins, the recent behavior of the targeted market (bullion-coin dealers and investors), projected costs of palladium and the special equipment necessary for coining it, and the capacity of the U.S. Mint to incorporate this new product line.

Because the language of the law did not expressly prohibit the issuance of these coins if an unfavorable study was submitted, at this point Congress could still decide to move forward with the palladium bullion program.

# C
# American Buffalo and First Spouse Gold Bullion Coins

The U.S. Mint currently has two programs of .9999 fine (24-karat) gold bullion coins. These offer purity of gold higher than the American Gold Eagle's .9167 fineness (22-karat). The higher purity is especially appealing to international investors.

## AMERICAN BUFFALO

American Buffalo gold bullion coins, authorized by Congress in 2005 and produced by the U.S. Mint since 2006, were the first .9999 fine gold coins made by the United States. These visually appealing bullion pieces are coined, by mandate, of gold derived from newly mined sources in America. They feature an adaptation of James Earle Fraser's iconic Indian Head / Buffalo design, first used on circulating five-cent pieces of 1913 to 1938.

One-ounce ($50 face value) coins were struck in the American Buffalo program's first two years, 2006 and 2007. In 2008, the Mint expanded the coinage to include fractional pieces of 1/2 ounce ($25), 1/4 ounce ($10), and 1/10 ounce ($5), in various finishes, individually and in sets.

The coins are legal tender, with weight, content, and purity guaranteed by the federal government. Investors can include them in some individual retirement accounts (IRAs). Proofs and Burnished (*Uncirculated,* in the Mint's wording) pieces undergo special production processes, similar to the American Eagle gold-bullion coinage, and can be purchased directly from the Mint. As with other products in the Mint's bullion program, regular bullion-strike pieces are distributed through a network of authorized distributors. Mintages range from fewer than 10,000 to more than 300,000 pieces, with the Burnished versions being the rarest.

**Design common to all American Buffalo denominations (shown enlarged).**

All American Buffalo gold bullion coins (Proof, Burnished, and regular bullion pieces) are struck at the U.S. Mint's West Point facility. The collector-format coins bear that facility's distinctive W mintmark.

## FIRST SPOUSE

The Mint's First Spouse bullion coins weigh one-half ounce each and bear a face value of $10. The coins honor the nation's first spouses on the same schedule as the Mint's Presidential dollars program. Each features a portrait on the obverse, and on the reverse a unique design symbolic of the spouse's life and work. In cases where a president held office widowed or unmarried, the coin bears "an obverse image emblematic of Liberty as depicted on a circulating coin of that era and a reverse image emblematic of themes of that president's life." For illustrations of all First Spouse gold coins, see the *Guide Book of United States Coins* (the annually issued "Red Book").

All First Spouse gold bullion coins (Proofs and regular bullion pieces) are struck at the U.S. Mint's West Point facility.

Designers:

*Martha Washington*—Joseph Menna (obverse), Susan Gamble (reverse)

*Abigail Adams*—Joseph Menna (obverse), Thomas Cleveland (reverse)

*Thomas Jefferson's Liberty*—Robert Scot / Phebe Hemphill (obverse), Charles Vickers (reverse)

*Dolley Madison*—Don Everhart (obverse), Joel Iskowitz (reverse)

*Elizabeth Monroe*—Joel Iskowitz (obverse), Donna Weaver (reverse)

*Louisa Adams*—Susan Gamble (obverse), Donna Weaver (reverse)

*Andrew Jackson's Liberty*—John Reich (obverse), Justin Kunz (reverse)

*Martin Van Buren's Liberty*—Christian Gobrecht (obverse), Thomas Cleveland (reverse)

*Anna Harrison*—Donna Weaver (obverse), Thomas Cleveland (reverse)

*Letitia Tyler*—Phebe Hemphill (obverse), Susan Gamble (reverse)

*Julia Tyler*—Joel Iskowitz; Sarah Polk—Phebe Hemphill

*Margaret Taylor*—Phebe Hemphill (obverse), Mary Beth Zeitz (reverse)

*Abigail Fillmore*—Phebe Hemphill (obverse), Susan Gamble (reverse)

*Jane Pierce*—Donna Weaver

*James Buchanan's Liberty*—Christian Gobrecht (obverse), David Westwood (reverse)

*Mary Todd Lincoln*—Phebe Hemphill (obverse), Joel Iskowitz (reverse)

*Alice Paul*—Susan Gamble (obverse), Phebe Hemphill (reverse)

*Frances Cleveland, Variety 1*—Joel Iskowitz (obverse), Barbara Fox (reverse)

*Caroline Harrison*—Frank Morris (obverse), Donna Weaver (reverse)

*Frances Cleveland, Variety 2*—Barbara Fox (obverse), Joseph Menna (reverse)

# D

## The MMIX Ultra High Relief Gold Coin

As discussed in chapter 3, the U.S. Mint's 2009 reprise of Augustus Saint-Gaudens's beloved 1907 Ultra High Relief double eagle was a wonderful success. My decision to return to the original high relief had been prompted, in part, by complaints of many collectors that the Mint (back in 1907) had ruined Saint-Gaudens's aesthetic by lowering the relief. That practical 1907 decision was made for the sake of commerce (so the coins could stack properly) and ease of production (because the technology of the day required multiple precise strikings). It didn't help that Mint engraver Charles Barber was vexed that President Theodore Roosevelt had commissioned Saint-Gaudens, and not him, to design the coin, making it the first time in history that a U.S. coin was designed by a non-Mint employee. Beauty gave way to function and politics.

Since a bullion coin is not intended for everyday circulation and since coining-press technology has come a long way, we had the opportunity in 2009 to return to Saint-Gaudens's original aesthetic. The first decision to be made was which version best represented the artist's purest vision. At the suggestion of my chief counsel, Dan Shaver, we had a conference call with numismatic expert Dave Tripp. He convinced us that the rarest example, and perhaps the most desired, was the 27-millimeter version. While the 34 mm versions were the standard diameter of the day, the larger the diameter, the thinner the coin would be, given that it had to contain one ounce of gold. The original 27 mm version had been made from melding together two $10 gold eagle planchets (which the Mint did not have the legislative authority to

The final model for the Ultra High Relief $20 gold piece. This was submitted by Augustus Saint-Gaudens to President Theodore Roosevelt for his approval in December 1906.

A plaster for the 1907 Ultra High Relief double eagle.

The extra-thick, small-diameter test strike of 1907. This pattern coin (an experimental piece) is 27 mm in diameter—the width of a $10 eagle instead of a standard $20 double eagle. "The purpose was to determine if a high-relief design could be better struck on a planchet of smaller diameter compensated by greater thickness," notes researcher Roger W. Burdette in *United States Pattern Coins*, 10th edition. "In effect, the force of the press was concentrated on a smaller area."

do). The finished planchet was twice as thick as the 34 mm planchet, and therefore had sufficient depth to create the highest relief possible. Only two test strikes of the original 27 mm remain today and they reside at the Smithsonian Institution.

Once I decided on a 27 mm coin, I sought and received approval to develop the project from Treasury Secretary Hank Paulson.

The next step was to visit the Smithsonian's National Numismatic Collection, located in the National Museum of American History. With permission from museum director Brent Glass and with the assistance of curator James Hughes, we studied the two 27 mm coins. Our team then selected archived plasters that most closely resembled the coin samples and scanned and digitally mapped them for unrivalled accuracy. In the past, a Janvier reduction lathe was used to trace the design from a plaster to a master die, but the machine could not transfer all the detail of the original plaster, nor was it consistent. The new method used digital technology to transfer the image directly to the production die (used for stamping the coins), and state-of-the-art die cutters to incise every bit of detail from the original plaster onto a master die.

Once the dies were made, Mint staff pursued the usual course of testing and adjustment. At the American Numismatic Association's summer 2009 World's Fair of Money in Los Angeles, we presented an exhibit of Saint-Gaudens's original plasters and some of the feasibility and progression strikes resulting from those experiments. As described in that exhibit,

This experimental pattern of the MCMVII (1907) Ultra High Relief double eagle was struck on a planchet 34 mm wide. The regular-production coins of 1907 to 1933 would be this width, but in lower relief due to technical limitations.

The first phase of the production process was testing the blanks and conducting "feasibility strikes" using geometric shapes to simulate the highest and lowest points of relief. The hardness of the blanks, metal flow to points in the design, and number of required strikes were all tested. The second phase was "progression strikes" which tested Saint-Gaudens's design at different tonnages. These progression strikes range from 15 to 55 metric tons, in increments of 10. During full production, only two strikes will be required with the tonnage set at approximately 65 metric tons.

Because the coin is edge-lettered with the legend E PLURIBUS UNUM, a three-part collar segment was made to wrap around the dies and create the edge lettering.

An example of the regular-production, lower-relief $20 double eagle.

The MMIX (2009) Ultra High Relief double eagle gold coin is 27 mm wide and 4 mm thick. This side view illustrates its thickness and depth of relief. The *Guide Book of United States Coins* observes: "It was made as a tour de force to demonstrate how technical advances in minting techniques can now accommodate manufacturing such a coin."

# E

# The Designer of the American Gold Eagle Reverse

## The Family of Eagles: From Beaumont to Bullion Coinage

### by Mike Fuljenz

Silver anniversaries are major occasions for every American family—and that includes the "Family of Eagles" nesting on the reverse of the American Eagle gold bullion coins.

The design has now appeared on the Gold Eagle coinage for a full quarter-century—and that's a source of humble honor to Miley Tucker-Frost, the talented sculptor who fashioned the now-familiar artwork back in the early 1980s.

"Having my design on the nation's gold coinage has been a tremendous honor," says the artist, whose name was Miley Busiek at the time the American Eagle bullion coins first appeared in late 1986.

The American Gold Eagles pair her design with Augustus Saint-Gaudens's magnificent portrait of Liberty from the obverse of the stunning double eagle (or $20 gold piece) of 1907 to 1933. Tucker-Frost takes special pride in this serendipitous pairing.

"I am thrilled that they did that," she exclaims. "I just consider it an incredible honor for my design to be on the reverse side of the coin that carries such a beautiful design."

The Family of Eagles' appearance on the gold American Eagles culminated a six-year journey for the artist, who came up with the concept after watching Ronald Reagan's acceptance speech at the Republican National Convention in 1980.

"The theme of his speech that night," she remembers, "was 'Together, A New Beginning.' He was encouraging

**Sculptor Miley Tucker-Frost, formerly Miley Busiek, designed the "Family of Eagles" that appears on the U.S. Treasury's American Gold Eagle bullion coins.**

Americans to be thankful for what we have in this country and to act upon that feeling. He was encouraging private-sector initiatives—a willingness to reach out and care about each other and pull together.

"Our national symbol, the American bald eagle, had only been depicted as a single eagle, and I liked the idea of thinking of America as a caring family. Therefore, I put together a sketch showing not just one eagle, but a whole family."

After seeing the design, the Republican National Committee asked her to create a sculpture based on this theme as the official commemorative for Reagan's first inaugural. President Reagan chose maquettes of the mini-sculpture as gifts not only for inaugural guests but also for the former U.S. hostages whose return home from Iran, after 444 days of captivity, coincided with his inauguration. He presented this sculpture to each of the 52 members of that group.

Soon after that, the artist saw an item in the Wall Street Journal reporting on efforts to obtain approval in Congress for a new U.S. gold bullion coin.

"I happened to see that article during an airplane flight," she said, "and, as an artist, it triggered an idea. 'Perhaps there's an opportunity here,' I thought. There couldn't be a more dignified, more positive opportunity for America to subtly state what we stand for in our country than on a gold bullion coin—a coin that would be sold all over the world."

She contacted the Treasury officials and offered her design for use on any such coin. They advised her that congressional authorization would be needed not only for the coin but also for the design.

At that point, she began a one-woman campaign to gain consideration for her concept. She had connections in Washington and had been there on occasion, but she started her campaign back home in Dallas, where she set about gathering bipartisan endorsements from key civic leaders.

"I showed them the design," she says, "and told them how I felt—that this was an incredible opportunity for us to honor what makes America great, and that's our people.

"I spoke with a balanced group of civic and religious organizations, all of whom eagerly wrote letters of endorsement."

Among the supporters she lined up was Tom Landry, longtime coach of the Dallas Cowboys. He, in turn, recruited Joe Gibbs, coach of the rival Washington Redskins, to contact members of Congress with whom he was acquainted.

After obtaining letters supporting her idea, she went to a copying machine, cranked out dozens of duplicates, and put together presentation packets. With these in hand, she traveled to Washington to continue her campaign in the halls of Congress.

Gradually patience, persistence, and passion for her cause began to pay dividends. She called on congressional staffs, lobbied their bosses directly when she could, and testified at hearings when coinage legislation was discussed—and little by little, she picked up important support.

"It's a good thing that my sculpting career is successful," she says, "because there were a lot of phone calls and a lot of trips to Washington. But every single one of them was important and necessary, because there were so many pivotal times."

The big breakthrough came in 1985, when simmering opposition to South Africa's racial policies reached the boiling point and President Reagan—pressed by Congress—imposed a series of sanctions. One was a ban on further importation of the Krugerrand, South Africa's popular one-ounce bullion gold coin. The Krugerrand's fall from favor sparked legislation giving U.S. citizens a bullion coin of their own as a replacement. (A bullion coin is one whose value is tied directly to that of the metal it contains; this distinguishes it from a numismatic coin, which can have added premium value as a collectible.)

The Senate passed the coinage legislation unanimously on November 14, 1985—just one day after South Africa had suspended production of Krugerrands. The House followed suit, also unanimously, on December 2, and Reagan signed the bill on December 17.

The legislation authorized the Treasury to strike four legal-tender gold coins in sizes of one ounce, one-half-ounce, one-quarter-ounce, and one-tenth-ounce. These corresponded exactly to the sizes already available for the Krugerrand. Each was assigned a face value. And while the denominations were (and are) far smaller than the value of the gold that the coins contain, their presence serves to underscore the fact that these are coins and not medals. The face values are $50 for the one-ounce coin, $25 for the half-ounce, $10 for the quarter-ounce, and $5 for the tenth-ounce.

Congress stipulated that the Family of Eagles design should appear on the reverse of the one-ounce coin. The Treasury wasn't required to use it on the three fractional coins, but chose to do so—and that decision gratified the artist.

The bill that authorized the coins specified that the reverse design must show a male eagle "carrying an olive branch and flying above a nest containing a female eagle and hatchlings." The bill didn't mention Busiek by name, but its wording precisely described the design that she proposed—and her design was clearly the one that members of Congress had in mind.

Congress didn't mandate a particular design for the coins' obverse, except to say that the one-ounce coin should carry a "design symbolic of Liberty" on that side. Treasury officials subsequently decided to resurrect a classic coinage portrait by using a "slenderized" version of Lady Liberty's likeness from the obverse of Saint-Gaudens's majestic double eagle.

The artist was given a close-up look as Mint craftsmen worked to transform her basic design from a drawing into an engraving.

"The Mint staff did the actual engraving," she said at the time, "but the Treasury and the Mint were gracious enough to let me have some input. I now have a much greater appreciation for what goes into the production of our coinage."

Her dream was fulfilled on September 8, 1986, when the very first one-ounce American Gold Eagles were struck in special ceremonies at the U.S. Bullion Depository at West Point, New York. She and her sons Matthew and David—then 12 and 8, respectively—got to strike examples of the coin. And, she now recalls, it was "the thrill of a lifetime."

Her sons' classmates were among her most enthusiastic supporters during her successful campaign to secure a place on a coin for the Family of Eagles design. She showed her appreciation in a very tangible way after the dream became a golden reality.

"My older son's class worked so hard to bring this about, writing letters and helping in other ways," she noted. "The whole legislative process was a literal civics lesson for them. I would report to them regularly on the progress of the legislation, and they followed it carefully and were just so excited about it. So when they graduated, I gave each one of them a coin with a little note wishing them well for the future."

Through the years, she has purchased Gold Eagles on numerous occasions "purely as gifts." But, she says, "I've never bought any to hold for investment or anything like that."

At the same time, she's aware—and fully approves—of the bullion coins' role as investment vehicles.

"It's gratifying," she says, "to see that our statesmen made a wise decision in bringing back gold. It's there today at a time when people need the sort of comfort it provides and need to have choices on ways to invest their money. It gives our country a balance that I don't think we ever dreamed that we would need."

For her, the greatest comfort provided by Gold Eagles is not their investment value—although that is considerable—but the way they remind Americans every day of family values.

"The spirit behind this design was to honor our family and America," she says, "and this is a time when people need to be encouraged and affirmed—particularly our young people, with so much uncertainty clouding the future. We need to have an optimistic vision of the future.

"I'm really thankful," she adds, "that this is an ongoing design that won't be changed periodically. There's just a nice consistency behind the story it tells, and I'm especially happy about that."

The future coin designer got her start in art—and enjoyed her first success—while attending Beaumont High School in Beaumont, Texas, which is also my hometown and where we have a number of mutual friends.

"Beaumont," she recalls, "was a small, wholesome East Texas town—and because of the conservative culture, it was an ideal place to be a teenager. It was while in high school there that I really began to appreciate how much I enjoyed art. The art teacher there encouraged me and said, 'I really believe you have talent.'

"In my senior year, the art teacher encouraged me to enter a competition to design the yearbook cover. I thought that would be fun, so I jumped in—and I won. That turned out to be my first venture in taking a chance and doing something artistic.

"Beaumont High School was the place where I really came to realize that I could just step right out and enjoy doing art."

She's largely self-taught.

"After high school," she says, "I was an early childhood major and never took any formal art classes. I took one art class at an evening community school in Dallas while we were living there, but nothing beyond that."

She taught herself well—for over the years, she has received a number of important sculptural commissions from government agencies, educational institutions, and private clients. One of her favorites is a larger-than-life monument of three running wild mustangs which occupies a place of honor on the campus of Southern Methodist University in Dallas. The mustang is SMU's mascot.

Though her Texas ties are strong, she has lived for the last 15 years in the Washington, D.C., area, where her husband, Howard Frost, a doctor of political science, works for the federal government.

For the last several years, she has spent considerable time in Germany, helping to sculpt a monument she designed honoring the patriots whose peaceful demonstrations brought about the fall of the Berlin Wall in 1989.

A non-sculptural project close to her heart is the "Habitat for Humanity Veterans' Initiative," where efforts continue to create a one-stop interactive web site for veterans—particularly disabled veterans—that will offer assistance to military personnel returning to civilian life after serving their country.

"This is aimed at all veterans," she says, "but especially the ones that are coming back from service in combat zones. It's based on private-sector investment putting money into start-up small businesses and refurbished houses and property. The veterans returning now are coming back to a poor economy, and they need jobs and houses. There's a huge need for this, and filling that need is the purpose of this web site."

Last year, Tucker-Frost had a chance to meet one of the Iranian hostages who received her original Family of Eagles replica from President Reagan in January 1981.

**Monuments by Miley Tucker-Frost are commissioned by government, corporate, and educational institutions across America. This 15-foot-high monument of the Wild Running Mustangs, for Southern Methodist University, occupies a place of honor on the SMU campus in Dallas, Texas.**

"I was so privileged to be there," she declares. "I thanked him for all that he went through and did for us while he was being held captive. It was just a real pleasure to get to say hello and thank him in person. He told me how much the sculpture meant to him—and that's one of the most gratifying things about this whole experience.

"I get such satisfaction from knowing that my Family of Eagles is making people aware of their own family values as Americans, and that the coins have become an ongoing part of our culture."

Despite the time and effort she has devoted to make the American Gold Eagle bullion coin a reality, she has never realized one cent of profit.

"This," she says, "was a gift to my fellow-Americans.

"It's really the most wonderful feeling," she adds, "to be able to give a gift to your country."

**The artist's stainless-steel depiction of the Seal of the President of the United States is now at home in a newly dedicated presidential library.**

# F

# Illustrated Catalog of Coins of the Moy Era

This catalog illustrates the coins released by the U.S. Mint during the tenure of Director Edmund Moy, September 2006 to January 2011. It includes silver, gold, and platinum bullion coins; a variety of circulating coins (including several entirely new series); and copper-nickel, silver, and gold commemoratives. In addition to these legal-tender coins, the Mint issued many national commemorative medals, as well as auxiliary products (e.g., booklets and coin-related jewelry), not pictured here.

**Lincoln, Memorial Reverse, Cent (2006–2008).**
Mint Director Edmund Moy presided over the final three years of the Lincoln Memorial type of the Lincoln cent, with its obverse design by Victor David Brenner and reverse by Frank Gasparro.

**Lincoln, Shield Reverse (2010–2011).**
From 2010 to date, the Lincoln cent reverse has featured a Union shield "emblematic of President Lincoln's preservation of the United States of America as a single and united country." It was designed by Lyndall Bass and engraved by Joseph Menna.

**Lincoln, Bicentennial, Cents (2009).**
2009 brought four new reverse designs to the Lincoln cent, each symbolizing a major aspect of Abraham Lincoln's life: Birth and Early Childhood in Kentucky (designer Richard Masters, sculptor Jim Licaretz); Formative Years in Indiana (designer and sculptor, Charles Vickers); Professional Life in Illinois (designer Joel Iskowitz, sculptor Don Everhart); and Presidency in Washington (designer Susan Gamble, sculptor Joseph Menna).

**Jefferson Nickel (2006–2011).**
Jamie Franki's innovative new portrait of Thomas Jefferson, sculpted for coinage by Donna Weaver, was introduced to the nickel five-cent coin in 2006. The reverse was a "Return to Monticello," resuming Felix Schlag's view of Jefferson's home. (In 2004 and 2005, four new reverse designs had commemorated the westward journey of Lewis and Clark.)

### Roosevelt Dime (2006–2011).

A modern-classic U.S. coin that has circulated since 1946 (minted in .900 fine silver until 1964), this dime was designed by Chief Engraver John R. Sinnock to honor fallen president Franklin D. Roosevelt. More than 7 billion dimes were struck at the Denver and Philadelphia mints under Edmund Moy's direction, 2006 to 2011.

### State Quarters (2006–2008).

The U.S. Mint's State quarter program started in 1999. The first design officially debuted by Mint Director Edmund Moy was the final entry for 2006, South Dakota, which was launched that November. Five coins were rolled out each year in 2007 (Montana, Washington, Idaho, Wyoming, and Utah), and the program's final five coins in 2008 (Oklahoma, New Mexico, Arizona, Alaska, and Hawaii).

### District of Columbia and U.S. Territories Quarters (2009).

Following up on the popular State quarter program, the U.S. Mint released six new quarters in 2009 to honor the District of Columbia and the five U.S. territories (the Commonwealth of Puerto Rico, Guam, American Samoa, the U.S. Virgin Islands, and the Commonwealth of the Northern Mariana Islands).

### America the Beautiful™ Quarters (2010).

The America the Beautiful quarters program was launched, and its first five coins were released, under Edmund Moy's directorship of the U.S. Mint. Popularly known as "National Park" quarters, they honor sites of natural or historic significance in each state, district, and territory of the United States. The program will run through 2021. The 2010 coins were for Hot Springs (in Arkansas), Yellowstone (in Wyoming), Yosemite (in California), the Grand Canyon (in Arizona), and Mount Hood (in Oregon).

### Kennedy Half Dollar (2006–2011).

Another modern classic of U.S. coinage, the Kennedy half dollar has been minted since 1964 (in .900 fine silver in 1964, .400 fine silver from 1965 to 1960, and copper-nickel since then). It was designed by Chief Engraver Gilroy Roberts (obverse) and Frank Gasparro (reverse). More than 20 million Kennedy half dollars were struck at Denver and Philadelphia when Edmund Moy was director of the U.S. Mint, 2006 to 2011. They were made available to the public through direct purchase from the Mint in rolls of 20 coins or bags of 200 coins.

**Sacagawea Dollar (2006–2008).**
The final three years of the Sacagawea dollar were minted under Edmund Moy's direction. The coin (designed by Glenna Goodacre, obverse, and Thomas D. Rogers Sr., reverse) would transform into the Native American dollar starting in 2009.

**Native American Dollars (2009–2011).**
The first three coins of the Native American dollar program, which started in 2009 and has run to date, honored native agriculture, the Great Law of Peace, and the Wampanoag Treaty.

**Presidential Dollars (2007–2010).**
The Presidential dollars debuted in 2007, and the program will run through 2016. Each coin honors a former president of the United States, in the order that they served. The program was launched and its first 16 coins issued while Edmund Moy was director of the U.S. Mint.

**American Eagle Silver, Gold, and Platinum Coins (2006–2011).**
The U.S. Mint produced a remarkable suite of silver, gold, and platinum bullion coins under the tenure
of Mint Director Edmund Moy, from late 2006 to early 2011. These coins are studied in the present
volume and in John M. Mercanti's *American Silver Eagles: A Guide to the U.S. Bullion Coin Program.*

**American Buffalo .9999 Fine Gold Bullion Coins (2006–2011).**
The nation's first 24-karat gold coins were struck several months before Edmund
Moy took over as director of the U.S. Mint in September 2006. The coins would
be minted throughout his tenure and to date, in a variety of sizes and formats.

**Commemorative Coins (2006–2010) (opposite page).**
A wide variety of commemorative coins was offered to collectors by the U.S. Mint from
September 2006, when Edmund Moy was confirmed as director of the Mint, to January 2011,
when he left office. These coins honored Benjamin Franklin; the historic San Francisco Old
Mint; the 400th anniversary of Jamestown; the desegregation of Little Rock Central High
School; the recovery of the American bald eagle; the birth bicentennials of Louis Braille
and of Abraham Lincoln; disabled American veterans; and the Boy Scouts of America.

**First Spouse $10 Gold Bullion Coins (2007–2010).**
The First Spouse 24-karat (.9999 fine) gold-coin program was inaugurated in 2007, during Edmund Moy's first full year as director of the U.S. Mint. Under his leadership the first 17 coins in the series were released. Each contains one-half ounce of gold and has a face value of $10. The Mint also issued a series of bronze medals with designs similar to those on the First Spouse gold coins.

**MMIX Ultra High Relief Gold Coin (2009).**
"The 2009 Ultra High Relief Double Eagle Gold Coin represents a new era in coin design," Mint Director Edmund Moy said in February 2009. The coin was made as a tour de force to demonstrate the U.S. Mint's expertise in technology and design.

**America the Beautiful Silver Bullion Coins (2010).**
The first year's coins in the America the Beautiful silver bullion program debuted under Edmund Moy's leadership at the U.S. Mint. Mirroring the designs of the circulating "National Park" quarters, but with greater detail and depth, the coins measure three inches in diameter and contain five ounces of .999 fine silver each. The program will run through 2021. (Coins shown reduced.)

# Notes

## Preface

1. As compiled in *100 Greatest U.S. Coins* (Jeff Garrett and Ron Guth) and *100 Greatest U.S. Modern Coins* (Scott Schechter and Jeff Garrett), various editions.

## Chapter 2

1. Berk, Harlan J. *100 Greatest Ancient Coins* (Whitman Publishing, Atlanta, GA, 2008), p. 12.

2. Bowers, Q. David. *A Guide Book of Gold Dollars* (Whitman Publishing, Atlanta, GA, 2011), p. 3.

## Chapter 3

1. These "expatriate coins" eventually made their way into the hands of many European families, and from them to coin dealers. They are the primary source of supply for collectors of the rare early federal U.S. gold issues.

2. Heritage Auction Galleries press release announcing the sale of the original letter of President Theodore Roosevelt to Secretary of the Treasury Leslie M. Shaw, December 27, 1904:

    My dear Secretary Shaw:

    I think our coinage is artistically of atrocious hideousness. Would it be possible, without asking the permission of Congress, to employ a man like St. Gaudens to give us a coinage that would have some beauty?

    Sincerely yours,

    Theodore Roosevelt

3. Web site of the Saint-Gaudens National Historic Site, www.nps.gov/nr/twhp. "On the other side would be some kind of a (possibly winged) figure of Liberty striding energetically forward as if on a mountain top, holding aloft on one arm a shield bearing the stars and stripes with the word 'Liberty' marked across the field, in the other hand perhaps a flaming torch; the drapery would be flowing in the breeze. My idea is to make it a living thing and typical of progress. . . ."

## Chapter 4

1. Matthews, Dylan. "Michael Castle: Unsuspecting godfather of the $1 trillion coin solution," January 4, 2013, *Washington Post Wonkblog*, www.washingtonpost.com/blogs/wonkblog/wp/2013/01/04/michael-castle-unsuspecting-godfather-of-the-1-trillion-coin-solution/

2. Castle became a true believer in coin collecting for enjoyment, educational purposes, and seigniorage when he sponsored the legislation for the incredibly successful 50 States Quarters® Program of 1999 to 2008. The total profit from that issue, reported by the Mint in 2009, was a staggering $6.3 billion! See "50 State Quarters Program Earned $6.3 Billion in Seigniorage," Coin Update, February 1, 2010, news.coinupdate.com/state-quarters-program-seigniorage-0133/

3. U.S. Mint. "Mint Releases First Proof Platinum Vistas of Liberty™ Design," www.usmint.gov/pressroom/?action=press_release&ID=42

# Bibliography

Augsburger, Leonard D., and Joel J. Orosz. *The Secret History of the First U.S. Mint*, Whitman Publishing, Atlanta, 2011.

Balfour, David M. "The Past and Future of Gold," *The Bay State Monthly*, volume 2, issue 6, March 1885, pp. 359–366.

Bowers, Q. David. *A Guide Book of Double Eagle Gold Coins*, Whitman Publishing, Atlanta, 2004.

————. *A Guide Book of Gold Dollars*, Whitman Publishing, Atlanta, 2011.

————. *Expert's Guide to Collecting and Investing in Rare Coins*, Whitman Publishing, Atlanta, 2005.

————. *Grading Coins by Photographs: An Action Guide for the Collector and Investor*, second edition, Whitman Publishing, Atlanta, 2012.

Bressett, Kenneth, and Q. David Bowers. *The Official American Numismatic Association Grading Standards for United States Coins*, 7th edition, Whitman Publishing, Atlanta, 2013.

Bucki, James. "U.S. Mint Releases Palladium Bullion Coins Market Study," about.com coins, coins.about.com/b/2013/03/23/u-s-mint-releases-palladium-bullion-coins-market-study.htm

Carter, Howard, and A.C. Mace. *The Tomb of Tut-Ankh-Amen*, George H. Doran Company, New York, 1923.

Galvez, Brad J. (chief sponsor). H.B. 157 Currency Amendments, 2012 General Session, State of Utah.

Garrett, Jeff, and Q. David Bowers. *Gold: Everything You Need to Know to Buy and Sell Today*, Whitman Publishing, Atlanta, 2010.

Garrett, Jeff, and Ron Guth. *Encyclopedia of U.S. Gold Coins, 1795–1933*, second edition, Whitman Publishing, Atlanta, 2008.

————. *100 Greatest U.S. Coins*, third edition, Whitman Publishing, Atlanta, 2009.

Goldberg, Ira, and Lawrence Goldberg (editors). *Money of the World: Coins That Made History*, Whitman Publishing, Atlanta, 2007.

Judd, J. Hewitt, and Q. David Bowers (editor). *United States Pattern Coins*, 10th edition, Whitman Publishing, Atlanta, 2009.

Matthews, Dylan. *Washington Post* "Wonkblog," www.washingtonpost.com/blogs/wonkblog/wp/2013/01/04/michael-castle-unsuspecting-godfather-of-the-1-trillion-coin-solution

Mercanti, John M., with Michael Standish. *American Silver Eagles: A Guide to the U.S. Bullion Coin Program*, second edition, Whitman Publishing, Atlanta, 2013.

Moran, Michael F. *Striking Change: The Great Artistic Collaboration of Theodore Roosevelt and Augustus Saint-Gaudens*, Whitman Publishing, Atlanta, 2008.

Mui, Ylan Q. "Virginia Coin Moves Closer to Reality," *The Washington Post*, February 5, 2013, online edition.

"Palladium Eagles," American Palladium Eagle Coin Information, www.palladiumeagles.us, April 2013.

*Precious Metal: Investing and Collecting in Today's Silver, Gold, and Platinum Markets*, Whitman Publishing, Atlanta, 2012.

Public Laws: All public laws cited were found in full text online at the web site of the Government Printing Office, www.gpo.gov

"Read Before Investing," Investment Guides, California Numismatic Investments, www.golddealer.com

Reagan, Ronald. Statement on Signing the Gold Bullion Coin Act of 1985, December 17, 1985, presidency.ucsb.edu/ws/?pid=38178

Reed, Fred. *Abraham Lincoln: The Image of His Greatness*, Whitman Publishing, Atlanta, 2009.

Roach, Steve. "33 Double Eagle Trial: At Long Last, a Conclusion," *CoinWorld.com*, July 21, 2011.

Russell, Corie. "Gold Investments Can Provide Long-Term Gains," *plansponsor.com*, February 8, 2013.

Schechter, Scott, and Jeff Garrett. *100 Greatest U.S. Modern Coins*, second edition, Whitman Publishing, Atlanta, 2013.

Sheldon, William H. *Early American Cents, 1793–1814*, Harper & Brothers, 1949.

U.S. Congress. "An Act Concerning the Gold Coins of the United States," Statutes at Large, 23rd Congress, First Session, chapter XCV, June 28, 1834.

Steinberg, Julie. "Where to Put All That Gold," *The Wall Street Journal online*, Weekend Investor, January 18, 2013.

Unser, Mike. "2013 American Eagle Bullion Coins Robust in First Quarter Sales," coinnews.net, April 5, 2013.

Yeoman, R.S., and Kenneth Bressett (senior editor), *A Guide Book of United States Coins*, Whitman Publishing, Atlanta, various annual editions.

# Index